Music & Literature

Kaija Saariaho

Stig Sæterbakken

Can Xue

Number Five

Music & Literature

Number Five

ISSN: 2165-4026
ISBN: 978-0-9888799-4-2

Publisher: Taylor Davis-Van Atta
Editors: Taylor Davis-Van Atta & Daniel Medin
Associate Editor & Director of Publicity: Madeleine LaRue
Digital Editor: Jeffrey Zuckerman
Editorial Assistant: Chloe Elder
Cover Design & Visual Identity: EA Projects, Brooklyn, NY

Kaija Saariaho's writings appear courtesy of the author and by permission of Stéphane Roth, editor, *Le Passage des frontières. Écrits sur la musique*, 2012, and the publishers of Éditions MF; an excerpt from *Birds* appears by permission of Gallery Press; "A Conversation with Kaija Saariaho," "Conversations with Three Conductors," "A Conversation with Anssi Karttunen," and "The Flute Music of Kaija Saariaho—A Personal History" appear courtesy of Clément Mao-Takacs and *Symétrie*: earlier versions of all four texts appear in French in *Kaija Saariaho: l'ombre du songe* (*Tempus Perfectum* no. 11); "A Discussion and a Monologue" was originally published in Finnish in *Aistit, uni, rakkaus, Kaksitoista katsetta Kaija Saariahoon*, edited by Pekka Hako, LURRA Editions, 2012, and appears courtesy of the editor; all photographs in the Saariaho portfolio courtesy of Kaija Saariaho and Jean-Baptiste Barrière; "The Terrifying" originally appeared in English in *Smug* magazine, and accompanying illustrations by Sverre Malling appear courtesy of the artist; portions of "The Wind from Outside" were previously published in Norwegian in *Morgenbladet*; "Enthusiastic and Merciless" and "Twenty-Five Years of Tenderness" originally appeared in Norwegian in *Vagant* 1/2012 and 4/2009, respectively, and appear courtesy of the authors and *Vagant*; an excerpt from *The Last Lover* reproduced by permission of Yale University Press; all photographs in Can Xue portfolio courtesy of Can Xue and Jonathan Griffith.

Music & Literature, Inc. is a 501(c)(3) charitable organization.

U.S. subscriptions: US$20 (single issue); US$35 (one-year, two issues); US$65 (two-year, four issues) / International subscriptions: US$30 (single issue); US$55 (one-year, two issues); US$100 (two-year, four issues)

Music & Literature no. 4: Clarice Lispector / Maya Homburger & Barry Guy / Mary Ruefle
Music & Literature no. 3: Gerald Murnane / Vladimír Godár / Iva Bittová
Music & Literature no. 2: László Krasznahorkai / Béla Tarr / Max Neumann
Music & Literature no. 1: Arvo Pärt / Hubert Selby / Micheline Aharonian Marcom

For more information visit www.musicandliterature.org

Acknowledgments

The editors wish to recognize the writers, translators, and other artists whose work appears in this volume. Special thanks as well to the following people for their invaluable efforts: Jean-Baptiste Barrière, Elina Bloch, Matthew Campbell, John Donatich, Jonathan and Jeri Griffith, Paul Griffiths, Pekka Hako, Reijo Kiilunen, Audun Lindholm, Alexandra Pearson, Stéphane Roth, Clément Mao-Takacs, and Annelise Finegan Wasmoen.

Our sincere gratitude to Can Xue for her kind cooperation and careful attention to the peculiarities of this project, down to its finest details.

We wish to acknowledge Stig Sæterbakken, who was a friend, an enthusiastic supporter, and one of *Music & Literature*'s first champions. The results of his thoughtfulness are still being realized and will be felt and appreciated for the lifespan of the project.

Our heartfelt gratitude as well to Elizabeth Sunde for her recommendations and attentive editing of texts, her aid in obtaining rights, and above all, her courage and friendship.

A warm salute to Aleksi Barrière, whose assistance on multiple fronts made the Saariaho portfolio a far more robust and—we trust—enduring collection of work than it otherwise would have been.

Finally, we are indebted to the collaborative efforts of Kaija Saariaho, whose music has long thrilled and inspired us. Her openness and trust in this project was essential, and we are very grateful for the time she devoted in service to it. We are honored to celebrate her work in these pages.

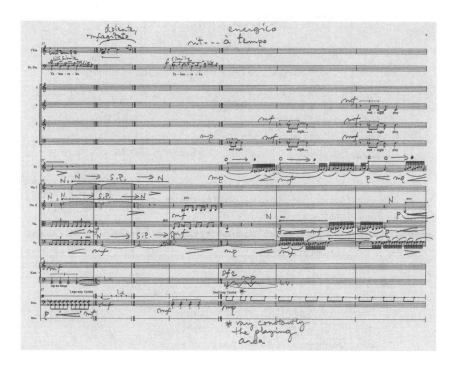

From *Tsunemasa*

Contents

Selected Works of Kaija Saariaho

Bruden, for soprano, two flutes, and percussion (1977)
Suomenkielinen sekakuorokapple, for soprano, baritone, and mixed chorus (1979)
Study for Life, for female voice, dancer, tape, and lights (1980)
Preludi—Tunnustus—Postludi, for soprano and prepared piano (1980)
Im Traume, for cello and piano (1980)
Laconisme de l'aile, for flute and electronics (1982)
Verblendungen, for orchestra and tape (1984)
Lichtbogen, for nine players and electronics (1986)
Io, for orchestra, tape, and live electronics (1987)
Nymphéa, for string quartet and electronics (1987)
Petals, for cello (1988)
Du Cristal..., for orchestra (1989)
...à la Fumée, for alto flute, cello, live electronics, and orchestra (1990)
Maa, ballet for chamber ensemble and live electronics (1991)
Nuits, adieux, for vocal quartet and electronics (1991)
Amers, for solo cello, orchestra, and electronics (1992)
NoaNoa, for flute and electronics (1992)
Nocturne, for solo violin (1994)
Lonh, for soprano and electronics (1996)
Château de l'âme, for solo soprano, eight female voices, and orchestra (1996)
Graal théâtre, concerto for violin and chamber orchestra (1997)
Couleurs du vent, for alto flute (1998)
Oltra mar, for chorus and orchestra (1999)
L'Amour de loin, opera for soprano, mezzo soprano, baritone, chorus,
and orchestra (2000)
Sept Papillons, for cello (2000)
Aile du songe, concerto for flute and orchestra (2001)
Orion, for orchestra (2002)
Quatre Instants, for soprano and piano (2002)
Je sens un deuxième coeur, for viola, cello, and piano (2003)
Dolce Tormento, for solo piccolo (2004)
Adriana Mater, opera for voice quartet, chorus, and orchestra (2005)
La Passion de Simone, oratorio for soprano, spoken voice, chorus,
and orchestra (2006)
Notes on Light, for cello and orchestra (2006)
Mirage, for soprano, cello, and orchestra (2008)
Émilie, opera for soprano and orchestra (2008)
Laterna Magica, for orchestra (2008)
D'Om le vrai sens, concerto for clarinet and orchestra (2010)
Sombre, for bass flute, percussion, harp, and double bass (2012)
Circle Map, for orchestra and electronics (2012)
Maan varjot, for organ and orchestra (2013)
La Passion de Simone, oratorio for soprano, spoken voice,
and chamber orchestra (2013)
Light and Matter, for violin, cello, and piano (2014)
True Fire, for baritone and orchestra (2014)
Only the Sound Remains (2016), opera

Kaija Saariaho (center) with Dawn Upshaw (left) and Gidon
Kremer (right) at the Maison de la Radio, Paris, 1995.

An Introduction to the Saariaho Writings

The following selection of Kaija Saariaho's writings, appearing here for the first time in English, spans three decades, from her days as Paavo Heininen's student at the Sibelius Academy in Helsinki to a remarkable and recent essay exploring her major works for large ensemble. In this collection, Saariaho examines a few of her earliest pieces for solo instruments and small ensembles, and reflects on her formative time researching electronics at IRCAM (the Institute for Research and Coordination in Acoustics/Music) in Paris. Her companion passions for fine art, cinematography, poetry, and literature—and their integration into her musical thinking and development as a composer—are present in these essays, as are frequent reflections on her childhood and on the writing process itself. These articles document what Saariaho calls her "slow evolution toward a deeper consciousness" and offer rare glimpses of the true work of an artist who remains ever obedient to the "urge to plunge deep into oneself, by one's senses and by one's dreams, all to produce a physical movement through time while remaining conscious of the past."

Kaija Saariaho (center, arms crossed) at one
of her first concerts, in Helsinki, circa 1978.

Scream If You Wish, But Fly! (1980)

Kaija Saariaho

Translated from the French by Jeffrey Zuckerman

My natural tendency toward music has always been driven in large part—and perhaps too much—by intuition. Of all the arts, it's music that has remained a purely intuitive experience, for the specific reason that it mixes different sorts of sensations. As a child, I liked listening to Johann Sebastian Bach's music for organ. It filled my eyes with movement and color as much as it filled my ears with sound. When I learned that the German word Bach meant "river," I began associating this music with perfumes and with the springtime sun, not to mention the small stories that unfolded on the banks of this river.

Engaging with the other arts allowed me, early on, to understand the importance of technique for attaining a final result—I examined colors, surfaces; I practiced. And in my eyes, this approach was clearly different from what I was able to produce with a musical instrument: I wanted to feel the music in all its nuances. This difference was magnified by an environment in which music was less familiar than pictures and books.

The second chapter of my relationship with music opened with my studies in composition with Paavo Heininen. It's impossible to exaggerate the importance of his teachings on my slow evolution toward a deeper consciousness, and on my ability to account for several simultaneous options—the aerial perspective and (I want to put it precisely this way) free flight. Coordinating my heart and my mind isn't always straightforward, but my capabilities as a composer and my ability to thoroughly focus on my own music keep growing.

Musical thoughts often come to me as if they are responses to a stimulus, whether there has actually been one or not. A stimulus might be a word or a sentence that I hear or remember, a text, discovering a new direction, a surprising connection, or even a sound that reminds me of something familiar.

As far as the birth of my musical pieces, the most important story to date is that of the piece for horn and percussion entitled *Yellows*. Paavo Heininen was the one to suggest pairing these two instruments. I began by gathering material aimlessly, gropingly, without even knowing what I was looking for. At the end of the spring [of 1979], I did nothing at all; in the summer I moved a few brief notes from one place to another, with a guilty conscience, all while I was working on a choral work that had been commissioned.[1] I put up with this mess through the fall, until I suddenly felt at the end of the year a strong urge to finish the piece. I managed, at last, to figure out the first part. The result wasn't satisfying, but I didn't know how to fix it, and didn't have the heart to do it all over again. I had a far clearer idea of the second part, though it took some time before I wanted to undertake it. For no good reason, I finally felt the urge to finish this part. I was terribly sad once the second part was done. I had just realized that my project, including the third part, which had to connect to the section that was already mostly done, didn't have any overall coherence. The thing was far from being done.

Now it's already March [1980] and I'm sick and reading the third volume of Proust's *In Search of Lost Time*, which has just come out in Finnish translation. I'm doing my best to read as carefully and slowly as possible; I want to keep this forever; I dread coming to the end. I don't want to think about my composition in progress. Nonetheless, one day, while reading Proust, that composition comes to mind and I understand at once how to finish it.

The clarity and perfection of the text I was reading had taken me much further than ever before, and had even partly transformed me. At least that's how it seemed. Now it was easy to compose the end of the piece. And then it was done…but I was still unhappy with the composition as a whole.

Over the summer, I went through the piece with a very different mindset, and the first part still seemed unfinished and powerless. So I tried to recompose it and, once I was done, I was finally satisfied with it. The piece was all ready.

Yellows is a particularly important piece right now, as I've become interested in the organization of very different, even totally opposed, musical sequences, cheek by jowl in a single composition. Nonetheless, I'm starting from the premise that they will constitute a uniform whole. (Besides, I'm more and more interested in concrete sounds, in technology and recorded music, in Monteverdi's *stile concitato*, in the atmospheres that can give rise to a sound, in musical timbres, and in the psychology of listening. I'm also studying combinations of music and movement, new literary associations, colors and lights, the total work of art, the meticulous construction of acoustics, the Greek language, and even phonetics.)

This reflection began with *Yellows*. The approach is different in each part; even in whom the notation is meant for. The little trilogy of *Preludi—Tunnustus—Postludi* ("Prelude"—"Confession"—"Postlude"), composed not long after *Yellows*, takes up the same idea on the structural level.

At the moment, I'm working on a duet for cello and piano.[2] With this piece, I'm trying first to refine the principle that I have just described. I envision a total independence of parts—composed such that they may be played in any order. At the same time, they must remain full of detail and offer more depth than my previous music.

Another very important thing I learned while composing *Yellows* is the negative influence of my own impatience. I think I'll be able to get rid of it bit by bit—and I must, because some ideas only flourish with time.

While thinking about my career as a composer and about my motivations, I tell myself that if I weren't a composer, I would be a painter or practicing some other art. No other activity has real importance for me. That might seem pathetic, but it's true. My motivation for art isn't just to communicate, even if I think that art transmits unique and irreplaceable fragments of the reality of our time, and of all time. The more important thing for me is to try to bring together all that life brings me and to do new things, things that end up making independent and living parts of our world. When I do so, everything seems clear to me: in a single moment, all intentions and meanings have found their places, even though it won't take long for them to fall once more into disarray.

The title of this text, borrowed from Elmer Diktonius, perfectly reflects the ideas about art that I now put my faith in: breathing freely; opening the heart; seeking the new. The artist should not, must not, give in to habit or comfort. Good souls often create mechanisms that, despite protecting them, dull their visions and limit the range of what is possible. We cannot contradict them; the arrows will hit those whose hearts have no armor. Our cultural climate is tough both for the young artist and the elder, at least if she has managed to establish herself. The circles are small and the elite are few. That's why one should only look in oneself. As for the media, they're dominated by a few despots for whom contemporary creation is outmoded and who place intelligence and technocracy on the same level. A thought's importance and freshness is deliberately reduced to nothing. I can understand the composers who, in this atmosphere, because they're broken down, stop creating. However, I refuse to sympathize with those who have agreed to sell themselves to keep this senseless go-around moving.

I hate moralizing, and I don't want to seem completely naïve either. However, despite all these obstacles, I wish to keep my innocence and believe in the artist's honesty with regards to her work. Against the spirit's narrowness, I'll stand up for purity of intention and of action.

Credo (1984)

Kaija Saariaho

Translated from the French by Jeffrey Zuckerman
Elmer Diktonius poem translated from the Swedish by Benjamin Mier-Cruz

Art is, in itself, merely art: words, lines, colors, and tones. But what it awakens in us is what truly matters. We often speak of the concreteness of reality and the abstractness of art. To me, however, art is our most profoundly authentic reality: it's what digs into our innermost being. The forms change…

At the moment that I write these words, after a year of work, I have just completed *Verblendungen* for orchestra and tape. At the end of this tunnel, coming back to the world and to life, I feel carefree. I answer my friends' letters, I watch the news, I read some books.

The impending spring is a portent of another task entirely: I'll keep expressing my musical ideas by using technology. I have this passion that forces me to penetrate sound to its core, the very substance that I want to change. More concretely, that means that I'm analyzing sound using digital means, in search of new applications of dissonance and consonance borne out of manipulating harmony. This time, I'll pay particular attention to the internal structures of sounds and to the harmonic solutions that they contain. This does not necessarily imply enslaving timbre to harmony; on the contrary, I'm looking for new internal structures that could engender vaster musical entities.

I'm also asking myself this question: how do I integrate silence into a composition? And in what way can it influence the timbre, the granular and porous characteristics of sound?

…but the heart from which art springs…

I'm trying to get further, to get deeper. Lately, I've been wondering what I need to do to keep the will and the strength necessary for exploring, wondering if all that really matters, or if it's just about nurturing a natural aptitude from childhood, and perhaps about other, equally important skills eventually replacing that aptitude.

The strength of youth and faith, and the riches they contain, all become visible once the goal has been reached. It is surprising to see how a reputable artist, having achieved the social stature he's struggled to attain, can lose the will to continue his development, how he lets himself become complacent and absorbed in the goals he has achieved instead of setting his sights on new horizons. Paralysis. Once the goals are achieved, do fossilization and emptiness irrevocably set in?

Art has always had its detractors. But in our time it risks sinking in the waves of commercialism that are submerging our visual and auditory perceptions everywhere. A new art emerges as a substitute, all tied up, with no technical faults. But it remains soulless and degrading.

After having familiarized myself with electronic music, I now know that the best studios, the ones with the greatest means, only produce ads and entertainment. Technical innovations are chiefly intended to buttress the consumerist industry and society, to promote a yogurt or the latest disco hit. It's only at the moment when mass production has brought down costs that artists will reap the benefits of this new marvel. This is deeply indicative of the structures of our time.

...and the heart into which it flows...

In Finland, the traditional figure of the composer has been relegated, with some benevolence, to the reassuring mythical image of the artist (which isn't always positive), as if people wanted to banish it from everyday life. Here, as elsewhere, some budgetary concessions have guaranteed many artists some peace in their work. But this situation can prove controversial. The atmosphere is far from being as free as we'd hope, and economic problems perpetually threaten that liberty. They're jealous, they're exhausted, they're fed up, then they become selfish... The critic plays a vital role here in terms of how instinctively and negatively he reacts when he's confronted with something truly new, rather than welcoming it fearlessly and enthusiastically. It doesn't take a trained psychologist to understand that the fear of someone else's superiority, a bad conscience, and jealousy are destructive.

The critic is omnipresent, but in Finland intellectual life is sidelined because of the country's geographical remoteness (which isn't entirely a bad thing). New currents appear, intensify, and bring about radical transformations, whether people know about it or not.

…are…

For now, official judgment doesn't mean anything to me. I know the future will open its doors to me. In my work every day as a composer, I try to free myself of other people's opinions, which are only obstacles, and I make myself challenge old truths and old certainties, in the hope as well that these points of view can change and that the movement may continue.

…always…

I don't want to complicate things, and that's why I give sound and music an essential role on the physical, auditory, and visual levels. The more I work through numbers and digital devices, the more it seems important to be attentive to sensitivity; the more our era values a world as measured by hard cash, the happier I am to map sensory abstractions.

…the same…[1]

My Library, from Words to Music (1987)

Kaija Saariaho

Translated from the French by Jeffrey Zuckerman

At the heart of my library is a shelf filled, in no particular order, with my favorite books. Surrounding this shelf, in perfect order, are my books on music and all of the other books. I come back to the shelf with my favorite books every time I want to take a retrospective look at my life. I choose books that are dear to me, flip through them, and reread them while paying attention to the feelings they arouse in me: what has changed?

In my childhood, poetry captivated me above all, and when I seriously began to set down on paper the music that came to me, this music often took form thanks to a poem. I felt particularly close to the poet Edith Södergran. Her collection *Runoja* (*Poems*), translated into Finnish from the Swedish and assembled by Lauri Viljanen, was one of my nightstand books until adolescence. When I began to read Södergran's poems in Swedish, the colors and the rhythm of the original texts inspired me in a new way and, around some of them, musical ideas were created in my mind. As a result, in 1977, I composed a small collection of songs entitled *Bruden*. One of the songs' first verses described the collection rather well: "I am nothing but infinite will, / infinite will, but to what end, to what end?" These words came from the poem "My Life, My Death, and My Fate." This was my first "serious" composition. Aside from these songs, which I composed ten years ago, when I was still a student, I didn't compose any other music based on Södergran's texts. These poems, for me, were part of my childhood, which I couldn't and didn't wish to touch again. They encouraged me while I was trying to find a path and a goal for my ideas. When I read them again today, these poems which once transported me now bring back these feelings from my childhood. I'm surprised to realize that, after that point, there wasn't any possibility of transforming poems into music, and that I had already set that aside in the interest of developing an abstract musical language.

Virginia Woolf's *The Waves*, a novel in which creative intelligence and complex metaphors combined, reflects particularly well what I was looking for in my music. The richness of Woolf's language escapes simplistic interpretation, and I sought ways of achieving a similarly prismatic language in music. This question was amplified by my reading Proust's *In Search of Lost Time*; I was more and more interested by the exactitude of language. I still remember those sunlit April days when, recovering from a throat infection, I savored Swann's love while telling myself: I don't want to reach the end. Behind me, I heard Pierre Boulez's *Structures II*, which, aside from those few days, I have never appreciated. The cold intelligence of this music mixed with Proust's text, and the text illuminated Boulez's French world in a new way, by giving him the heat that had otherwise been missing.

This idea of a synthesis between language and sound became a goal. This goal was to develop an abstract reflection and, by means of this reflection, gain control over my sensibility, and establish equilibrium between the mind and the heart.

In reading Proust, somehow, I also regained my childhood, this time when I didn't yet know how to read and when, to me, language only corresponded to a freewheeling combination of sounds, colors, and feelings (I remember trying to mark on paper sounds that were "yellow and nervous"). Proust's text is conducive to experiencing the world synesthetically. Although this was my own attitude, I tried to shunt it aside to become "solely" a musician. The images brought forth by the Madeleine allowed me to find this singularity again. I accepted it and began to develop my own way of seeing, of expressing myself, in spite of a frequent feeling that I had been broken into a thousand pieces by listening to these calls from all around…When I tried to remember the best path for myself, my goal, the words that often came to me were "forward and deeper still." They retain this feeling of stretching, tensing, and burning that engender a simultaneous urge to plunge deep into oneself, by one's senses and by one's dreams, all to produce a physical movement through time while remaining conscious of the past.

At the beginning of my compositional studies, I tried in vain to find a model in the world of music; female composers were few and far between. No doubt this is why I was interested in the lives of female writers, and took pleasure in reading their diaries, letters, and biographies, in addition to their works. Besides Virginia Woolf, the two figures who meant the most to me were Sylvia Plath and Anaïs Nin. While Woolf and Plath's lives both ended in a desperate act, by reason of their urge to combine — at least that's what it seemed to me — "a woman's life," meaning their roles as mother, and their artistic careers, Anaïs Nin, in her permanent youthfulness, vain but powerful, pursued her path using all the means at her disposal through to the end of her long life. As I kept leafing through Nin's diaries, I was doubtlessly looking for a confirmation, even a justification of my own decisions. I was searching for a way of life, and was reading these diaries as survival manuals.

Once Nin's luxurious (even superficial) life had begun to bore me, I found a new passion for asceticism; in this lifestyle, work was tantamount to life. My favorite book from that time was Simone Weil's *Gravity and Grace*. The solidity of Weil's world, the mysticism of her work, and her religious convictions resulted in incredible aphorisms: "A double movement of descent: to do again, out of love, what gravity does. Is not the double movement of descent the key to all art?"

Books are omnipresent in my work, even if not necessarily in the words of my vocal music. When I am looking for a title for a new work (in order to crystallize the identity of the music for the composition in progress), I look imploringly at my library, especially at the section holding my dearest books. On that shelf are not only the books I've just mentioned, but also treasures of other sorts, such as *The Oxford Book of Death* (which I read every time I'm sick!), David Foulkes's *A Grammar of Dreams*, Vassily Kandinsky and Paul Klee's books, and even Roland Barthes's *A Lover's Discourse: Fragments*.

Sometimes, while working on a composition, I search desperately for books which, in one way or another, convey the same feeling as the piece, in order to clarify an idea. Part of that text will be integrated into the final work. This was what happened with my piece for flute, *Laconisme de l'Aile*, which opens with fragments from Saint-John Perse's *Birds*, recited by the musician. That's the source of the piece's title. Or here's a more recent example: at the end of *Lichtbogen*, the flutist whispers a poem into her instrument, even if in this case the text remains unrecognizable. It's from the English author Henry Vaughan's poem "The World," which I came across in Louis Vax's book *La Poésie philosophique*. I used the sounds, particularly the consonants from the first verses of the French translation, for the part the flutist recites ("J'ai vu l'Éternité l'autre nuit..."). The poem describes a vertiginous view, a view of infinite light and space; in this eternity of light and peace, time flows in the form of hours, days, and years. I was astonished when I found this poem; its tone corresponded perfectly to the one I was trying to express in my work. At the time the first ideas were born, I was spending a December night in Lapland watching the northern lights, and this experience somehow illuminated the entire piece. When I found Vaughan's poem, the work was almost done, and only the end was unfinished, although it had been resolved. Even if the public would never realize the significance of the whispered verses, it was important for me to use a text that was in harmony with the music in order to generate the phonetic material. I believe that its atmosphere was transmitted through the entire final part.

Lately, my interests have turned toward books on natural science and those that describe the universe. I especially appreciate Hubert Reeves's books. The first, and most awe-inspiring, of Reeves's books that I read was *Poussières d'étoiles*. This book is, in the author's words, "an ode to the universe." Reeves takes on nature's structures, life in all its forms, and astrophysics. The book is filled with images, every one as interesting and stimulating as the text. In the pages of this book I found the title of the work I labored over this winter: *Io*, the name of one of Jupiter's moons. My intention crystallized with the name of this particularly dynamic and richly colored satellite: to create a work in which the external strength would be even more present in the music than I had ever been able to compose before. As a general rule, reading about the planets' composition and their climate, or about geometric forms within nature, or the simple act of looking at images of nature, allows me, in the middle of a period of intense work, to forget tiresome routine and transcend it all.

I think that this "nature" period can be explained, aside from my fear of our planet being destroyed, by a need for duality—this desire to examine through new forms, through my thoughts and all my senses—but also by the research that has been done on the similarities between microcosms and macrocosms. I'm constantly looking for new dichotomies that allow me to structure thought and time—in other words, music.

An Excerpt from *Birds*

Saint-John Perse

Translated from the French by Derek Mahon

In an early composition for flute, Laconisme de l'aile, *Kaija Saariaho integrates the following excerpt from the epic poem* Birds. *This fragment is uttered by the flutist into her instrument.*

Ignoring their own shadows, knowing of death only the immortality implicit in the noise of distant waters, they vanish, they leave us, their lonely thoughts traversing space, and we are changed for ever.

The Four Poems of *Bruden*

Edith Södergran

Translated from the Swedish by Stina Katchadourian

MY LIFE, MY DEATH, AND MY FATE

I am nothing but infinite will,
infinite will, but to what end, to what end?
Darkness looms all around me,
I cannot lift a straw.
My will wants one thing only; I do not know what it is.
Once my will breaks through, I will expire:
I hail you, my life, my death, and my fate.

LUCKY CAT

I have a lucky cat in my lap,
he's spinning lucky yarn.
Lucky cat, lucky cat,
offer me three things:
Offer me a golden ring,
that tells me that I'm happy;
offer me a mirror,
that tells me that I'm fair;
offer me a soothing fan
to waft away my pesky thoughts.
Lucky cat, lucky cat,
Spin me more yarn about my future!

The Bride

My circle is narrow and the ring of my thoughts
goes round my finger.
There lies something warm at the base of all
                            strangeness around me,
like the vague scent in the water lily's cup,
Thousands of apples hang in my father's garden,
round and completed in themselves—
my uncertain life turned out this way too,
shaped, rounded, bulging and smooth—and simple.
Narrow is my circle and the ring of my thoughts
goes round my finger.

The Grieving Garden

Oh, that windows see
and walls remember,
that a garden can stand grieving
and a tree can turn around and ask:
Who has not come and what is not well,
why is the emptiness heavy and saying nothing?
The bitter carnations cluster by the road
where the fir tree's gloom grows deep and dark.

Earth and Air (2005)

Kaija Saariaho

Translated from the French by Jeffrey Zuckerman

On the occasion of her residency at the Strasbourg Conservatory in 2005, Kaija Saariaho wrote the following responses to several words and phrases that were given to her.

CHILDHOOD

When I was a child, I was already imagining music. It was already part of me, but I didn't know it. When I tried to sleep in the evenings, I heard music and I believed that it came out of my pillow. I asked my mother to turn off the pillow.

TIME AND LIGHT

We often speak of the concept of time in my music. It certainly has to do with my culture, with the light in my country. During the winter months, it's very dark in Finland. When spring comes, it's the opposite: the sun never sets. Nordic time can be very painful. It's so slow. I've always felt it very deeply in my body and in my spirit. Time is light: the light indicates the time, gives the rhythm, influences nature. I've always needed daylight when I work. I can't compose at night. For me, each instrument's sound has a different intensity of light. The whiter the light, the purer the spectrum.

THE FOREST AFTER RAIN

In nature, there are many extraordinary acoustic phenomena. One thing particularly struck me when I was young: I loved walking in the forest after rain. I didn't know why I loved that so much. Years later, I realized that the combination of wet leaves and the birds' first song after the rain created something truly resonant that completely changed the forest's sound. It was absolutely magical.

THE SILENCE OF SNOW

Nature produces particular sounds just after snowfall. Snow is incredibly absorbent; it creates an enormous silence. Each snow is different: there is the snow of very cold weather; soft snow; there is also the noise of footsteps in snow, which is not unlike that made by pressing the bow hard on the strings near the bridge. Then it melts and the earth appears after months of living under the snow, a strange smell pervades: a smell of rot, agreeable because it announces that it's all finally over, that life is coming back after a long trip. That's how everything is with nature up there; the seasons are so strong. My music is certainly imbued with that. I know there are such places that we spend our lives looking for!

DEPTH AND INVENTION

More than twenty years ago, I wrote a little text in which I said that my goal was to go straight, but also to go deep, and to try to take advantage of the tension that resulted from this double movement. That's still my goal today. The experience that I've acquired hasn't made writing any easier or any faster, because I've never wanted to repeat myself. I'm nowhere. I don't understand anything at all.

There are very powerful things in music. Where does this power come from? Where do the technical solutions I choose when I write a piece come from? I really don't understand! When I go to a concert of my own music, I'm never moved. It's strange. I can't be touched by my music, even if the concert and the musicians are extraordinary. When hearing the music, I cannot enjoy it again. When I listen, it's even painful because I'm constantly trying to reevaluate my compositional choices.

BEING A FEMALE COMPOSER

At the beginning of my career, I saw the fact of being a woman as an enormous handicap. I wanted people to listen to my music, and not a woman's music. I tried to scrub away the feminine aspect: I smoked cigars; I dressed like a man. I was jealous of my male colleagues, who were far more free. I found it unfair that they could calmly withdraw to work in quiet, which was nearly impossible for a woman with children. To be a female composer was to share the everyday struggle of most women today: to reconcile work and family. It has to do, I think, with the psychological structure of a woman to be able to do several things at once. A man can't pull that off; that's also a strength. That's what I learned from men: to do one thing at a time. This way of functioning definitely helped to free me from stress. I could never have anything against men; after all, it's women who raise men. In any case, all the obstacles confronting me along my path I set aside to focus solely on my music. That's the advice I can give to all young people: the most important thing for a composer is to try to find his or her own music.

EARTH AND AIR (MOTHERHOOD)

As a mother, I have access to many things that men could never experience. Before having children, I really was up in the air most of the time. The earthly aspect became more present with children.

Has my music changed with motherhood? Of course. At the same time, I don't like to say that, because I really felt some people's suspicions when I had my first child, suspicions like: this is the end of her serious music, she'll become too sentimental. Music changes all the time, and it's possible that this earthly side could have appeared anyway. An artist's work is above all a way of life. If I had a religion, it would be music. I have always had only one desire: to go back to my music.

In Music, of Music, toward Music (2005)[1]

Kaija Saariaho

Translated from the French by Jeffrey Zuckerman

Sunday, July 4 — AT REST

Finally out in the countryside. There's a wind outside. The huge trees' glittering green leaves are shaking. I'm thinking of a young Japanese flutist, Keiko, who recently played my piece *Couleurs du vent*. I asked her how she saw it as a whole, since it often seemed to be missing a common thread, but she'd still mastered it wonderfully. Because the title is *Couleurs du vent*, she answered, she imagined the wind in nature, at various speeds, in a whirlwind, the wind catching on leaves and other things. "Why not?" I thought to myself. All that matters is that it works. And besides, it's doubtlessly about one of the huge trees I was listening to and looking at while composing the piece.

I've strived toward this calmness: complete silence, no social life, nor daily routines, nor city crowds. All that remains is the essential: the music, the possibility of burrowing into it once again, going farther. Years have gone by in this way: the desert of urban routines, regularly interrupted by the oases of life in the countryside, which I eagerly await and where I compose so much, so much more easily than in the city. It used to be that I thought I could compose anywhere and that my surroundings had no influence on my music. Then one year I came back to Finland, and I experienced the four seasons there, especially wintertime, with snow, darkness, and endlessness. Everywhere I heard people speaking Finnish. Now I think exactly the opposite: everything that has an influence on me as a person also has an influence on my music.

Did I actually compose in a different way before, or did this fact simply escape me?

*

Long ago, my orchestration professor, Kalervo Tuukkanen, described the viola's character by saying that "it holds dandelions and resembles a young boy." I had trouble keeping a straight face. Over the years, I've gotten closer to Tuukkanen and found that all metaphors are permissible when trying to define something as complex as the sensations brought about by a musical instrument. Whatever the instrument, whatever one does, the result leaves something to be desired. Every instrument houses a rich and multidimensional world that the musician must awaken and breathe life into. It's true that this world isn't manifested in the same way for every person: "my cello" in particular makes use of the high register and the noise of a bow that glides from the bridge to the fingerboard; the clear sound of "my flute" frequently transforms into whispers and hums. Stretching out its usual recognized and established sound broadens the range of colors and expressions; the musician produces a sound in a different way that isn't used in classical repertoires.

On the other hand, I often hope that the colors I'm looking for will be played with the same ferocity as, say, a Beethoven sonata or a Bach concerto. Last year, the Berliner Philharmonic opened a concert with *Orion*. Magnificent. However, it was only after the intermission, when Brahms' Second Symphony had started, that the violinists actually began to play. They were freed, they breathed with the music. The difference was so great that tears were running down my cheeks, and it wasn't just because I was frustrated, but also because I thought: how wonderful that they can play this symphony, because it gives them so much pleasure!

For me, it's necessary to delimit the range of each instrument and, in the orchestra, the farthest instruments each have their own responsibilities. The piccolo sketches its glissando above all the others; the contrabassoon makes its entrance only when the woodwinds need a moody and robust base, or maybe a melodic detail that should be played very low. Among percussion instruments, the crotales and the celesta on one hand, the bass drum and the timpani on the other, frame the orchestra, define and extend its ambit.

An orchestrated page is especially satisfying once it corresponds to the idea I've dreamed up for its sounds, but also once it pleases my eye.

I've never analyzed these visual criteria. I'm happy to intuitively declare once a page is ready and turn to the next one. Beyond technical savoir-faire, the instruments and the orchestra deal with a number of feelings and experiences—I'm certainly afraid to overanalyze these delicate and intuitive canvases.

Wednesday, July 6—THE NEED TO COMPOSE

Sometimes I wonder where this necessity to compose, to begin a new work of any size, comes from, and how it starts more or less from nothing. There's pleasure and a feeling of fullness once music comes to me, sleepless nights when everything suddenly seems trite and pointless.

Even if most of the time I'm sure that this is the best way for me to live and that I'm lucky as a composer to be able to devote myself completely to my work, I often feel insignificant when faced with the sheer immensity of the world. I'm also wondering what kind of picture of life I'm giving my children. The list of my priorities is so particular: silence and a great deal of time to work. Beach vacations and amusement parks are pretty far down on this list...

It's been years since I have taken a break from composing, even just for a few days. Needless to say, during tours or orchestra rehearsal periods, I don't compose very much, but even then, some internal necessity keeps pushing me to create.

In reality, there are different sorts of needs. The most important is this one: "I compose, therefore I am." In other words, there is some sort of existential trauma there, even though I always have a passionate wish to develop and give concrete form to my musical ideas. Of course, having been raised in a Protestant culture, I also feel a moral need to work; sometimes I ask myself this question to figure out how separate these two needs are.

Some of my needs have to do with my working conditions. In the beginning, the position of the light source and the room I was in were very important. At some point, I realized that the only necessary condition was that my head follow and that it be more or less ready; all the rest didn't matter. Today, I don't even try to figure out where my head is, and I can handle plenty of interference; the only external factor I can't bear is the presence of other music or defined-pitched sounds. It's not always easy to screen those out in Paris, and that's one of the reasons working in the city is much harder than here in the countryside.

There are also social necessities: I might have promised something or signed a contract. I try to make sure the pressure doesn't get too great, to have enough time for everything so that panic doesn't overwhelm it all. That doesn't happen too often, actually. So, when I "need to finish a piece," that usually means that I have an internal urge to rid myself and relieve myself of musical matter; it's not about irritated sponsors or any impending concerts.

When the internal urge becomes especially pressing, I think of a Finnish rock 'n' roll phrase: *pakko ku kuolla*—in life, the only thing we must do is die.

Thursday, July 7—MUSIC IS ENERGY...

...like love or hate, but music has more dimensions. If I try to distinguish them, the first thing that comes to mind is specifically mental energy, immediately followed by all the others: music is also physical energy, like waves or light, but it's also above all a sophisticated language.

Music is a language that has several dialects, some more interesting than others. I'm trying to decipher its grammar and teach it, and even if we understand several aspects of it, I think that the core only opens up to the senses.

If it really is fun to listen to your favorite music, that's because music stimulates both the intellect and the senses; it offers a total experience. Of course there's music with its intellectual or sensory aspects reduced to a minimum, but I'm usually not interested in that.

This multidimensional character makes the compositional act so complex. The composer works hard to find technical solutions, but technique, which of course is the basis of everything, isn't the most important thing.

But what is, then?

Indeed, that's one of the questions driving my compositions, so I'll get closer to music's mysteries, so I'll burrow into music. The large works seem better suited to exploration, because staying with the same subject for such a long time allows me to go further—at least that's what I think. Nonetheless, sometimes a totally intuitive bit will come close to the miracle of music. When that happens, music seems to be vast, and I, the composer, very small. It can't be possible that this music comes out of me. But where else would it come from?

For me, religious doctrines and dogmas have nothing to do with music, because music has no limits. I see music more as a part of nature's vast mystery, closer in this way to love or death. What do we really know of that?

After the trio concert,[2] Hannele [Segerstam, a Finnish violinist], my friend, phoned from Finland and told me that it "opened up space." After a good concert, I often feel the same way myself: space stretches out and time disappears.

And sometimes this feeling overwhelms me. Here, in my office, each note finds its place on the page, within the humming exaltation of existence, far from this time and this place.

Friday, July 8—BOUNDARIES

Even if, when I was Paavo Heininen's student in the seventies, I had never written this piece for snare drum that he usually asked his students to compose, I would still have learned so many essential things from him about setting boundaries around my material. Everything begins there: delimiting the material, developing it after settling on the essential and paring away the superfluous. Contrary to several younger colleagues who enthusiastically developed their own systems, I tried to find the right notes by listening to my heart. It was a very cumbersome process that Paavo's teaching very gently began to mollify. As my musical identity became clear, the choice of material grew easier.

Today, "the minimum" has become a challenge. I want to keep reducing the material I have when starting a piece; it's a recurrent obsession... Although it's not my goal, it's almost minimalism.

Another necessity consists of keeping an eye on musical boundaries, of stretching out the moment where the vowel becomes a consonant, where a cello's natural sound becomes an extremely high pitch harmonic, or even where light becomes shadow—as if life's slow metamorphosis became clear at those moments, as if in this way we could finally understand something.

Paring away the excess in these extraordinarily small details can be thought of in two completely opposed ways: it's possible to think that with time I'll focus on the essential and eliminate what is useless, or perhaps with time the world will grow smaller and become ever more clearly bounded. Indeed, older artists' works are often simpler and more rigorous than their earlier creations. There are certainly exceptions: one of Henri Dutilleux's last works, *Correspondences*, is a particularly rich and plentiful piece.

Saturday, July 9—A TYPICAL WORK DAY

People often ask me what my typical work day is like. Usually, I describe my day as if everything was going well, or as I wish it went: once the children have gone off to school, I sit down in my office, I eat lunch without taking a break from work, and I keep working through the afternoon. On days like that, I'm at peace because the work goes at its own pace, I feel free, and in a single day, it's possible for me to look at the same musical section from several different angles.

Here, in the countryside, is where I have days like that, and those are my best periods of work. However, reality is far more complicated, so complicated that I don't even have the energy to talk about it. It's become more and more difficult to find quietness in which to breathe.

Isn't it strange that once people can choose their way to work, their ideal comes down to a routine much like the one others usually hate and try to escape? Honestly, I don't see any difference between my pleasant routine and the routine that kills, aside from my desire and motivation to do this work, and the fact that I chose it myself.

Sunday, July 10—MUSICIANS AND THE NATURE OF MUSIC

Although I experience music as textures, colors, and feelings, at the moment that I compose, it takes on a far more concrete dimension, when I envision the musician, the singer or ensemble, their instruments, their breathing. When I'm writing for a solo instrument, I often think of a specific musician and her instrument even if someone else ultimately plays the piece. When I write for singers I know well, I don't just imagine their voice in different registers, but also their throat, and I try to keep in mind the way singing is produced in their body and how to find the different colors of their voice. Nonetheless, I also try to protect my music from these physical constraints because, naturally, I tend to avoid traditional virtuosity with its high notes and fast scales. On the contrary, while watching a singer's larynx moving, I run the risk of overly limiting my expression. While writing my first opera, for example, I was very careful not to put the vowel *i* too high in the singers' registers. During the whole composition process, I had in front of my eyes, pinned up over my work table, a page from *Tristan und Isolde*; it was their meeting in the second act ("Isolde! Geliebte!—Tristan! Geliebter!"), which I framed when I was a student and which, in the intervening twenty years or so, collected dust in a closet. I took it back out to give me strength, because in this act there's an incredible energy. One day, glancing at it, something else leaped out at me: the *i* sung by Isolde is very high, just like the *i* in "Geliebte," and even if the vowels had to be a bit extreme, the piece had reached its apex and it was one of the most beautiful acts in the history of opera.

In a way, I associate the virtuosic tradition with something superficial, characteristic of street music, far from my musical universe. Some might say the distance is too great.

These last years, I've wanted to physically get closer to my music. So I've tried to find new aspects of my musical expression, aspects that I hadn't known, like playfulness, joy, or movement. Each of these aspects is tied to the joy of performance, something different from music that's *misterioso* or *doloroso*, where I expect the musician to concentrate wholly on the music's structure or on interpreting a particular world of sound or a text.

Ten years ago, I wouldn't have thought even for a minute that one day I would look for the key to musically interpreting joy; twenty years ago, I wouldn't have imagined that one day I'd use octaves, not even for orchestrating a large ensemble piece. In other words, I've changed with the world, and so has my music—not necessarily in the right way, only in some way. I just read a review that clearly missed my previous compositions and connected my current aesthetic to an interpretation of the Celtic myths about King Arthur.

The title of an article I wrote nearly twenty-five years ago and which considered the work of composition, was borrowed from Elmer Diktonius: *Kirkua saat, mutta lennä!* ("Scream if You Wish, But Fly!"). If I remember correctly, I expressed an idea in this article that, despite my evolution, is still essential to me: the desire to go as deep and as far as possible and to take advantage of the tension that results from this double movement.

Five Acts in the Life of an Opera Composer (2010)

Kaija Saariaho

Translated from the French by Jeffrey Zuckerman

I. Memories

A small, overheated, cramped room; fat singers standing upright, straight as a post, downstage; it's all rather funny, although it's not supposed to be. Beautiful voices, occasionally sublime music, but overall a stifled feeling.

More enjoyable were the ballet performances. I specifically remember *Swan Lake* and *Sleeping Beauty* in the sixties. Tchaikovsky's music was otherworldly, the dancers were beautiful, and I may have even had my first crush on Prince Charming.

Liisa Tuomi in *Annie Get Your Gun* at the Finnish National Theater: I absorbed the comedian's onstage freedom and compared it in my mind to the opera singers' stiffness. The film version of Bernstein's *West Side Story* was broadcast in Finland a short while after it had been released, in the very early sixties, and I was given a recording for my birthday—one of my first vinyl discs.

And then the Saturday afternoon I spent listening to *Tristan und Isolde* for the first time, my eyes riveted to the sheet music, in my childhood home. This was decades before I first saw the opera performed, but the passion, the suffering, the anticipation conveyed by the music and the score have been so deeply carved into my mind that no subsequent performance could have tempered it. It was disorienting to identify love with music. For about twenty years, I pinned up in my room a photocopy of Act II, Scene 2: "Isolde! Geliebte!—Tristan! Geliebter!"

And finally the Savonlinna opera festival in 1975, Aulis Sallinen's *The Horseman*, and, in fall of that same year, Joonas Kokkonen's *The Last Temptations* at the Finnish National Opera. These masterpieces were, in their musical language, far removed from the universe I was interested in then (that was when I was studying composition), but their truth and profundity deeply impressed me. In *The Horseman*, Paavo Haavikko's superb text spoke to me, and in my opinion, the *Four Dream Songs* drawn from opera are among Finland's most beautiful song cycles.

In 1991, I entered an opera house for the first time in a professional capacity with *Maa*, composed for the Finnish National Ballet in collaboration with the choreographer Carolyn Carlson. This seven-part work wasn't just my longest piece to date, but also my first work intended for an opera stage; it was my first time being involved in the production of a performance, with all its components, especially the lights. This experience was so striking that I began imagining a work for voice and lights that in some way followed upon one of my first pieces, *Study for Life*, composed for soprano, voice recording, and lights. I was used to the idea of an abstract work that didn't have any linear narrative—just a voice, lights, maybe a stage with different colors and textures. I admired the new digital means for controlling light—especially useful for rock concerts that I watched rebroadcast on television—and I imagined similar apparatuses for a luminous polyphony, which would accompany sensitive and precise music. I discovered Jacques Roubaud's poetry, which I often turned to at other times, in *Maa* and in my vocal quartet *Nuits, adieux*. In terms of a work for stage, I especially had in mind his book *Exchanges on Light*— quoted in snippets in that last piece—a book where each chapter reads like the transcript of imagined evenings where people from different realms come together to talk about light, each from his or her point of view.

I also thought again and again about my various operatic experiences, which have only increased since my move to Paris, and even more so after my studies in Germany. The staging I saw of Peter Sellars's *Don Giovanni* in 1989 completely torpedoed the idea I'd had of opera as a precious and dusty form. This experience, like Patrice Chéreau's staging of Berg's *Wozzeck* or Luigi Dallapiccola's *Il prigioniero* allowed me to see how opera could be thought of as a place where disciplines intersected, where the other arts could reinforce and intensify the music. I realized with astonishment that an evening at the opera could, on the contrary, be a powerful, modern, and intense artistic experience that speaks to all our senses and interrogates our own existence like no other art form.

II. *L'AMOUR DE LOIN*

Little by little my abstract project receded into the background, and I grew interested in creating musical characters. I became aware of how important it was to be able to identify with opera—and how this could only be done with a story. I looked for fairytale-like stories that, even if they were transparent, would correspond to my musical language. I hesitated to start writing because my music was hardly dramatic. Flipping once again through Jacques Roubaud's work, I came across his *Inverse Flower*, in which he alludes to Jaufré Rudel's life as a troubadour in the twelfth century. These few lines about him stuck with me:

> Jaufré Rudel of Blaye was a very noble man, the prince of Blaye. And he fell in love with the countess of Tripoli, whom he had never seen, because of all the praise that he heard said of her by the pilgrims who came from Antioch; and he made many songs about her, with good melodies and few words. And for the sake of seeing her he took the Cross and set out to sea. And on the voyage a grievous illness fell upon him, so that those who were in the ship with him thought he was dead, but they brought him to Tripoli and carried him to an inn... And it was made known to the Countess, and she came to him, and took him in her arms, and he knew she was the Countess, and recovered consciousness, and praised God and thanked Him for having let him live to see her. And so he died in the Lady's arms. And she had him honorably buried in the Church of the Templars, and on that same day, she became a nun, through the grief that she felt by reason of his death.[1]

Jaufré Rudel's vida stayed in my mind, and when I was talking to people about the endeavor of an opera, I made them read it too, and asked them if they saw an operatic subject there. But the answer was almost uniformly negative; nobody saw the dramatic density needed for the opera form.

I also had to resolve several technical problems. First of all, at that point I had only set preexisting texts to music, which I had chosen carefully, or rather, as I liked to say, which had "chosen me." Few texts "spoke" to me, and I couldn't see any other way of unfurling narrative than by using a narrator. I mentally replaced Mozartian recitatives with a spoken text; the singers would only be singing because the poetic texts were similar to arias. Mozart's example was the one I usually took, and little by little the idea of two couples grew on me: on the one hand, the troubadour and his lady, and on the other, an earthly, even silly, couple, who could be friends at first, or servants, or who knows what else. For a narrator, whose role consisted mostly of recitatives, I envisioned a low voice—perhaps a pilgrim.

The original story grew in my imagination into visual and chromatic ideas, and feelings. Once I sketched the structure of my music, I kept on constructing oppositions—in this case, these oppositions were even outside of music: the green French coast and its chilly stone castle, contrasted against a hot, exotic, and fragrant Tripoli, and so on.

My formal starting point was the combination of a mirror and a circle that closed on itself. At this stage of creation, I was in touch with Jacques Roubaud, who I considered the librettist of my opera and who was very interested in the project. Together we developed the synopsis; Jaufré's death became the midpoint of the opera, which would continue from that moment in the realm of the dead, before a dreamlike loop brought him back to the original spot.

The opera project developed in my head and I began to prepare for it by composing several works that comprised my first forays into the subject. I wrote *Lonh*, an Occitan piece for soprano and electronics; Jacques Roubaud recorded Jaufré Rudel's poem "Lanquand le jorn" for me, a text that was my point of departure and which I'd found at the National Library of France while looking for Rudel's manuscripts. This piece was intended for Dawn Upshaw, whose voice and interpretations I'd loved since the late eighties. She presented the creation in Vienna in fall 1996. In August of the same year, she had already performed the cycle *Château de l'âme*, my first piece for voice and orchestra, as part of the Salzburg Festival with the Philharmonic Orchestra under the direction of Esa-Pekka Salonen.

The first lyric cycle went well, and, screwing my courage to the sticking-place, I contacted Gerard Mortier to propose my opera project. He was immediately enthusiastic about the idea, but in the meantime Jacques Roubaud had pulled out from the project and I found myself without a librettist. I focused once again on the original text of Rudel's vida and the multitude of possibilities it offered. I thought I might dream up a libretto drawn from various sources about Jaufré Rudel's life (Heine and Rostand, among others, had tackled the topic). I actually imagined a text in several languages and several levels. Up until then, the librettos for my vocal pieces mostly consisted of "homemade" collages like this—certainly that was the case for the *Château de l'âme* and *Lonh* libretti.

Doubtlessly for the best, Gerard Mortier didn't want to hear anything about a libretto under my name, so we went looking for a potential librettist, as well as a director. Over the years, I'd fallen in love with Peter Sellars's stagings, most of which had contributed to the development of my idea of an opera. The aforementioned production of *Don Giovanni* had been a sort of breakthrough for me; then I had watched his *Rake's Progress* (with Dawn Upshaw in the role of Anne Trulove), and the revival of Messiaen's *St. Francis of Assisi* born out of his collaboration with Esa-Pekka Salonen (in Salzburg, 1992). This interpretation of Messiaen's opera left a deep impression and gave me the impetus and the confidence I had been lacking: there was a massive difference between this version and the original one, which I had seen in Paris, and which had struck me in its stiffness and lack of dramatic energy.

The names Sellars and Salonen seemed obvious when thinking about bringing together a team, but because of their overfull schedules, we had to make the decision to replace them with other collaborators. Amin Maalouf's name had already come up in my conversations with Sellars. I'd read his novel *The Gardens of Light*, as well as his famous essay *The Crusades through Arab Eyes*, but I never would have thought of him myself. Gerard Mortier reached out to Amin; he was interested in the project, but first he wanted to finish the novel he was working on.

Little by little, Peter Sellars found the best place for himself within the project, and he played a crucial role in putting together the libretto. One day when all three of us—Amin, Peter, and myself—were talking about the libretto, Peter asked me to tell him the story again, and he noticed after I'd done so that at no point had I mentioned anybody other than the troubadour Jaufré, Clémence, and the Pilgrim. I realized that I only had musical ideas for these three characters, and that musically distinguishing two more characters would be tedious. Amin was just as interested in reducing the opera to three characters. And so the remaining musical material found its place in the choir.

Collaborating with Amin Maalouf turned out to be easy. I worried that the text, for one reason or another, wouldn't "match" my music. But that wasn't the case—quite the contrary. Amin's libretto also resolved the problem of the narrator: having one wasn't necessary, since the natural dynamic of the responses didn't call for any other kind of storytelling.

Thanks to several years of preparation—while waiting for the libretto, I'd composed *Oltra mar*, a piece in which I'd also used the opera's material—the composition period was relatively quick, although dense, and lasted a year and a half.

The musical material was split into three parts with various structures and patterns, distributed among the characters. I envisioned three harmonic universes, three orchestrations, and three different styles for the vocal parts. The most important passages, dramatically, were marked with "harmony of fate," in which Jaufré and Clémence's respective harmonies would be combined. Throughout the opera, Jaufré and Clémence's harmonies would overlap until they evolved in a layered way. At the end, just before his death, Jaufré's material would join completely with Clémence's music. In terms of the text for voices, the Pilgrim's musical identity perpetually oscillated between Jaufré and Clémence's music. This character's orchestration was far easier to identify: a microtonal carpet of strings and a motif of a descending flute always signaled the Pilgrim's arrival. *L'Amour de loin* also included an electronic component, produced at IRCAM with Gilbert Nouno. Each character in the opera and his or her music was associated with an acoustic universe which the orchestration illuminated.

While I was composing, I finally understood, at least a bit, why I had chosen this subject, a question people had frequently asked me but which I had never known how to answer. I often compared my vague motivations to the ones that guided Olivier Messiaen to choose St. Francis of Assisi: he was a Catholic, he was an ornithologist... What other subject could have been more appropriate for his own opera? But contrary to this foregone conclusion, the fixation I had on this troubadour's story seemed odd, as if it had come out of nowhere. Yet while writing the opera, I realized that each of the three characters corresponded to me in some way: the troubadour Jaufré was the musician; Clémence was the nostalgic woman living far from her birthplace; and the Pilgrim wanted to bring these two fates together.

The opera was finished in fall 1999 and performed in August 2000 at the Salzburg Festival, conducted by Kent Nagano. Going to the first rehearsals of my opera was a difficult experience. It was exhausting to be there for five weeks in the energetic crossfire of powerful artists, since the bulk of my work up until then had been the solitary labor of composition, interrupted only by professional trips of a few days' length and performances of my pieces. Now, each note was weighed up and interpreted. They begged for modifications, they looked for solutions, the various visions of the piece were conflicted, and the atmosphere was, at certain moments, extremely strained. Sometimes I could almost see the entire group struggling with my music. I actually fell sick several times, doubtlessly due to the anxiety, and had many sleepless nights. During these hours of insomnia I composed my solo cello piece, *Sept Papillons*.

When I came back to my work table in fall 2000, starting to compose a new work seemed terribly difficult. I was subdued by the experience of collaborating, and of the result, which had been an extraordinary premiere. All throughout the period during which I composed my flute concerto, *L'Aile du songe*, the feeling of loneliness grew more intense than ever. For the first time I realized just how solitary the composer's work is, just how different my life was from those of performance artists who play every day within a network of human relations and all the positive and negative energies that float in the air around rehearsals and performances.

III. *Adriana Mater*

During the years of its creation, it seemed clear to me that *L'Amour de loin* was the only opera I would ever compose. I never, at any given moment, thought of myself as "an opera composer." As far as I could tell, I was just a composer who had notably written an opera. But when Gerard Mortier was named the general director of the Paris Opera, he contacted me to start thinking about a second project.

I hesitated for a long time, because it seemed to me that a second opera would have to be weaker than the first one. There was no rational explanation for my feeling, other than my personal preference for Berg's *Wozzeck* over his *Lulu*, and for Ravel's *L'Enfant et les sortileges* rather than his *L'Heure Espagnole*—and it didn't even occur to me that one day I might write more than two operas! Why would I compose another opera, since I'd already done one? On the other hand, collaborating with other artists, particularly with Peter Sellars, had been so interesting and inspiring that I ended up accepting the proposal. As I imagined a theatrical work, I yearned more and more strongly, from my isolated composer's perch, to open my music up to the world and let my music be influenced by and imprinted by the world. The urge to write an opera reflecting the world around me was doubtlessly born out of the events of September 11th. The relationship to music I had had up until then, like an intimate and protected universe, was shattered. Cracks had already started to appear during the rehearsals for *L'Amour de loin* in Salzburg, when I distanced myself with compositional work while listening to my own music from sunup to sundown those five weeks. Peter Sellars's influence here had certainly been decisive; he was always trying to push open the doors of real life.

By accepting the Paris Opera's request, I was making the general decision to pursue my investigations into the possibilities of the operatic form, but also, at the same time, the possibilities of composing concert music, specifically chamber music. This allowed me to keep my close and wholly personal relationship to music, while, working on opera projects, I had to force myself to broaden my horizons with external influences and collaborations—even if the long hours spent at my table meant equally solitary work for both endeavors.

The *Adriana Mater* team was obvious: the libretto could only be written by Amin Maalouf, and Peter Sellars, to whom I dedicated the opera, was present from the project's start. I had looked for a subject and musical material that would be as different as possible from those for *L'Amour de loin*. As a starting point I suggested to Amin that we construct a story connected to the question of motherhood; I told him about how strong the experience had been for me when I was pregnant with my first child, the feeling of two hearts beating in my body. Amin, in turn, introduced a motif that was just as crucial to him on a personal level: war and its inherent violence.

Musically, I imagined an expression that would be gloomier and heavier than the ethereal orchestration of *L'Amour de loin*, and I wanted to use types of voices that were new to me, such as a tenor. For the protagonist, Adriana, I decided on a deep mezzo-soprano voice. Contrary to *L'Amour de loin*, in which the two female characters had been written for Dawn Upshaw and Lorraine Hunt (who unfortunately hadn't been able to perform the role, due to chronic illness), none of the roles in *Adriana Mater* were written for particular singers. I also wanted to start with a clean slate after my previous experience, and imagine the characters without constantly thinking of this or that singer's voice.

Adriana Mater's synopsis was dreamed up by Amin, who wrote the following summary:

> *Adriana Mater* takes place in a country at war. It has no name, but strongly echoes some region of the Balkans or elsewhere at the end of the twentieth century. Adriana, a passionate young woman, is the victim of a rape: she is pregnant, but refuses to have an abortion. "The child is mine, not the rapist's," she says to

her sister. It's also to reassure herself: this being will be born with two bloodlines: the victim's, and the torturer's. "Will he be Cain or Abel?" Adriana wonders. As an adult, her son Yonas learns that his progenitor, who fled the country at the end of the war, has come back. He promises to kill him, but cannot steel himself to do so. "This man deserves to die, but you, my son, you don't deserve to kill him," Adriana tells him. *Adriana Mater* asks the eternal questions about the human condition: can you give life during war? Should you always forgive? Is forgiveness cowardice or courage?

Even if this libretto seemed to be diametrically opposed to the almost mythic narrative of *L'Amour de loin*, which was anchored in the past, the two stories had much in common, in particular the interplay of archetypal situations and emotions that humanity has always had to confront. It's also important for me to create rich characters, each being a mélange of personality traits, various thoughts and feelings, both good and bad, that drive their sometimes-ambiguous actions. It seemed critical to try in this opera to illuminate from within (as George Tsypin's décor, filled with James F. Ingalls's lights, literally did) the infinitely complex intricacies of the familial and personal relationships we are enmeshed in, relationships which often drive inexorably toward outbursts of violence.

Structurally, *Adriana Mater* is composed of two hour-long acts, in which the events are separated by a seventeen-year gap. While conceptualizing and developing the musical material, the idea of having the characters— as well as their respective musical styles—transform over time became a central focus. The nature and degree of that transformation of course depended on what the characters had gone through in the time gone by. As such, the man/father Tsargo's music transforms radically, reflecting the change he undergoes from being a young, uncertain man who was a violent and impulsive soldier to being a broken wreck of a man, blind and eaten away by remorse. The other elements, in contrast, changed less dramatically, such as the relationship between Adriana's music and her sister's. However, a new character's arrival in the second act (Yonas, Adriana's son) affects the two tempos. The idea of two hearts and their polyphonic rhythm was one of the first thoughts I had incorporated into this opera, and so it naturally became an omnipresent musical element. The different relationships between various characters' rhythms and tempos were always in my mind. I sketched them out early on and used them as precise matrices.

Just as in *L'Amour de loin*, the four characters of *Adriana Mater* live through their own material. Adriana's orchestration is moody and dramatic, very rich on a harmonic level. The sister, Refka, has a diminished harmonic texture, but a greater range. Whereas Adriana often sings at the apex of her range, Refka's vocal part is written in the middle of the orchestration, between the high and low instrumental lines. Tsargo's music is rhythmical, grayer in its timbre than the others, and his vocal line is often followed by shadows cast by the deep strings. Yonas's light and energetic music, colored by trumpets, illuminates and softens the second act.

I began the work of composing the opera in fall 2002, and the opera was finished at the end of winter 2005. During this time we also recruited the singers. Finally, Esa-Pekka Salonen confirmed that he would participate as conductor. The rehearsals began a year later, in February 2006, at the Bastille Opera.

The rehearsal period for *Adriana Mater* was laborious and culminated in a canceled premiere, due to a last-minute technicians' strike at the Opera. The singers were already in their greenrooms and people from around the world were waiting in front of the building. More than one hundred twenty foreign journalists had to pack up and leave, as most of them couldn't stay for later performances. I watched the distraught crowd in shock and bewilderment through the windows of the bus that was driving me to what was supposed to be the first production of my opera, and consoled myself by saying that, contrary to what I was feeling right then, this wasn't the worst thing that could happen to a composer. So I thought of worse things while peering at the compact crowd that was waiting in vain, and thought about the death of Janáček's daughter and the way he had inscribed her last words and their melody on a musical staff...

IV. *LA PASSION DE SIMONE*

In 2004, while I was still hard at work composing *Adriana Mater*, a job that would take almost three years to finish, Peter Sellars suggested another project, which had grown out of several discussions since the performances of *L'Amour de loin* in Salzburg. Peter often deepened our reflections on opera by reading from texts by the philosopher Simone Weil, who had special standing in my eyes—so much so that *Gravity and Grace* was the only non-musical book I had taken with me upon leaving for Germany in 1981 to continue my studies in composition. When I asked Peter what had driven him to Weil, he told me that he suspected Amin Maalouf of having taken inspiration from her work while writing the libretto. When I broached the subject with Amin, he claimed not to know Simone Weil nor her writings, but he grew interested after our conversation.

Peter approached me with the idea of a work about Simone Weil for his New Crowned Hope Festival at Vienna. Adriana Mater was finished on Wednesday, March 2, 2005, and I began composing *La Passion de Simone* the next Saturday. Oddly, going back to work wasn't difficult. Simone Weil's world was very familiar to me, and I was delighted to be writing once more for Dawn Upshaw. The work was finished nearly a year later, just before the rehearsals began for *Adriana Mater*.

It was also important for me to focus on a concert work that wasn't theatrical, because I was utterly fixated on composing an opera when the foundations of this new project were established; the idea of switching immediately to a new work for stage seemed unbearable (the two works were first produced in 2006). However, according to Peter, this new opus had to take place in some kind of theatrical space, and so he suggested integrating a dancer. At first, I protested against a dancer being present, because it was very important to me that the soprano be alone on stage, in an atmosphere that was as abstract as possible. Maybe I was also unconsciously recalling my old dream of a pure combination of a soprano and some light effects. During the entire composition process, *La Passion de Simone* assumed the form of a concert that would to function musically without the element of a stage performance. Even though the subject was Simone Weil, the soloist wasn't her, but rather was addressing her. Quotations from Weil's writings were prerecorded, and I tried to place the speakers as closely as possible to the audience, as if her thoughts had come out of our own mind.

The form and content of the piece were sketched out after a now-customary meeting with Amin and Peter. Each of us had a particular point of view on Simone Weil's life and work. Peter specifically underlined her social activism and compassion for the disadvantaged, while Amin was intrigued by various biographical elements, and I was fascinated by the fervor and thoroughness with which Simone Weil had searched for truth, as a philosopher, as a mathematician, and as a writer. Each of these visions found a place in the libretto.

As always happens with me, the earliest real progress was made by searching for a formal solution, which was also the fruit of these collective brainstorms. Simone Weil compared her life to that of Jesus, her true idol. Over the course of our conversation the dramatic genre of the Passion Play came up, with the *Via Dolorosa* and the sequence of places connected with events leading up to the death of Jesus. After having compared Simone's life to the Fourteen Stations of the Cross, we connected each to different themes that we felt were relevant. Based on this idea, Amin finally wrote a libretto in fifteen stations, each station representing both a distinct aspect of Weil and another step in a linear progression. Here is how Amin presented the subject and the synopsis:

> At thirty-four years old, between Christ's age and Mozart's, a young girl chose to leave this world. It was in August 1943, and mankind had just reached the apex of barbarism. Simone Weil went out noiselessly, as if in silent protest, in the anonymity of a British hospital. What her voluntary death tells us is that she refused all forms of slavery: those of violence and hate, those of Nazism and Stalinism, but also those of a dehumanizing industrial society that empties beings of their substance and pushes them toward nothingness. Simone's writings, most of which were published after her death, are specifically an attempt to find a way out of nothingness. Her passion is a compass, simple but powerful, for our wayward world.
>
> *La Passion de Simone* is a musical path in fifteen stations, which cross her life and her work. On stage, a woman—Dawn Upshaw—is speaking to Simone and describes her course with a tenderness that still permits reproach; in voiceover, Simone Weil's own phrases are recited—by Dominique Blanc—in the rhythm of her writing; in addition to these two voices is a choir which is often used as an echo, but which, at other moments, doesn't hesitate to transcend its role and become a third character.

La Passion de Simone's *dramatis personae* consisted of a solo soprano, a choir, an orchestra, and an electronic component (the actress Dominique Blanc reading Weil's texts) that constantly fluctuated. I asked Amin to create a minimalist libretto where the texts would be sung in parts by the choir, in parts by the soloist, and would stretch out to different lengths. It seemed important, after *Adriana Mater*, to delimit the textual material, mostly to put the focus on the music, but also to constrain the piece's length, given that the demands of the text would rest almost entirely on a single singer. After receiving the definitive text, I sketched the fifteen parts of the piece to assign each of them an appropriate tone and to decide how they should be composed. The orchestra is indeed present in every part, with a different role in each one, while the soloist (*chant*), the choir (*chœur*), and the recording (*electro.*) aren't necessarily present from one part to the next.

I *molto espr., passionato*	chant		électro.	*(attacca)*
II *doloroso*	chant	chœur		
III *molto intenso*	chant		électro.	
IV *espressivo*	chant			
V *molto energico*	chant	chœur		*(attacca)*
VI *con violenza (tutti) ff*		chœur	électro.	
VII *più calmo, ma intenso*	chant	chœur		
VIII *lento, misterioso*	chant		électro.	
IX *passionato, doloroso*	chant	chœur		
X *intenso, meno mosso*	chant	chœur	électro.	
XI *più mosso, passionato*	chant		électro.	
XII *intenso*		chœur	électro.	
XIII *lento, dolce*	chant	chœur	électro.	
XIV *calmo*	chant		électro.	
XV *tutti, molto espr.*	chant	chœur	électro.	

La Passion de Simone quivers through the opposition of orchestral textures; its fringes are at one end ethereal and fluid, and at the other consist of variations on a rhythmic ostinato that feels more abstruse and moody. The relationship between the soloist and the orchestra modulates throughout the oratorio, and the choral part consists almost wholly of a self-contained text—in contrast to my other operas, where the text is often used as a vocal extension of the orchestra, a sort of bridge between the orchestra and the soloists. In this work, it's only in the fifth part that the choir joins in the din of a factory suggested by the orchestra.

During the opera's first production in Vienna in fall 2006, it was ultimately Pia Freund, and not Dawn Upshaw (who had fallen ill), who took on—brilliantly—the soloist's role. Susanna Mälkki directed the Klangforum Wien orchestra and the Arnold Schönberg choir. Peter Sellars's mysterious staging included an angelic character, as fleeting as a shadow, who was performed by the dancer Michael Schumacher, and who added a new dimension—now integral to the piece to the point that it has only once to date, in 2010, been performed as a concert. The solution that was finally used—stage positioning that could be adapted depending on the concert hall—certainly seemed to be the best one. The subsequent performances were done alternately by Pia and Dawn, and new adjustments to the setup on stage were made according to the location.

V. Émilie

My most recent opera was performed just a few months before I started writing this text, and I worry that the dust of the premiere still hasn't completely settled; the mental image I have of this experience is too fragmented and emotionally charged for me to analyze it—it's too early to assess it.

As with all my opera projects, Émilie is the fruit of several years of thought. The idea of writing a monodrama for Karita Mattila and the 2001 Aix-en-Provence Festival was originally Stéphane Lissner's. Even though the premiere didn't happen then, the seeds had been planted. A few ideas had already been scribbled down with Amin Maalouf, under the provisional title Elsa, la Nuit. Several years went by as I composed Adriana Mater and La Passion de Simone, as well as a lyrical cycle for Karita Mattila titled Quatre Instants. This was our first collaboration, and Karita's incredible intensity inspired me from the compositional work all the way through to the last performance.

Most of my works, including instrumental music, have been composed for specific musicians, whose imprints are evident on the pieces they perform, even if others perform these same works later. Émilie was composed especially for Karita Mattila, whom I'd had in mind during the entire process of composition, both in terms of music and in terms of the stage. I'd kept an eye on Karita over the years, and I'd seen her in numerous and varied roles. Her performances always seemed convincing to me, whether she played Janáček's Jenůfa or Strauss's Arabella. Karita is a natural artist who demands the very best of herself. She constantly plunges the depths of her roles and brings them fully to life. Every concert, every theatrical appearance of Karita's is a singular experience.

Coming back by train to London, where I had gone expressly to see and hear Karita on stage—this time as Fidelo in Jürgen Flimm's acclaimed version at Covent Garden—I wondered if I could find a female character who possessed enough strength and who would give her enough material to work with as an actress. And I thought of Émilie du Châtelet, whom I'd learned about in a book by Élisabeth Badinter. I was most interested in du Châtelet as a female scientist ahead of her time; I was also intrigued by her stubbornness and her extraordinary life. I realized that this character would be a tailor-made role for Karita, and a stimulating challenge. In the meantime, the idea of an opera for Karita cropped up again when the head of the Opéra de Lyon, Serge Dorny, made a point of reviving the project and taking it under his wing. I brought up my thoughts about the subject with several members of the group: Karita, Amin, and François Girard, the director suggested by Dorny. They were all enthusiastic, and Amin suggested, after having read through Émilie's letters, creating a libretto in an epistolary style; in the last months of her life, Émilie wrote many letters to her lover Saint-Lambert, whose child she was carrying.

The endeavor of a monodrama was somewhat extreme, but in this way it suited Karita. My first idea was even more radical: I imagined Karita alone on stage, accompanied solely by a digitally-controlled soundscape, and something visual along the lines of a video or a film. However, this seemed too ambitious for a single singer, even Karita, because the piece would last at least an hour.

The opera was broken up into nine sections, each of which illuminated a different conflict within Émilie's tormented life as a scientist, a lover, a mother, and a spouse. In the program for the Opéra de Lyon's performance, Jean Spenlehauer gave the synopsis of *Émilie* as follows:

I. Premonitions
Monday, September 1st, 1749. Evening. Émilie begins writing a letter to Monsieur de Saint-Lambert, her lover, the father of the child she is carrying; the lover who, no matter what he said before, doesn't love her very much, doesn't love her anymore. Émilie has premonitions that keep coming back as she awaits her child; a premonition: "death, death, death."

II. Grave
She wonders: what will be inscribed on her gravestone? "Here lies Gabrielle-Émilie Le Tonnelier de Breteuil Marquise du Châtelet-Lomont..." or maybe simply "Here lies Émilie." She recalls Voltaire's words: "The divine, the sublime Émilie." Voltaire her lover; Voltaire and Émilie: "The poet and the surveyor."

III. Voltaire

Émilie addresses a bust of Voltaire. She looks back—in Voltaire's language and in Newton's language—on their ten years in an intense romantic and intellectual relationship: "Ten years for us to love and theorize"; then her cooling toward him, her amorous feelings transmuting into amiability.

IV. Rays

In front of her library, Émilie conjures up her passion for science, which she loves "furiously"; the nature of the sun, and of color and light; physics, optics, astronomy, algebra, metaphysics; literature and languages. The Aeneid and Dido's anguish, Alexander Pope's *Essay on Man*.

V. Meeting

She goes back to writing the letter to Monsieur de Saint-Lambert. She remembers their meeting, her passion for him when she was already past thirty . . . "And I loved you, I loved you furiously. I've never learned to love any other way."

VI. Fire

Émilie sets down her pen. In confusion, she speaks—in French and English—about fire and the fire that burns in her. She speaks to herself, to Saint-Lambert, to Voltaire. In her pregnant, female body, she feels trapped: "The closer I come to childbirth, the more I feel death coming."

VII. Child

Émilie addresses the soon-to-be-born child—maybe a girl—as well as her father, the Baron de Breteuil. She wishes for her child to have a father like her own, who teaches her about the world, who offers her the world, and who sings with her. She gives her child advice: take on passions, even at the cost of suffering, don't dwell on old things; don't have regrets. "I, I refuse to curse my delayed passion, even though it drags me toward nothingness."

VIII. Principia

Émilie goes back to her letter to Saint-Lambert. She tells him about her anguish at not being able to finish her translation of

Isaac Newton's book, *Philosophiae Naturalis Principia Mathematica*, to which she has devoted days and nights and the last of her strength. "But the most important thing is done. Soon, I will hold my book in my hands."

IX. AGAINST FORGETFULNESS
Émilie talks to herself, but also a bit to the others. The book will appear, even posthumously. In the end, death conquers all. "But let me finish my book, so I will be remembered." Émilie dreads disappearing, "with book and child," into the depths of oblivion...

Émilie's character particularly interests me because of her unusual intelligence, her feminine intuition, and her wild passion for men, games of chance, and finery, passions for which one might say she destroyed herself, since she died giving birth to the child conceived by her lover—a pregnancy too late in her life (she was forty-three years old). I intended to create a portrait reflecting these apparent contradictions, like a set of photos taken from different points of view, which despite their dissonance merged into a singular portrait in the minds of the audience.

In the operatic tradition, the woman is typically presented as an object of love, or as its suffering and betrayed victim. As a woman, I of course wanted to present a different perspective, though I wasn't interested in a risqué and almost excessively realistic confession by a woman (nor by a man, for that matter). Nor was I interested in any sensational revelations seen from a female point of view or shattering all forms of gentle intimacy.

In the western world, stories are often told in a linear way about a fight between good and evil, without much of a gray area. Whenever I depict human beings and their feelings in my operas, I simply try to show the nuances of these beings and these feelings as everyday experience. As I often invoke frontiers metaphorically, as I do the space between shadow and light, I'm interested in the nuances of the human spirit, these often-narrow boundaries that divide different feelings from one another.

For this reason, the drama I seek in my operas is rooted less in external events than in the internal dynamics of the characters. *Émilie* is the most extreme manifestation of this search, because the entire opera centers on Émilie's thoughts; although she's sitting at her work table at the beginning of the piece, busy writing a letter, the place doesn't matter. In that sense, my first impulse toward an ethereal electronic accompaniment and a wholly filmic décor wasn't lacking in logic. François Girard, despite being a filmmaker first and foremost, or perhaps for exactly that reason, somehow wasn't interested in using such a machine in his staging; with his decorator, François Seguin, he dreamed up a wholly different stage design based on astrolabes from Émilie's era.

I have gradually grown accustomed to the fact that directors wouldn't follow my ideas about the visuals to the letter, and I accepted it, believing them to be professionals in their fields. How would I respond if a director gave me instructions about the music? The idea of bringing together film and opera was something I'd dreamed about since *L'Amour de loin*. For that matter, in the eight versions of the opera that have been performed to this point, two have abandoned the stage directions in favor of this technology. Jean-Baptiste Barrière, with whom I had produced several "visual concerts," most frequently around my chamber-music pieces, thought up the first of those installations; it was performed first in Berlin, and then at the Théâtre du Châtelet in 2006. This video sought to be an extension of the orchestral material by using colors, textures, and abstract motifs as well as occasional images of singers being filmed in real time. It was the most beautiful performance of that opera in concert version, the image continuous and seamless with the music. The second video/ film version was made by the artists Elmgreen and Dragset. This time it was an animated film, but it was also to be projected concurrently with the concert version of the opera. The premiere was in 2008 at the Bergen International Festival in Norway.

I imagined that in *L'Amour de loin* the video could increase the feeling of spatial breadth and depth, whereas in *Émilie* it could have accentuated the intimacy of the work. The singer's voice was amplified whenever she whispered, a feeling of proximity which I intended to be similar to that created by a close-up in cinema.

Even if my opera scores don't consist of any thoughts that aren't musical, nonmusical influences certainly affect the compositional process. For instance, the visual and symbolic space I imagined for *L'Amour de loin*, the warm and cool colors, and the smell of exotic spices, had a direct impact on the orchestration. In the case of *Adriana Mater*, I had in mind a psychological space, the characters' interactions, and the development of their relationships; the pattern of different tempi, of various heartbeats and their polyphonic superimposition, gave shape to this space. In *Émilie*, the orchestra had to be completely subordinated to the singer's breathing, yet remain an extension of her, a reflection of her thoughts and her emotions.

The score for *Émilie* is written for a small orchestra, which specifically requires an amplified harpsichord. At times, the soloist's voice has to be modulated in real time. The orchestra represents Émilie's mental landscape, and its components vary according to the topic at hand. The harpsichord's nervous ostinato accompanies her anxieties; the orchestra, colored by microtones, opens out onto new and expansive territory as Émilie discourses on the properties of light rays or the nature of fire. The child's motif, which echoes a music box, is associated with memories of Scarlatti's harpsichord pieces, which I've always loved.

Émilie has often been compared to Schönberg's *Erwartung* and Cocteau and Poulenc's *La Voix humaine,* for the sole reason that each features a woman singing on stage alone. In the same way, *L'Amour de loin* has often drawn parallels to *Tristan und Isolde* or *Pelléas et Mélisande.* With *Adriana Mater,* everybody seems to assume Janáček's operas as models. Such comparisons are certainly useful for listeners, but seem vague to me. My productions bear traces of all the music that has struck me, and the masterpieces I've mentioned are included among many others. But every time I undertake the composition of a new opera, I have in front of me a blank page, which historical models won't help me to fill. Of course, every creative gesture is conditioned by a particular relationship with tradition, by an openness to influence or a categorical refusal thereof, by erudition or ignorance, and anybody can certainly compare their first opera to other works in the same genre. However, I see my last operas more clearly through the prism of my first attempt. And it's the same for the other forms: my first concerto, *Graal théâtre,* was extremely difficult to write, specifically because of the weight of tradition. The ensuing concertos had the first one as a point of departure, and I felt far freer in composing them. It reminds me of the relationship parents have with their oldest child— and adults in general—in contrast to their relationships with subsequent children, who immediately benefit from the space their older sibling has carved out and the lessons their parents have learned about the ways a child can be!

Am I interested in composing an opera again, or even a few more? At this precise moment, I don't know. In any case, I don't feel any pressing need to accept the proposals opera houses have been making. All of my projects are born out of meetings and have grown over many years in my mind before being set down on paper, and then staged. Sometimes I feel an urge to write an opera in Finnish. Sometimes I imagine an operatic form composed of many small roles, in a manner diametrically opposed to my previous operas. Sometimes I'm overcome by the desire to return to my first ideas of abstract light-operas. We'll see…

A Conversation with Kaija Saariaho[1]

Clément Mao-Takacs

Translated from the French by Sophie Weiner

CLÉMENT MAO-TAKACS: *I would like to begin by clearing up a few clichés that seem to have attached themselves to you and your music. To name a few: You're from Finland, therefore, you love and are inspired by nature; you are "a fiery volcano beneath ice"; since you live primarily in France, you inevitably subscribe to French music. Can we try to make sense of some of these preconceptions? Let's start with the nature-Finland parallel.*

KAIJA SAARIAHO: I think there is some truth to the connection between nature and Finland. The country's population is so small and nature's presence there is so pronounced, it's impossible to lead the kind of urban life you can in a big capital—even though some people try desperately to pretend that they do. Nature is one thing, but what's more important is light. Changes in sunlight throughout the year are so drastic that they affect everyone. You can't escape its influence. And because of this experience— which is so physical, we feel it in our body—we, as individuals, have a very special relationship with nature. We have respect for it, we are aware that it's something larger than us; further, its influence is part of our broader culture and can be found, for instance, in Finnish epic poems, where nature is truly sacred, which was the case for many early cultures. For me, its importance comes from the experience of living in the "period of darkness"—there's a very specific term for this in Finnish: *kaamos*—all the while retaining hope that the sunlight will start strengthening again until it is fully restored. Springtime is extremely long, and since the earth has been covered in snow for such an extensive period, there's a kind of rotting—though pleasant—smell, which gradually gives way to spring vegetation. My relationship to nature isn't about admiring the aesthetics of a sunset; it's something much more physical that I carry inside me.

I get the impression that you're interested in light as a phenomenon as well as a source of inspiration. Reading the titles of your works and the indicators you use (luminous, translucent, brilliant, sparkling, bright, etc.)—usually disguised as tempo markings—it feels as though light has a very important place in your imagination, though not in the tone-painting way, as it is in Bach or Wagner, where light is symbolic.

I think that's just how my mind works. I don't actually try to find metaphors; they come naturally. It's true that I'm very sensitive to light and that I'm inspired by it. Sometimes I genuinely do think about orchestra in terms of light. When I picture certain orchestrations, I make instant connections with light. I feel like the senses are mixed together, but I'm not interested in analyzing why or how that may be. What matters most is that it works and that it inspires me. At any rate, for a long time, I've believed that the senses are not compartmentalized, but are in fact far more connected than we realize.

Interestingly enough, nature and light are elements that are often associated with French music—with Debussy, Grisey, and Messiaen, for instance. And you've become connected to French music in several ways: you've lived in Paris for many years, you've worked at IRCAM (the Institute for Research and Coordination in Acoustics/Music), your pieces contain some elements connected to the French spectral approach; plus, the affinity between your music and Debussy's, Ravel's, and Messiaen's is so strong that almost every conductor interviewed about your work has pointed it out.

It is interesting how everyone's said that! Because, of course, I very much admire the music of Debussy and Ravel, who are so different from each other. When I was younger, I was really drawn to Debussy because his music is so fluid in form, and yet, so difficult to analyze. His fantastic ear has created things that move me on a very personal level. But he's not the only composer I love…

Messiaen, for instance?

Messiaen, of course…

Your thoughts on Debussy are perhaps a subtler key to this underlying connection, and the same can be said for some of Sibelius's pieces (beyond your shared nationality). There's a search for organic solutions where form and material aren't two distinct elements, but are in fact complementary and inseparable, even from the start of the piece's creation. In fact, your music cannot be analyzed using classic criteria (many works are neither in sonata nor rondo form, and variational form only appears to a certain extent), since their process is very much metamorphic.

Yes, from the very beginning, my work has sought to unify material and form. I don't know why, but I feel like I have to reinvent the form for each new piece. The idea of taking a predefined form and saying, "Okay, let's write a sonata or compose something according to a classical, predefined form"—it's just not possible with my music. It can't survive like that; it would be dead before it was even born! Every piece of music must live its own life because each one is utterly its own. Of course, from one work to another, I might come up with similar solutions in form, given that it's my style. But I either use them consciously, or sometimes I go against my intuition, because I feel like you have to open up the possibilities, try new things. But to come back to material and form, once again it's like the five senses—for me, there's a back-and-forth between thought and intuition when composing, which makes it impossible to separate the two.

It does sometimes feel as though, from one piece to another, you fixate on the same material until you've found different forms and solutions for it. This has created a sign of continuity—a kinship—between your works. Is this something that you do consciously?

It's both conscious and subconscious. I'm completely conscious about reusing a piece of material. When I'm writing a larger piece, I usually feel the need to attack it from different angles, and in some cases go through several revisions. Sometimes, it's simply because I love a work so much that I don't wish to let it go...but this can also be a challenge. I'll create something with certain material in a certain format and then I'll try to do something else with it because I feel as though I haven't explored or realized the material's full potential. In these instances, I think it's really interesting to work within limits and constraints. When I reuse material, I set limits on my possibilities, and this can be very inspiring because it forces me to go in new directions. First, there's whatever comes naturally, then I have to come up with something else.

Though in no way repetitive, your music often uses forms of repetition, iteration, rhythmic figure, or reoccurring melodies that create a quasi-ritualistic dimension. Your music is comfortable with what you could call a kind of prayer or incantation—I'm thinking particularly of L'Amour de loin, Château de l'âme, *and* La Passion de Simone. *I don't necessarily mean in a Judeo-Christian way, but in the shamanistic sense.*

Yes, that's true. But I'm not a religious person. For me, music is a study of my own self and of the human spirit. I've always believed music to be very deep, or at least it can be very deep. It's like a liquid that can go into the depths, spread out in all directions, and take on various shapes. Words, on the other hand, are choppy and basic, and the grammar and understanding of sentences can just as easily serve as barriers. Music often speaks much more directly, both to the heart and mind. Certain harmonies are like smells that you recognize instantly. With music, you can have an intellectual perception, but also a sensitive and yet very profound understanding. Feelings and sensations are immediate. I don't think about all this as I'm composing because it's such a complex and absorbing activity. But through my music, I experience all those things. So I think that if I had a religion, it would be music, because I find it to be so rich, so universal, so profound.

You mentioned "words" just now. The human voice is very important to you, especially as a vehicle for texts. The words that you set to voice may come from poems or literature, and are sometimes reorganized (like a collage)… Could you say that you have a special fondness for voice as an instrument?

I have such an affinity for the human voice—and a personal predilection for texts! Everything I just said about music can be found in voice, and in an extreme way. In a sense, it's the richest form of expression because the instrument is inside a human being and there are many things that cannot be falsified when using your voice. Whether or not a work for voice originates from a text, it's necessarily a different mode of communication than instrumental music. Of course, using a text adds another layer of richness and meaning. I really love using voice, but it was difficult for me to write for it at first, probably because the historical context was difficult. I've always loved Berio, for instance, and what he did with voice, but I don't like music that imitates Berio—and at some point, it felt as though you could only write for voice in that way, you had to write that way. So it took time for me to find a certain freedom and my own way of writing for voice—and to accept it.

Your operas and some of your pieces are written in French, though you've also used German, English, and Finnish. Which language do you prefer to write in? Or is language simply a tool with its own characteristics?

Yes, it's a musical tool. Every language is different. I think my pieces are written in the languages that surround me. When I lived in Germany, I automatically gravitated toward German texts. Last year, during my stay in New York, naturally I used texts written in English. When a language is spoken around me, I think I'm influenced—maybe subconsciously—by that environment's particular sound. What I'm sure of is that each language encourages me to think about the orchestration, the different colors. But I think I'm going to stop writing in French. I've already written too much with it. I have to mix things up.

Everyone is aware of your interest in poetry, literature, fine arts, and cinematography. However, most people don't know that you have a diverse range of reading material—that you read Proust as well as scientific journals.

I have to admit that I read Proust in Finnish! It was one of the first translations of Proust published [into Finnish]. That translation was remarkable. Anyway, I didn't speak French at the time. Now I'll have to read it again in French to compare the two versions. But you're right about the diversity of what I read. I enjoy reading in different languages too. When I was little, I read a lot of Russian literature—which was normal at that time. Now I have access to so many books. What I look for above all else are ones with originality and ones that describe human experiences in a smart—but not necessarily formalistic—way.

Lots of creative people are introverts who live in their own inner world. Yet, like Mozart and Liszt, you travel a lot, you write about troubled individuals, such as Simone Weil and Émilie du Châtelet, and about painful subjects, including the rape of a young woman in Adriana Mater. *What is your relationship with today's world?*

At first, I spent a lot of time living inside my music. When I was little, my inner world was so strong that I couldn't really leave it. Little by little, I came out of my shell, but what I learned was that the world could be a very hurtful place, and music became a kind of refuge. It was only after becoming a parent that I established a true connection with the real world. It simply forced me to get out of myself. In France, I started living differently because there were all kinds of necessary social relationships. Over time, I started opening myself up, meeting people who weren't musicians, watching young people play my music... So I became more sensitive to the outside world. Maybe I've become stronger too. I think I had less of a need to seek refuge in my music and had more and more of a desire to see the world with my music. There are a lot of reasons for this, but one undeniable reason is Peter Sellars, whose artistic credo is to always engage in a dialogue with the contemporary world.

People frequently draw attention to the fact that you're a female composer. I remember a conversation we had in Helsinki in which you told me that, at the time, when speaking French, you preferred to use the word compositrice *[as opposed to the masculine* compositeur*]. Could you tell me a little more about this? Is there something particularly feminine about your process? Because there are indeed elements of your music that stem directly from your experiences as a woman.*

Throughout my entire life I've had to prove that I am, above all, a composer, and one who is as serious and as smart as any of my male colleagues. My music has been very successful, and I think it's despite the fact that I'm a woman, while my colleagues have thought it's clearly because I'm a woman! I've said to myself, "Fine, I'm a woman and I accept the fact that people say I'm a *compositrice*." But of course, this term doesn't work as eloquently in other languages as it does in French. In English, you'd have to say "woman composer," but you'd never say "man composer." So I don't consider myself a compositrice. It's more of a silly quip that makes people think.

As for my material emerging from my experience as a woman, that's just a point of departure. Once I begin composing, I transform it into pitch and rhythm. So whatever that experience is, it simply becomes an element of my work and not a personal story—that's all that matters. The material can come from our own lives, the lives around us, or wherever. But at some point, it simply becomes music. That's why my music is not descriptive. Of course, you can hear the beating hearts of Adriana and the son she is carrying [in Act 1 Scene 3 of *Adriana Mater*], but more than anything else, it's a rhythmic issue: how do I vary an unchangeable rhythm, how do I make it not tedious, how do I create a process that will distinguish the child's heartbeat, how do I make this transformation noticeable—these become questions of a purely technical and musical nature.

It's quite clear that this question of transformation—of a gradual process—is at the center of your studies. In your music, there are often spans that appear to be static on the surface but are actually innerly dynamic due to different variables—textures, for instance. And this metamorphosis occurs slowly, sometimes so slowly that we don't even notice until it's over. This was the case, if I'm not mistaken, for your study Vers le blanc, *and you could almost say it's a defining trait in your compositions.*

Certainly, even if there are more dramatic aspects to my music than there were twenty-five years ago. [Indicates a cup sitting on the table and its shadow on the wooden surface.] I'm definitely always intrigued and interested by the place where the shadow starts and ends. I've looked long and hard at it, but in reality, there is no exact spot. At what moment and how does this shadow disappear? It's as though I'm tempted to see just how far I can go without stopping the movement. It's connected to our perception of time. A composer—or *compositrice*—works with time; this assumes a specific awareness of the way in which we manipulate the listener's ear. And in my temptation to stop time, I have the irrational feeling that, if I succeed, time will become space and I'll be able to enter a secret realm where I've never been before. It's something along those lines. Once again, the physical parameters are muddled; it's like a secret invitation to find the celestial pattern that would contain the solution, which I know to be an impossible quest.

"You see, my son, time here becomes space." That's one of the most famous lines in Parsifal. *Connections can be made between your work and Wagner's, one of which is this interest in sound spatialization, which, with his work, may be hidden (in the orchestra or in Brangäne's voice) or in motion (the English horn solos in* Tannhäuser *and* Tristan*); and in your work, it's found, for instance, in the chorus in* Adriana Mater *or in the use of electronics.*

I am interested in spatialization, but under the condition that it's not applied gratuitously. It has to be necessary—in the same way that material and form must be linked together organically. Truthfully, I don't really like it when musicians move around the room because most of the time it's unnecessary or distracting. I was really surprised that it worked so well at the end of my clarinet concerto. Actually, what matters most for me is the acoustics of the venue. I don't know if there's a connection with Wagner—not an intentional one, at any rate—even though I do love certain works of his.

Misterioso is a term that appears regularly in your scores. When Peter Sellars talks about you and your music, he also uses the term mystery. *As for me, I'm reminded of paintings by Khnopff, which are so packed with meaning yet remain so mysterious, and so similar to your world. Why the fascination with mystery and the repetitive use of the word* misterioso?

Evidently, there's an aspect of my music that's mysterious, but when I use the word *misterioso*, it's mostly intended as a message for the musicians. I feel like musicians create sound differently when I give the indication *misterioso*—they're more focused and involved. In contemporary music, interpretation is often very unemotional and I've always wanted to do the opposite, to reawaken the interpreters by inviting their feelings and sensations; that's why I use words like *misterioso, dolce, con violenza*, and so on. When I was younger, lots of people teased me for using *con ultima violenza*, but it was precisely because I wasn't able to find the level of commitment that I wanted from my musicians.

Could you talk about the way in which you compose? I get the impression that, no matter what, you're at your workspace everyday. Is writing music a daily necessity?

I'm very happy when I write on a daily basis. Of course, so many things are going on in my everyday life that it's a nearly impossible feat. But that's my goal. When I'm able to establish this kind of regular work routine, I'm very happy. But in the end, it's a pretty rare occurrence, and when you mentioned Mozart and Liszt earlier, who worked while traveling, it's important to point out that they had good reason for doing so—they were also performers who played and conducted their own music. That's not the case for me. I only travel to attend rehearsals and concerts, which is both frustrating and gratifying. I want to do it, and I have to do it, but every time it means I'm leaving my workspace and interrupting my process.

Isn't it also frustrating because, even for composers who are as successful as yourself, rehearsal time is awfully short and you're given very little opportunity to provide feedback?

Certainly. Sometimes it feels as though I'm traveling to the other side of the globe to hear *Le Sacre du Printemps* rehearsed, when I'm in fact attending the world premiere of a work that will only be read two or three times before its performance during the same concert.

You've been prolific as a composer, and always have new projects coming up. Can you talk to us about that? How do you envision your future? And what's your take on your productivity and musical evolution?

I have many projects lined up through 2020. We can never predict what tomorrow has in store for us. I always allow enough time for a project to mature, so that's why I really like having projects for the somewhat distant future. All of my projects, even the smaller works, have taken time and have required a period of maturation. I don't look back very often and I'm not interested in arriving at intellectual conclusions about how my music has evolved over the years. It has evolved with me; I've had a lot of experiences that changed me and, as a result, my music changed. What's important to me is to always be writing music in the present while envisioning the future.

If you had to define yourself, how would you do it with words and not with music? Who are you, Kaija Saariaho?

That's a very difficult question...I'm someone who has always lived deeply through my feelings, someone with great sensitivity and an inner imagination—especially for music. I'm a composer with a lot of technique and experience, but I feel very humble because I am not a musician or a performer; sometimes, I'm really amazed by the music that's created from within me... In the end, it's all very *misterioso*...

Could you tell us more about this new chamber version of La Passion de Simone*?*

I created this new version on the proposal of young artists from La Chambre aux échos. As I was thinking about it, I realized that it was a very good idea, and I was tempted to see how it could work. I had already realized some reductions of my other works, and I knew it could work well. To convert a large orchestra into an ensemble of nineteen musicians means that the piece will be more focused on the individual energy of each musician, because everybody plays an important role, and has to be a very active part of the work.

The best surprise came from the modification of the choir into four individual singers: it was not obvious, but the result was good, especially in this version proposed by La Chambre aux échos, which is a stage version. I do mean "stage version," but not in an usual operatic treatment: the orchestra was not in the pit, the chorus far at the bottom of the stage, and the solo singer in front of the audience! Everybody was on stage; all of the movements, the gestures, which is to say, all of the "action" was led by the music, and even the musicians were sometimes moving on stage, or standing up for a solo. It was very organic.

Another important thing: in the original version, there is an electronic part, which mostly consists in some sentences by Simone Weil, recorded by the French actress Dominique Blanc. It was like a ghost-voice, without body, that summoned the words by Simone Weil and created a kind of balance between the live musicians and singers. But in the chamber version, upon suggestion from the company's artistic team, I gave up on electronics altogether, so it seemed a natural choice to incorporate a live actress instead of a tape. I was very happy with this solution, which brought more humanity and emotion to the performance. This actress is of course not acting as Simone Weil (neither is the soprano soloist), but one more human presence on stage, a part of this collective ritual between live people addressing their culture and their past.

You have had a few premieres recently: Sombre *(for bass flute, baritone's voice, percussion, harp, and double bass);* Maan varjot (Earth's Shadow) *for organ and orchestra; and you are working on* Only the Sound Remains, *a musical theater piece inspired by the Noh plays. Let's discuss these new items in your production, which are—as has been the case so often in the past—inspired by painting or poetry.*

When Sarah Rothenberg proposed that I write a piece for the Da Camera ensemble, to be premiered at the Rothko Chapel in Houston, a space entirely dedicated to some of the late works of Mark Rothko—an artist

whose catalog I have felt close to for a long time—I immediately began
to imagine a dark instrumentation that, I believed, matched the paintings
in the chapel. The color of the bass flute sound became a center of this
palette; it had in my mind a close connection to Rothko's work. The
title *Sombre* appeared naturally from the character of the instrumentation,
of the texts, and above all, of these last paintings by Mark Rothko. I also
wanted to include a baritone voice in the ensemble and began to look for
texts.

During my residency at Carnegie Hall, I read more English and
American poetry, and there I came across Ezra Pound's final *cantos*, or,
more precisely, fragments of them. Their minimal form as well as their
heartbreaking content seemed to suit this piece perfectly, and the language
(English) helped me to renew my vocal conventions: I was able to explore
new paths in my vocal writing.

Your new lyrical project, Only the Sound Remains, *is also based on texts
translated and adapted by Ezra Pound.*

As usual, one thing often leads to another. Soon after reading Ezra Pound's
poems and adapting them, Peter Sellars proposed a work on two classical
Noh plays adapted by Pound in collaboration with the translator Ernest
Fenollosa.

My creation of a version of *La Passion de Simone* for chamber orchestra
also influenced this new project, because it consists of a vocal ensemble of
four voices, instrumentation for only seven instruments, and electronics.
The main character will be a countertenor, and we will collaborate with
the French singer Philippe Jaroussky. I already finished the first part of
this work—"Tsunemasa." This project is co-commissioned by three Opera
Houses—Amsterdam, Paris, and Toronto.

*In fact, in the same way English language renewed your vocal writing, using
the bass flute renewed your approach to the flute, an instrument you know quite
well, and for which you had already composed so many pieces—most notably,
a concerto. Perhaps you've entered a new period, with new colors suggested by
new instruments, such as the bass flute* (Sombre), *organ* (Maan varjot), *and the
kantele* (Only the Sound Remains).

Sombre is not a concerto, but rather a chamber music piece with a very important solo part for bass flute, which is an instrument rich in effects. I felt I was breaking new limits of my own world with this piece. Also, I have been wanting to explore the bass flute more deeply for a long time with Camilla Hoitenga, for whom it was written.

With *Maan varjot*, which is, once again in my opinion, more a work with a prominent solo organ part than a concerto, I was pleased to write for organ, because it has long been an important instrument for me. I enjoy listening to the organ—the repertoire of organ music is so extensive, from Bach to the present—because it was my instrument before I became a full-time composition student. I felt very comfortable, since you could play it and still remain hidden to the audience! My relation to this instrument can also explain the use of a Finnish title for the work.

But despite my intimate relationship to and affection for it, I haven't written much music for organ. For *Maan varjot*, I was attracted by its richness, its polyphonic tradition. Organ is a powerful instrument (from *ppppp* to *fffff*). I like its ability to produce rich and very precise textures that are in turn controlled by a single musician. I also like its long sustained notes, which are free of the constraints of breathing or the length of a bow. Registration is also a kind of orchestration; you can obtain so many various colors and mix them with the orchestras. The organ part in this work is very graphic, and as every organ is different, the part sounds different with every performance. To realize the registrations with Olivier Latry, who has performed the organ part so far, has been greatly inspiring. I learn enormously from the musicians I collaborate with!

As for kantele, it's rather different: it's a traditional Finnish instrument, and many contemporary composers have written for it, searching for new manners of playing, mixing it with electronics...but I had never wrote for kantele before. Two things led me to include it in the ensemble for *Only the Sound Remains*. In my third opera, *Émilie*, I added a harpsichord to the ensemble and it brought a special flavor to the identity and instrumental colors of the work. It was inspiring to use it with amplification and electronics. So I wanted to continue this experience with kantele, to explore it more extensively. Also, kantele may be considered a Finnish version of the Japanese koto. Last summer in Finland I started to work on the instrument with a prominent kantele artist, Eija Kankaanranta. She will also perform the part in the opera. Of course, the sound is fragile, but that's precisely a part of the beauty and charm of the instrument.

You've spent some long periods in recent years in the United States, particularly in New York City. Has the spirit of that city changed anything in your music?

Changing cultures can affect my work in a good way, and I feel that the time spent in New York has done so. Having lived most of the second part of my life in Paris, I enjoyed the welcoming spirit in New York. For example, even after all these years in France people start speaking English to me, as if to emphasize the fact that I am a foreigner or a second degree citizen, or that they do not understand my French—and perhaps they don't, since I have an accent… But in New York, because the city has always been a melting pot of emigrants, there are so many people speaking with different accents that it is not important. People are more focused on communicating, and you're not considered an outsider simply because of your origins. Sometimes, I come to think that the spirit of openness and richness of culture I experienced in Paris at the beginning of the eighties is now to be found in New York.

Conversations with Three Conductors

Clément Mao-Takacs, with Esa-Pekka Salonen, Ernest Martinez-Izquierdo, and Susanna Mälkki[1]

Translated from the French by Sophie Weiner

Esa-Pekka Salonen[2]

CLÉMENT MAO-TAKACS: *Can you tell us about the form of Saariaho's orchestral pieces?*

ESA-PEKKA SALONEN: I don't think we can use the term "symphonic works" to describe Kaija's orchestral music.[3] I'd say that Kaija's formal method has very little to do with the dialectical method of German music and its logical development, as seen in Beethoven's work, for instance. Kaija's music is formed largely by processes that are hard to qualify verbally. The linguistic or visual concepts that inspire her are expressed through purely musical means, especially in pieces from her earlier period—*Lichtbogen*, for example. The principles of form concerning her later pieces are based more on the concept of metamorphosis. Metamorphosis is not variation. We might compare this to the life cycle of a butterfly and the variety of possibilities that may emerge from a cocoon. The same is true of Kaija's music: the intrinsic structure is exactly the same, but the results are unique. The frame for this metamorphosis is fixed. It's the empty space inside of this frame where something is created, but the space itself remains unchanged. Think of romantic paintings by Caspar David Friedrich, and the way in which he always depicts a witness—a spectator—in his landscapes. The content is formed by our observation of this spectator who is witnessing the landscape. We are forming a space that is regulated by a principle of immutability, and inside this space, things are created. We are forming a question.

What do you think about her orchestration and instrumentation?

[*Laughs.*] They're good! The main characteristic of Kaija's orchestration is that it doesn't have the appearance of an orchestration. Melody, harmony, texture, and color are all on the same plane. This is the same compositional principle that can be found in Debussy's music—starting with *La Mer*— and in Sibelius's work. It's impossible to consider the different levels of compositional work as distinct factors. When interpreting or listening to this kind of music, you don't think in terms of orchestration, but expression. You don't think to yourself, "Hey, this idea is orchestrated in such and such a way." It's the clear mark of an experienced composer to mask her art in this manner.

As for her instrumental writing, one thing in particular deserves to be said. While Kaija's music does not attempt to test an instrumentalist's technical limits, it does require musicians to feel—so to speak—certain mental limits. They have to maintain extreme concentration for long, static intervals. That's the strength and the danger of Kaija's music. There's no physical climax for the musician, so they have to find the energy to sustain tensions for long durations. This is rarely practiced in Western music, but much more typical of Asian music—Indian, for instance.

You have conducted several works by Saariaho. Do you think that genres or types of works influence her style of composing?

I think Kaija is an outstanding vocal composer. And it's because there's a certain intrinsic narrative quality to her music, whatever the genre may be. What's more, even the titles of her instrumental pieces evoke narrative ideas for anyone who interprets or listens to them.

In your opinion, what makes Saariaho's work unique in today's world of contemporary music?

One of the most difficult things for a composer to do is create their own syntax—a language that identifies them. It's something Saariaho has managed to do brilliantly. It only takes twenty seconds to recognize her music, which can also be said of Schubert and Berlioz. Creating a strong musical identity with a personal syntax and grammar may be her biggest achievement as a composer, or at least it's what separates her from other contemporary composers. And even if her language can be qualified as esoteric, or elusive at any rate, Kaija has a real audience that supports her and loves her music. This isn't a topic that is often discussed in contemporary music because it generally isn't something to brag about.

But it's no minor detail. After all, we have to ask ourselves: what's the point in doing all this if no one's going to hear our work? So that's another accomplishment of hers that deserves recognition.

Where do you place Saariaho within the history of Finnish and European music? Which composers do you like to conduct in tandem with hers and why?

I often play her music with that of Debussy and Ravel. That seems obvious to me—but also with Sibelius's work. However, I have no steadfast rules when it comes to pairing composers. It's like insisting this wine must go with this meal. In the end, it all depends on one's taste. As for determining her inspirations, I think it's too soon for that. We don't have enough perspective. We haven't seen all her cards yet.

What is your personal relationship with Saariaho's music? As a conductor and a composer, why do you like it and why do you enjoy conducting it?

It's interesting music for a conductor because it allows for considerable agogic freedom and even the freedom to reclaim it. Its rhetoric is flexible, not mechanical. Most music today, with its attempt to be arrhythmic, doesn't leave much of a place for conductors. Kaija's music, on the other hand, requires us to find a tempo and an ideal gestalt in every measure. This offers the conductor much more opportunity for self-expression than is often the case for most works by other contemporary composers.

As a composer myself, I have to admit that Kaija often finds interesting solutions in texture, especially for the strings. I've gleaned a few tips that I've used in my own work, even though they inevitably create different effects within the context of my music.

ERNEST MARTINEZ-IZQUIERDO[4]

CLÉMENT MAO-TAKACS: *Can you tell us about the form of Saariaho's orchestral pieces?*

ERNEST MARTINEZ-IZQUIERDO: I think it's difficult to make generalizations. I don't know if you can describe Kaija's music in "formalist" terms. Form is only perceived after a text is performed (this is especially true for operas, of course). You need context. When you play it or listen to it, you don't feel like there's a pre-existing, preconceived, entirely thought-out form; conversely, you feel a fluidity, a natural flow. It's hard to believe that her form is as much predefined as it is organic—the form seems to develop gradually before our eyes. I don't know, maybe her method of composing is the complete opposite—very thought-out and controlled—but this is just the impression I get from her music. Of course, there's an overall picture, but there's definitely no strict structure that's been conceived down to the smallest detail. In short, it has none of the negative and constricting aspects that you'd associate with the word "form."

What do you think about her orchestration and instrumentation?

What attracts me to Kaija's music is her poetry and the idiosyncratic language that she's developed over the years. This poetry clearly shines through all the instrumental colors, but is also expressed through a certain use of time. I find her music to be very dreamlike. It has a kind of magic that transports us into a far-off, suddenly accessible land. Her refined instrumentation and textures—all of it creates a rich universe that eludes all classification with its many different nuances. Her music is from another world. I can only approach it in a very sensitive and emotional way. A large portion of contemporary music is overly theoretical and lacks the sensuality and poetry found in Kaija's work. Not only that, but her music attracts much larger crowds than most music today. It's not only appreciated by so-called contemporary music audiences—more importantly, it's also enjoyed by people who don't necessarily have a musical background or theoretical and technical knowledge, but who are nonetheless capable of appreciating its refinement and sensuality.

You have conducted several works by Saariaho. Do you think that genres or types of works influence her style of composing?

I've been conducting her works from throughout her entire career, from the eighties to today, and in all forms—large orchestral pieces, concerti, operas, chamber music. When analyzing the evolution of her style, it's interesting to note that in *Lichtbogen*, even though the foundations of her very particular style are already there, her IRCAM education is still clearly evidenced through the piece's technical and structural complexity. Over time, Kaija's writing has become more fundamental (there are simply fewer notes). As for the notion of "genre," I'm not sure it really applies to her. Each piece is unique in its genre and Kaija's writing is quite fluid from this perspective.

I would also like to mention, more specifically, the success of her operas. They are proof that not only has Kaija found her own particular and multifaceted language, but she has also succeeded in reinventing a certain vocal quality—a natural vocality—that has been missing from operas ever since Berg and Schönberg. In many recent operas, singers' voices are treated like instruments, which leads to a loss of strength in the singer's idiomatic expression. Yet, Kaija writes beautifully for singers; her music doesn't wear the voice down, but nurtures it across fluid and natural vocal lines. That's why she's beloved by the public and singers alike. Her music doesn't overuse the singer's voice, thereby tiring out the listener's ear by the end of the song. Some people find it reactionary or conservative—but that's ridiculous. What really is conservative, is to continue to perpetuate a tradition that is proclaimed by those who consider themselves postmodern, or a tradition of post-Schönbergian, post-Lachenmannian vocality. What is truly modern is searching for a new and more individual vocality. Tonight, we are bringing *Émilie* to Lisbon, and the director of a Barcelona concert hall has made a deliberate point of coming. He's known for disliking contemporary music, but he's coming out of interest for Kaija's latest opera. Once again, this shows that her music knows how to incite desire and curiosity without compromising.

In your opinion, what makes Saariaho's work unique in today's world of contemporary music?

After a few seconds of Mahler or Strauss, you can identify the composer—that's the mark of a strong musical personality. It's the same for Kaija. She has an extraordinarily rich and imaginative mind. When I open up a new Saariaho score, I smile and think, "Okay, where is she taking me this time?" It's always an adventure. I never say, "Oh, I've already seen this somewhere," "she's repeating herself," or "this has been cut-and-pasted." Even though she's written so much and I know her music so well, she surprises me every time.

Where do you place Saariaho within the history of Finnish and European music? Which composers do you like to conduct in tandem with hers and why?

The easy answer is Sibelius, but I'd also say Strauss' *Eine Alpensinfonie*, or Brahms, whose orchestral textures have, in my opinion, the same misty feel and evoke for me that same Hanseatic haze. In February [2013], I'm going to try something a little less obvious—Schumann's Symphony No. 2 with Kaija's *D'Om le vrai sens*. Schumann is an equally unpredictable composer with an imagination that is often of another world.

Kaija is an independent figure who can't be pinned down to one school of thought, even though we could never imagine her without either Sibelius or electronic music, which has had a crucial influence on her remarkable sensibility for sounds—this can be heard in her instrumentation, and even in her purely acoustic pieces.

What is your personal relationship with Saariaho's music? As a conductor and a composer, why do you like it and why do you enjoy conducting it?

I ask myself this question all the time. Some people say Kaija's music is very feminine because of its sensitive and refined nature. But as far as I'm concerned, I'm not a very feminine person, so why do I feel so comfortable with it? I think this feminine label is too limiting for her music. It's actually the exact opposite: her music has incredible power and character. More importantly, she's able to create a strong contrast between one side that is truly dramatic and violent, and another side, which I call "cosmic bits." These are deep spans that are seemingly suspended in space, and are full of tenderness and sensuality. I like this contrast. I'm Spanish—I like the sun and the heat. But I also like Finland and the coldness of the Scandinavian countries... Actually, I like extremes—I am Gemini—I hate things that are average or mediocre, so I'm attracted to these strong contrasts in her music.

From a conductor's point of view, an interpreter has a lot of say with her music. In more mechanical and theoretical types of contemporary music, an interpreter can sometimes feel like a metronome. I don't enjoy that. Kaija's music, however, lets you participate in the creative process because of its extraordinarily flexible nature—and it's not just her music, by the way, but Kaija herself. When she attends a rehearsal or edits her scores, she knows just how much a piece of music can be fully realized as she's passing it along to an interpreter. Consequently, this music allows for an interpreter's work to be very rich because he can let himself get filled up by it, and he becomes, so to speak, the co-creator.

Susanna Mälkki[5]

CLÉMENT MAO-TAKACS: *Can you tell us about the form of Saariaho's symphonic works?*

SUSANNA MÄLKKI: If by "symphonic works" you mean "orchestral works" (which are very different), I think one thing they have in common is their sense of process. It is always about evolution, often evolution of a soundscape, but also that of harmony, which is a fundamental element even in modern music. In *Laterna Magica*, for example, the slow harmonic progress is almost Brucknerian. Therefore, the performers have a great responsibility in keeping the inner tension of the works alive. I think the slow pacing may be deceiving, since the music is never static, and of course there are many violent and explosive elements in her music too.

What do you think about her orchestration and instrumentation?

I hear quite a lot of French influence—in the way Saariaho uses spectral colors, for example. But it is definitely an orchestration that you recognize as being hers; it's very original. In terms of how she uses different forces of the orchestra, one of the striking elements is the frequent role of the strings as a textural surface; there is a great deal of shifting in the color of the notes (sul ponticello, sul tasto, harmonic trills, etc). In the winds, there are airy tones, glissandos, swaying chords. I think that in order to get a good performance, you need musicians who are willing to listen to the endless variation of sounds. Many expressive elements in the music demand that the instrumentalists do some research in order to produce quality sound projection. In the orchestration, there is always a rich use of percussion, both with and without pitch. Recognizable, but always well placed and functional in the context where it's used.

In your opinion, what makes Saariaho's work unique in today's world of contemporary music?

As with all important composers, having an individual and original language is the most important thing, and she definitely has one. I also very much respect and appreciate her search for subtleties and larger meanings in her work, especially now, when there's a lot of superficial, loud, and attention-seeking composing.

Where do you place Saariaho's work within the history of Finnish music and in relation to European music?

Kaija Saariaho is one of the greatest Finnish composers, and one of the most important composers of our time.

With which composers do you like to conduct her music and why?

Since her auditory world is so special, any work makes a wonderful addition to any program, modern or traditional, but of course the links to Finnish and French music are fascinating to bring forth as well.

A Conversation with Anssi Karttunen[1]

Clément Mao-Takacs

Translated from the French by Sophie Weiner

CLÉMENT MAO-TAKACS: *Anssi Karttunen, you've been collaborating with Kaija Saariaho for about thirty years now and you've maintained a real dialogue with her and her work. Could you talk about what makes her writing for the cello so special, or at least, what you think is most important?*

ANSSI KARTTUNEN: I have to say that for me it is harder and perhaps less interesting to talk about Kaija's writing for the cello (or what makes it special) than to analyze how she expands on tradition; I want to understand not what is different, but how she relates to her predecessors. We often fixate on a composer's or an artist's so-called "inventions" or "discoveries," but they're of no interest if they're not incorporated into a continuum. It's in this way that I believe Kaija has pulled off something very unique. For one, she has forged her own dialect, pushed technique further, used specific modes of playing, but most importantly, she's made these elements apart of a language that's been incorporated into the broader scope of music—not just contemporary. When I teach Kaija's music to young musicians, I try to make my students understand what in her phrases, movements, and forms is similar to those of Bach, Schumann, or Debussy. Naturally, she doesn't use the same classical forms, but in her pieces, you can find correlations or links between her modern language and traditional language forms.

There's an impression that her music has experienced a certain progression over the years. What's your take on the differences between her first scores and her most recent ones?

In hear early vocal music, she used to use a language that was rather removed from classical writing. In her most recent scores, she no longer feels the need to do that, but her music has lost none of its originality. For the cello, she started with very extreme scores, for example, her first piece for cello and piano, *Im Traume*, in which neither the piano nor the cello played a single note in a "normal" fashion. In a way, she studied everything that was technically possible, feasible, imaginable; then, little by little, she scaled back, analyzed, and synthesized these elements to see what was truly necessary for her music. Consequently, today the more "groundbreaking" elements are fully integrated into the discourse and while they're still present, they're now less prominent than in her earlier pieces.

The classic and romantic repertoire for the cello is particular. There are a few essential pieces like Bach's Suites, *lots of baroque music, chamber music like that of Schumann's, scores in which the instrumentalists take over (Schubert's* Arpeggione), *large concerti—especially those of the romantics—a few major sonatas, and then there are the twentieth century's very rich celloistic scores. How do you think Kaija fits into this world of cello music?*

I think that when she first started composing, Kaija certainly expressed a repertoire with a desire, not to break away, but to distance herself in order to find her own voice. That's every composer's mission—how to bring something new and original to the language while incorporating this work into a preexisting tradition. I think that today her relationship with her own language is very different. She has enough freedom to accept that there are occasional similarities—whether conscious or subconscious—to this composer or that one. With that said, for me, there are no composers or eras that work best with Kaija's music in a program. It's not about making a calculated decision, but about establishing a dialogue between her music and another composer. The question of her musical influences is secondary, even if we frequently arrange concerts that pair Saariaho with Debussy, for example. Nevertheless, the links that can be found in her work are as rich as those between Saariaho and Schumann or Saariaho and Webern. The most important thing is that there is always a sharing of emotions, even if they're manifested differently. What interests me is the fact that the same pieces by Saariaho will reveal different facets depending on the other composers in the program and that they'll have a dialogue, they'll bring out similarities as well as resonating—but also diverging—concepts. It's the whole wealth of music that comes to surface through this dialogue.

It could be said that Kaija Saariaho's music for the cello takes inspiration from baroque music, no doubt thanks to her work on sound (which brings to mind certain modes of playing we've now been hearing for the past sixty years) and her very elaborate and unique way of writing. However, it seems to me that, through her collaborations, she has also in a way restored the crucial bond between composer and "interpreter," which has existed since the baroque period (as they were one and the same) and which has slowly faded.

Yes, and this is also why I have a hard time analyzing her music by describing the specific techniques she uses, because our collaboration is so natural; it's a world that is so familiar to me that there are no longer any limits between composer and interpreter. I often wonder where the composer's work ends and where my life begins with her pieces. It's as if there's a blurred zone, a space that is shared by both the composer and interpreter. Ideally, I become the composer the moment I play her music. By the way, I don't like the word "interpreter." I'm not an interpreter who explains, translates or adds something to her music. I see myself more as a messenger through which the music passes in a fluid motion. Once I'm on stage, I stop asking myself questions, like "is this good?" or "would she have wanted this?" At that point, I am completely bound to her music; I've become her music. In the past, it was easier because the composer would perform his own music. Today, things are different. However, the collaboration I have with Kaija and a few other composers is practically ideal—but rare! Nowadays, you have to be attentive and able to work quickly and under tight deadlines; but for a musician, having this kind of relationship with a composer is a wonderful experience, and it has a positive effect on the other composers you work with, too. There's no longer a question of staying faithful to notes and respecting the writing because you don't have a desire to add something—you simply live with the music and everything becomes clear.

Aren't musicians indeed faced with significant time constraints? There's no longer the time to work attentively and at a comfortable pace? On the other end, the composer is often pushed to the sidelines for performances; they're only allowed to attend a few rehearsals and aren't to interfere too much (especially for operas and symphonies).

Unfortunately, I don't have the power to change certain realities. But for a musician, this dual life can be interesting. Working under tight deadlines, you may run into both good and bad surprises, but you always learn something, even from the bad ones. A concert is not a final culmination, but rather a single moment within a process, and every experience—good or bad—becomes a part of this trajectory. Kaija is a composer who's very aware of the fact that each concert is an adventure that may go down more or less smoothly, but that cannot be performed perfectly every time. Plus she trusts many of the musicians she's worked with for over thirty years, even if there's very little time to prepare the pieces; we pull it off because at some point, we've become immersed in her music. We've already taken the time to understand it, which gives us the luxury of moving more quickly at times.

You're more than immersed; you've performed an impressive number of her works.

I don't even know how many I've performed at this point! Counting her cello pieces, her chamber music, and her orchestras alone, it's probably been at least thirty!

This kind of collaboration, one that is equally personal and professional, has allowed you to know each other so well, that you could've eventually grown tired of one another. Yet Kaija continues to regularly write scores for you that are always different and inspiring.

It's a bit like that in life. There are people you want to stay in touch with and work with; I think that's why Kaija continues to write for the cello— and for me. I should also point out that Kaija has heard me play her music in different situations—with the very best conductors and with the not-so-good ones, from playing chamber music with people who were completely unfamiliar with her work as well as with musicians who've been playing her music for years. Because of all that, I've gained such an understanding of her music that when I teach it, sometimes I can help a student to learn ideas, skills, and techniques in only thirty minutes while it took almost thirty years to acquire them myself. Kaija knows that something surprising can occur from this exchange every time—my students will suddenly skip levels, and deliver a very mature performance without having to have lived with this music like I did. But to be able to teach them, I had to form this very deep personal and professional relationship, which continues to grow to this day.

When you teach her music, what exactly do you impart? Between those who are completely unfamiliar with her music, those who only play her repertoire, and those who know how to play it in a technical sense but not with heart, I imagine you have a whole range of students.

It's a bit of a paradox. Sometimes you can achieve faster results with a young musician who has no experience with Kaija's music because he or she has no preconceived notions. If I succeed in imparting my passion for her music and the desire to search for emotions, then all the technical issues become secondary because we've immediately reached what matters most. When I work with a musician who has already played everything under the sun, it's more complicated. We're all limited by our life experiences, our prejudices, our passions; usually this type of musician already knows which composers they feel close to and it takes a lot of work to remind them that we are not here to judge, but to react and to find the right emotions and movements, not in general, but for this music in particular. Because normally, when faced with a problem, a musician with a certain level of experience will try looking for answers in another composer's piece that they have already played before. Yet this isn't always the best approach. Differences between composers make it so we can't always play the same way—there are no standard solutions. If we're able to forget the solutions that worked well in the past and allow ourselves to enter this particular composer's world, then we can make a lot of progress.

Tell us a bit about the situation in Finland allowing for Kaija Saariaho's music to develop, as well as your collaboration.

What's unique about my generation in Finland—among both composers and instrumentalists—is that we weren't trying to form an exclusive group in terms of style, intellect, and nationality. The general attitude in Finland made it so that nothing was off-limits. We were more interested in finding the fascinating aspects of other people's work, rather than only what could be criticized. This relaxed attitude allowed me to work with many composers. If I had limited myself to finding one sole acceptable style, I'd have kept a relationship with only a few composers (including Kaija) and vice versa (there are lots of composers today who work exclusively with their "official" interpreters). In Kaija's case, it's different. She's established long-lasting trusting relationships with certain musicians, but she knows that it's beneficial for them to play music other than just her own. What's more, she herself is always open to new collaborations. At any rate, this kind of spirit was popular in Finland during the seventies and eighties. We preferred to try new things and make mistakes, and to accept the best and the worst in order to learn lessons, rather than have a fixed and stubborn attitude that would have restricted our fields of study.

You've developed several kinds of projects together: recordings, master classes, foundations, and so on. Could you tell us about these other sorts of collaborations?

Think about the world today. We're living in an era in which numerous possibilities are open to the creative process. However, over the course of the last thirty years, this world, and especially the musical world, has changed tremendously. The record industry is not thriving like it used to, the public is not the same, contemporary music is both supported and threatened whenever there are budgetary restrictions...Yet, if we want to remain as open as we were in the seventies and eighties, we have to go and find our fans and make it so they can find us. With www.petals.org, we've tried to bypass the steps defined by record production and establish a direct connection with the public. This has been proven successful, more so today than in the nineties. With that same intention, when we host workshops and master classes, we always try to teach not just how to play this music, but also about the way we live and work. Because today, these young musicians who are studying at the best schools in the world aren't being told what life is like after the conservatory. This is why we're trying to help them realize what happens once you're alone with your instrument, your music, your composer, your audience, and faced with the difficulty of earning a living. First you need to find what makes you happy, figure out what makes life exciting, and the solutions start coming to you. You need to really think seriously about all of this, and not just on an abstract level.

A Discussion and a Monologue

Esa-Pekka Salonen and Peter Sellars

Edited by Pekka Hako and Jaakko Mäntyjärvi
Transcribed by Jaakko Mäntyjärvi

ESA-PEKKA SALONEN: It was at some point in the mid-seventies that the word was out—

PETER SELLARS: I'm sorry, that's shocking to me already. I'm thinking of the mid-seventies and you and Kaija, I'm shocked already.

EPS: The word was out, the jungle drum was beating. There was to be a meeting, we—the young composers who were still studying—we had to do something to break out of the cultural isolation of Finland (as we perceived it). We all met in the apartment of a composition student named Kaija Saariaho, who had a nice place in the North Harbor of Helsinki with a painter named Olli Lyytikäinen. That was the first time I met Kaija. She had been a visual arts student before realizing that it was not really her thing; she then decided that composition was it, and applied for and got into the Sibelius Academy. She was maybe a first-year or second-year student when we met.

At that meeting, we decided to start the *Korvat auki!* (Ears Open!) society, which became an important force in the Finnish contemporary music movement in the 1970s and 1980s.

Kaija was a woman studying composition, which was rare in Finland at the time, or anywhere else for that matter. She had conditioned herself to be defensive about everything, because she felt that people would not take her seriously. I think the foundation of our friendship was that I did take her seriously. Not for one second did I think that a woman composition student would be any less believable than a man, because studying composition was a very utopian thing to do anyway. It doesn't matter whether you are a man or a woman, because you are pretty much doomed anyway. And we became friends.

The Ears Open! society was the main focus of everybody's lives, because we had this alternative reality thing going. There was the "official"

Sibelius Academy composition seminar, and then we would have our own. Because nobody was good enough to teach us, one of us always gave the lecture.

PS: That's fantastic, I didn't know this.

EPS: Eero Hämeenniemi was nominally in charge so that we could be part of the Sibelius Academy curriculum. But the point was that every week one of us would stand up and teach the others. On a subject you could choose yourself.

PS: What were the sessions like? What did you do? What did Kaija do?

EPS: For instance, I wrote a paper on Josef Matthias Hauer. He was this Viennese wacko composer who invented a kind of twelve-tone system before Schönberg. He wrote something like eight hundred pieces, and they were all called *Apokalyptische Fantasie* and things like that, in "cosmic relationship with the forces that move the universe" and that kind of thing.

PS: Oh wow.

EPS: He had his own notation, and I actually even learned that notation. And then I shared my knowledge with my friends.

PS: Your rapt colleagues.

EPS: Kaija did things on Alban Berg and maybe Nono. The idea was that we chose a topic and talked about it, and then learned everything there was to be learned about it. A bit later Kaija moved into a charming house in Marjaniemi, in eastern Helsinki by the sea, and that became the educational and entertainment center for us young composers. We had the seminars at the house, and the parties too. That was great, a wonderful time.

So, fast forward: I conducted the premiere of Kaija's first orchestral piece, called *Verblendungen*, which was on some level based on the Canetti novel *Auto-da-Fé*, which is one of the most devastating pieces of literature and deals with evil.

PS: Very intensely!

EPS: And I did this with the Finnish Radio Symphony Orchestra (FRSO). And then, the next big "Kaija moment" came several years later, in Los Angeles, when I conducted and recorded *du cristal...* And I think that at this point you met Kaija for the first time?

PS: Yes.

EPS: Late eighties, early nineties?

PS: I think early nineties.

EPS: 1991?

PS: Yes.

EPS: And of course the concrete, important, really crucial result of that meeting was the premiere of Kaija's opera *L'Amour de loin* in Salzburg in 2000.

PS: A long story to get there. Tell me one more thing. What went into this Canetti piece? First of all, what got you to conduct the FRSO? That was normal for you at that time?

EPS: Well, I had done part of my diploma with them, and I started to get some serious conducting work from them. In fact, the FRSO was the only Finnish orchestra to use my services. And they were fantastic, because not only did they give me all kinds of new music things and so on, but they felt I had to get real concerts as well, with repertoire, and this was my most important orchestra relationship when I was growing up. I think Kaija's piece was a commission from the Finnish Radio, and in those days they had an "afternoon world premiere" series at the University Hall, a very casual concert series at about four in the afternoon. Just one piece, or maybe one repertoire piece and then a new piece. It would only take about forty minutes or so. I don't think *Verblendungen* was particularly about the subject matter of the Canetti book, more about the idea of being blinded by a certain type of light.

PS: Was Kaija's music always, even from the beginning, conceived imagistically?

EPS: I think always. I think that was the identity of hers as a composer from the very beginning.

PS: I mean, while the boys were dealing with a lot of theoretical questions and scientific relations... I have a sense that Kaija is always focusing on her inner image?

EPS: Yes. In Kaija's work, the visual and the aural are linked.

PS: Synesthetically linked?

EPS: Yes, but not in terms of conventional synesthesia, where one color would correspond to a harmony or a pitch. It is more like if you were to translate a musical experience into another medium, in Kaija's case it would be a visual image, although for many others it would be verbal.

PS: Right.

EPS: So we guys were dealing with concepts, and by definition "concept" is something that you define in words.

PS: Right.

EPS: Even in the early days, Kaija was not interested in concepts; and now that you mention it, that was a profound difference. Then there comes a moment in life when you stop trying to translate between language and music and realize that music is in some ways like a butterfly: if you touch its wing, you will destroy something and then it cannot fly any more. Music has to be allowed to be its own thing rather than trying to organize it through another medium. But in Kaija's work these two kinds of expression breathe the same air, so to speak.

PS: I just do not know this first piece that you're describing. Is it an immersive, physical experience?

EPS: Well, it's a process. Kaija's early pieces were almost always manifestations of one process, so there was one formal idea, and that was the piece, to put it simple.

In *Verblendungen*, the dramatic arc of the piece is formed by a sort of textural metamorphosis. That sounds very theoretical, but it was very expressive. She had made a tape part at IRCAM, and this was at a time when the computer stuff that came out of IRCAM was not very expressive but kind of cold and theoretical, but hers was different. Her metaphor was a painter's brush, and the piece is one stroke of a brush, basically: the paint is thickest at the beginning of the stroke, and then it thins out and disperses into strands, and every strand is a different shape, and then they all run into nothingness at the end. That was the form, basically. The tape was loosely synchronised with the orchestra, so it was not a click-track job for me.

I remember a very funny thing about that concert. I was a guinea pig for the applied arts school at that time, and one of the classes had an assignment to create a conductor's outfit. So I was wearing this conductor's outfit in this concert, and it had a sort of tunic-style upper part that somehow just would not stay on. It was slipping down over my shoulder all the time, so I was conducting this piece, one of my first real concerts, and the world premiere of a really talented friend of mine, and I was fighting with my damn jacket at the same time. But it was fine.

PS: At that time, were you guys still involved in intense conversations and discussions about what everyone was making? Or by that time had she gone away to Paris and was no longer a part of ongoing conversation here?

EPS: Well, what happened was of course that everybody in the core group of the society went somewhere. Kaija went first to Freiburg. She was there for a year or something like that.

PS: Oh, with Ferneyhough?

EPS: Yes, and Klaus Huber, those two. And actually Magnus Lindberg and I, we made it to her diploma concert in Freiburg.

PS: No. No!

EPS: Yes. We took the train through half of Europe and made it to the diploma concert. At that point we had not slept for two days. Kaija was very touched by us being there, and so were her parents. It was kind of funny, because there we were, Magnus and I, we had made it, such a relief; and we were sitting in the first row, and the concert began, and we promptly fell asleep! Because we were so relieved. And Kaija was like: you guys are just hopeless.

PS: It is something special to have friends.

EPS: But we made it there! And that was the big deal.

PS: That's fantastic.

EPS: We kept closely in touch even after we were geographically separated and throughout our formative years, you know, the soul-searching years. I think every one of us could say that it was the most important feedback we got. Sure, there was criticism and there were suggestions, but there was also tremendous warmth and support, and that has continued over the years. We may disagree on things, but there is an overwhelming sense of being in this together.

PS: So when you got to Los Angeles, you felt that the first composer you would take up would be this one?

EPS: Right, it might have been.

PS: That's a huge statement.

EPS: It was a huge statement in many ways, but it was natural for me, because this was repertoire I knew, and one of my closest colleagues and collaborators. I felt that this music (*du cristal…*) had to be heard. It might even have been the first time any orchestra in the United States had played any of her stuff. A symphony orchestra, I mean; I am sure that some of her chamber pieces had already been performed there by then. Today, she is a household name, and every American orchestra plays her music, but this was not the case in 1991.

PS: But that is huge. What was it that out of all the group, all the young composers you hanged out with, what made you say: Okay, my first step is her? With this American orchestra and in California?

EPS: I actually did not even think in those terms, because it was the natural thing to do: I will play something by Kaija. I believed in this music, and I had seen it being created from close up, in a way, because I saw sketches, and in those early days Kaija also asked for my advice on orchestration issues.

PS: Right.

EPS: So I felt like some kind of a sous-chef.

PS: And even the title alone, *du cristal…*, suggests incredible image plays and a real physicality in the music.

EPS: Again, there is this metaphor thing. We are talking about a pair of pieces, *du cristal…* and *…à la fumée*—from crystal to smoke. That kind of metaphor can to some degree be successfully translated into music.

PS: Right.

EPS: Crystals are definite, clearly identified shapes that don't lose their identity regardless of where you put them. You can sink them into porridge or you can throw them up in the air, and they always retain their identity. And then, if you can imagine a process where a crystal becomes smoke, the process is about how these crystalline characteristics gradually dissolve into what smoke is, which is essentially chaos. It goes from order to chaos, which is kind of interesting, because usually we try to do it the other way around. Like Haydn in *The Creation*.

PS: And there is also this disappearing thing, because a crystal is transparent, translucent, and despite its hardness and its brittleness it is also elusive as a form. It keeps shifting form based on the perspective, and you keep seeing other worlds through it, depending on what the other world is it is next to. So it is also changing its character according to its environment. The bizarre and beautiful thing about smoke is that it is created by humans.

For me, the one really interesting thing that I always feel about Kaija's music is that its temperature is warm. I always feel there is heat in the centre of the music. And as you were saying a minute ago about IRCAM, there was this time in the history of contemporary music when it was cool to be cool. My feeling with Kaija, from the very beginning, has been that there is a heat, there is a fire burning somewhere. Her music always comes out of something essentially hot at its center. And there is no coolness of remove.

EPS: I completely agree with you, because from very early on Kaija developed her very sort of idiosyncratic set of instructions to musicians that nobody else since Tchaikovsky has been using. There are instructions like *disperato*, desperate, or *con ultima forza*, with the last strength, and these kind of highly charged, emotionally charged instructions that were really not fashionable. And amoroso, lovingly. She was the only one who wrote like that. I think Strauss wrote amoroso in places in *Rosenkavalier* as a joke, almost. Like when Ochs sings, that's amoroso, because he's a sloppy old drunkard.

So Kaija kind of re-invented the vocabulary of how to direct the performer. She wanted to make sure that you would not treat her music like "new music," with detachment and scientific precision, but with real expression, real emotional involvement. That was really essential from very early on, now when I think about it. In that, she was fairly alone among the new composers of the eighties, certainly.

PS: The other thing that strikes me even from early on is what she is asking string players to do. Most orchestras look at the score and say, "Oh, right, this is easy." And yet obviously what she wants particularly from the string texture is something that is not easy at all, but this is not reflected by the notes on the page.

We have done a lot of her pieces together, but was not until I had my first experience with Kaija and the FRSO—when we did *La Passion de Simone* at the Helsinki Festival—that I really heard Kaija's music for the first time; I mean, I heard a strings section that knew what to do with it. Suddenly those incredible textures were present in the strings.

I can understand it now that I know you had such a long history with the FRSO, but I felt I was hearing Kaija's music properly for the first time, like when you hear the Vienna Philharmonic playing Bruckner, and even with a bad Bruckner performance from the Vienna Philharmonic, you suddenly understand the logic of it. Suddenly I was understanding the logic of her music sonically when you conducted the Finnish Radio in *La Passion de Simone*. How do you cope with this as a conductor?

EPS: Well, the challenge is mental, not physical. As you said, what she requires physically or technically from the musicians is usually not anywhere near the limits of their abilities, but it is a mental challenge, because it is all about keeping things alive where there is very little material, and keeping the expression and tension going when superficially what we have is virtual stasis. You have to be able to discover the tension in things that sometimes approach silence. In order to do this, you have to have faith in the material, because the material in itself does not provide easy solutions or easy answers.

PS: For me, what is interesting is that so many other composers of that era were deliberately throwing in all kinds of things: their scores were ten feet tall and required three music stands to lay out, and they contained as many staves as possible, and the sheer number of notes per bar was just overwhelming. Kaija writes music that does not overwhelm you on the page with its complexity but is the opposite. In a strange way, it is taking you to some core experience, but it is something that is a vibration or an emanation of that core experience. There is a memory or a presentiment or something, it is not the experience itself.

It is kind of atmospheric, something like when you can sense it is going to rain soon, to borrow a Steve Reich title. That weird thing you feel in the air before it is going to rain, and you say oh, it is going to rain. It is impossible to describe but as soon as you feel it, you know, when you are out in that weather, you know. It is a knowledge that goes deeper than anything you were ever taught or have ever learned. You just know, as a human being, in the air, that it is going to rain soon. For me, so much of Kaija's music is like that air, like the atmosphere that surrounds something momentous. It is not the momentous thing itself, it is the sensation, this air we are breathing. It suggests a whole lot of other things that cannot be properly articulated, or even if you did properly articulate them, like the butterfly wing you mentioned, you would betray or devalue it in the act of trying to describe it.

EPS: That is actually a great metaphor, that rain thing, because how do we detect it? We do not know the mechanism. But I am sure that it is a twofold process. Partly we know it is going to rain because of something that is there, okay, but an equally important part is that we know it is going to rain because something is not there. Right? And Kaija has the courage and faith in her own material to be able to make these decisions—okay, now I'm not going to do anything but this. And this takes a lot of guts. In this way, she approaches Wagner in the sense that the hypnotic qualities of both of their music comes from this absolute faith in their material, the courage to do this and not that and to focus on this particular thing and not worry about something not being there. What you were describing, the five-foot score with ninety-four staves and black as the night, that is an expression of fear.

PS: [*Laughs.*]

EPS: It is lack of faith in what you are doing, because you have to fill the music with stuff. And we see this in the work of stage directors a lot also: if there is a quiet place in a play or in an opera, not a lot happening and not many words, then you have to get in a can-can group to fill the gaps.

PS: Cue the trapeze.

EPS: Yes, and I think this sensory padding is one the biggest curses of our time, and art has suffered very much from it, and we still have not quite recovered from the invasion of the padding. Kaija has actually been one of the leaders of the re-establishment of the essential. I think that the kind of following she has among listeners is very unusual for contemporary composers. I mean, the people who go to see and hear her work are not necessarily new music hardcore aficionados, they are ordinary people.

PS: At the same time, what is pretty interesting is a really young generation of composers, for who all of the rules are now finished, find a clearing in her work that lets them breathe and lets some air and light in and lets things be a little bit normal. At the same time, what always keeps going is the essentially poetic dimension, because, as you said, everything is always a metaphor. And to me that is the other really great gift of Kaija: her music never has one-for-one links or connections. Everything is linked poetically, because she has found a metaphor that unlocks a set of other things that don't have to be mentioned directly.

Her instrumental music has this quality… For instance, she says that she's doing Bergman's *The Magic Lantern*. What? How on earth can *The Magic Lantern*…? For me as a director, that book is filled with so many details that are so shocking and alarming—how can this be represented in music which is elusive rather than specific? What I always remember about that Bergman book is the details are horrifying. Bergman absolutely destroys you with this atrocious mean-spirited way in which he describes everything in hideous detail. And that is not Kaija's music. Kaija's music has a certain level of detail, yes, but it keeps itself alive exactly by insisting that there is something which cannot be detailed in sharp focus. Like with Bill Viola's low-light camera, the strange thing is you start to see something as its ghostly self, as something that the surface doesn't reveal. It is something that is either beneath the surface or is, again, a kind of atmospheric condition that hovers, but you cannot take a picture of it, you have to feel it in your nostrils, you have to feel it on your skin. There has to be a set of things that absolutely resist a kind of digital image. I think of Kaija's music a lot that way, of everything that resists description through other means.

Let me just say that meeting her in Los Angeles, those concerts were sensational for one thing just because they sounded so thrilling. I think one of the ways you know a real composer is nobody else sounds like that. When you hear one of their pieces, you say, oh, that is who that is. Like with, say, Haydn, there is a sound print that tells you, that is who that is, it is not Dittersdorf! And for me Kaija's sound print is so uniquely her own language.

EPS: I agree. The identity is incredibly strong. Now, a big turning point in Kaija's life, artistic life was of course the opera as a medium and collaboration with you and Amin Maalouf, and that kind of marked a new era in her artistic output, and everything she has done since has been kind of informed by this collaboration. Maybe you could talk about that?

PS: Well, I think one of the things that always happens in opera is first of all you have a larger canvas than you usually have as a composer. Obviously, working in opera lets Kaija move directly into a mode where you are creating an emotional atmosphere and you are working on a large canvas. And you are inevitably trying to describe physical realities. For me, that is one of the most powerful points of her music: the music is embodied feeling, but you feel that it is not primarily psychological, not primarily mental, but really what you feel in your body and what your body tells you. This kind of embodied knowledge is more like dance than literature, and that is the intense physicality of her music and the fact that it has to be totally inhabited by the performers. It is not enough to execute it, technically proficiently. It needs this other type of commitment where you plunge into it with your whole being.

That opera lets her go to that immersive, overwhelming place is not accidental. *Tristan* was a key work for her, and my own connection to *Tristan* is again through Kaija, but also my early experiences with her were through Wagner and Stravinsky, and really, Messiaen. Esa-Pekka and I first collaborated on the Messiaen *Saint François* with the Los Angeles Philharmonic at the Salzburg Festival after the death of Herbert von Karajan. This is a piece that really had not been performed except in the odd radio philharmonic concert in some European second- or third-tier city. To suddenly present it as the opening of a Salzburg Festival was a huge event, and at that time, as we were working on it, Messiaen died. And so, strangely, our work on this opera became a memorial in a certain way. When you do the work of a living composer, one of the most exciting things is having the composer there; and that did not happen with Messiaen. What was very moving was that Kaija was present, and I felt in some very deep way that we were making this work with Kaija and we were coming to Messiaen through Kaija, who was very much a guiding spirit as I was exploring and trying to understand Messiaen.

Similarly, a couple of years later I was working with Esa-Pekka on *The Rake's Progress*. Esa-Pekka had come out of a very Boulezian tradition of how to conduct Stravinsky, with this kind of sharp, pin-point focus, very rhythmically steely, unyielding and with a very dry sense of musical language. None of things could describe Kaija. There was a period where I was rehearsing the Stravinsky in the Châtelet in Paris, and Esa-Pekka could not be there, he had concerts in other cities. So I was working every day with my own revisionist approach to Stravinsky.

I actually feel that Stravinsky, like Beckett, had to lie every single day about what he was really doing, and in fact it was the opposite of what Stravinsky said in those conversation books, "my music doesn't require performers" and all that stuff. And at the same time, this dogma was so entrenched that you were attacked as being disrespectful if you tried to suggest that, well, in fact maybe the score speaks in a completely different way from those qualities. And maybe this music is lyrical. And maybe this music is tender. And maybe this music is heartfelt. And maybe this music isn't just a trigonometry problem. And what was so dangerous was to try and suggest Stravinsky was all of these things Stravinsky insisted he was not.

What was really moving was to have Kaija Saariaho in rehearsal every day, encouraging me to make the interpretation more emotional, more lyrical, with more rubato, more sense of inner life to every musical phrase. So one of the most important experiences for me was like coming to Stravinsky and Messiaen through Kaija and her giving us permission to hear this music in non-orthodox ways, or what at the time were not orthodox ways.

Now, this was before we were working on her piece together. She said to me, well, I have this piece about a medieval troubadour, and I really could not deal with that. I said, I am an American, this is not my world, I can only do American works; you really need to find somebody in Europe to work with. I was highly resistant. I love Kaija as a composer and as a person, but I did not feel that I was the person to work with her music, to create the visual and emotional world of these pieces in a European context, because I am not European. But strangely, Kaija really drew me out of my own rather limited sense of identity and really invited me to work in deeper waters and in a way that was not overtly American. The first of my pieces that are not overtly American are the stagings that I made of her works.

I am really sure that culture is very, very specific to where you grew up and how you grew up, and your parents, and what they said or did not say, and what you overheard, and what was kept from you, and all of those sorts of things. And to me, Kaija's music is absolutely informed by all of that, and of course when you know Finland—the skies here and the sunlight, the lack of sunlight and all that, then you can understand Kaija's music in a certain very specific way.

At the same time, one of the reasons I think Kaija lives in Paris is to suggest to herself that there is a larger identity and that music is not simply a form of nationalism as it was for the nineteenth-century composers. Now, in the twenty-first century, not all of us are wrapped in the national flag doing our victory lap like in the Olympics. There is something that is on behalf of a larger swath of humanity that is not geographically defined.

Look at the context where Kaija is working with Amin Maalouf, who was born in Lebanon, and is one of the great Arab writers, also insisting on living in Paris, also insisting on not writing in Arabic, also insisting on a larger identity than simply an Arab or a Lebanese writer. And insisting on writing in French. Interestingly, he shares this outlook with Kaija. They are two people living consciously in exile and consciously proposing a kind of wider culture. Could you say these are Finnish-Arab operas? Well, no! They are about different geographies. They are about the East imagining the West in the case of *L'Amour de loin*, they are about the Balkans in the case of *Adriana Mater*, or they are about an incredible intensity of spiritual, mystic tradition as with Simone Weil. In each case, these works are flowing beyond the borders that are usually used to define culture and are suggesting a culture in the twenty-first century that can speak multiple languages in multiple geographies.

I think part of the breadth of Kaija's compositional development is that she has moved outside of anything that can be regarded as a school, and she is no longer in dialogue with any particular musical language. She has really evolved so deeply into her own world, and at the same time the work with Amin Maalouf has meant that the sensibility is extended in terms of the large emotional scope of sustaining an emotional argument across two and a half hours. The first two operas have this incredible, long emotional scope with only three characters in the first opera and four in the second. Usually a large-scale opera like that has a large cast of characters across which there is a lot of diversity of texture and interruptions and detours, but not in these pieces. You are in a kind of claustrophobic relationship with three individuals in *L'Amour de loin*. You are in a complete tunnel of experience and history with four individuals in *Adriana Mater*. So each of these pieces is so intense and is so concentrated and is presented in the most concentrated possible form.

I think this is exactly the opposite to trends in the cinema, trends in literature and trends in music that are happening in these same decades, where you are usually seeing this massive sense of anything to distract, anything to create constant interest and distraction so that your eyes are always channel-surfing and you are always surfing on the Internet, no idea is ever complete before you are already on to the next one. And Kaija and Amin have created these works that have this incredible tunnel focus of a deep, deep unrelenting intensity that moves across a two and a half hour span. Nobody is doing anything like that. It is extremely unusual and it also is only possible if you really turn your back on the world. You are not making what is on television, you are not making what is in the newspaper, you are not making this world around us which is of nonstop event, event, event, event. These operas are almost event-free. There are only very few events, and in that sense they are like *Tristan* or like the Messiaen *Saint François*: it is not about the events; it is about the spiritual path and journey that each of these characters is on, and you're really with them in their moral struggles and in their spiritual yearning.

Amin's words are so stripped back, are so elegant, beautifully formed and yet naked, I mean really naked. And then Kaija has clothed them in music of unrelenting self-examination that does not let up. These characters are their own most severe judges. Kaija creates this music of what Peter Handke would call self-accusation, of a sense that you are responsible. The music carries this incredible sense of responsibility, and then once you are in this state of heightened awareness, self-awareness, and self-absorption and delusion, suddenly everything is about the climate change of your own moral and emotional course, and your actions have these incredible, huge implications for global climate change. Kaija has the orchestra and chorus constantly beam this reading of the shifts in the climate, of the temperature adjustments, of the extremes of weather, of the extremes of spiritual reversals and intensity of the spiritual struggles. Now, that is very different from any other opera being written, and as I said I think the lineage is *Tristan*, is *Saint François*, are these operas that are really depicting inner states in a way that becomes palpable, but again cannot be reduced. I think is that the power of Kaija's language.

And also, like Wagner, material you would not initially consider promising is developed across three hours, and over and over again, the same chords, the same patterns; and like Wagner, it becomes hypnotic, and it becomes emotionally overwhelming in ways that at the beginning you do not sense. You do not realise how far this material is going to go. And nothing prepares you for its devastating impact two-and-a-half hours later. It is not that new chords have been introduced. You are hearing the same patterns all night long in these operas, but these patterns develop a kind of hypnotic momentum and inner necessity that takes you to a place that is completely overwhelming. And I would just say that each of these pieces, and I include *La Passion de Simone* in this, each of these pieces traces a deep and emotional arc. There are not that many composers whose music traces that depth of emotion across that span of time or whose work is not primarily entertaining but really quite the opposite and invites you to a place where there are no distractions and invites you to a place where just facing the most basic parts of your existence becomes the most important thing you can do.

We were talking earlier about Kaija's visual artistry and the music working in terms of imagery and having this synesthetic dimension to it. I want to emphasize again that when Kaija is painting this psychological or spiritual portrait, it is not in terms of the standard psychology of movie music, it is really another set of colors, it is another set of images, and those images are always some kind of light from a world beyond, like in the title of Messiaen's last piece, *Éclairs sur l'au-delà*. It is always a world that is impalpable and ungraspable. This is the opposite of most film music, which is psychological and very, highly directive and manipulative. I want to emphasize when I am talking about these incredible emotional arcs that Kaija traces, they are so impressive exactly because they avoid the usual psychological signifiers that we know from film music and the kind of predestined sense of emotional manipulation that we are surrounded with all the time.

Another strange thing with Kaija's music is also that we are in this place of mystery, which Bill Viola spoke about so beautifully; like with a medieval artist, the task is to enter and explore the mysterious. Kaija elevates each of the operas by never writing music that is simply practical or that simply paints the picture of the scene but always insists that what is really functioning is this invisible dimension that is invisible even to the characters and that the music is there to remind you of the power of invisibility and that all of the things that are moving are actually invisible. But Kaija moves them imagistically. And so it takes you into this other world of visual art which is not about things as they appear but their secret existence shimmering in the dark. And that is where Kaija's music lives.

(Left to right) Peter Sellars, Kaija Saariaho, and Esa-Pekka Salonen.

The Flute Music of Kaija Saariaho—A Personal History

Camilla Hoitenga

In 1982, Kaija Saariaho and I were participants at the International Summer Courses for New Music in Darmstadt, Germany. We met in the first week while waiting in line for lunch at the canteen. I don't know what we discussed, though Kaija remembers I spoke to her first. I recall her as a striking figure in a long black dress and long, flat, black shoes. (The rest of us were in shirts, jeans, and sandals). Be that as it may, I learned that she was a composer, and she that I was a flutist. The composer-teachers that first week were what we called the "French Contingency," notably Gérard Grisey, Tristan Murail, and Michael Levinas, and we enjoyed visiting their courses and concerts and socializing with them afterward. Kaija had just moved to Paris to study at IRCAM, and I was also a big fan of Paris, so already we had common interest in this city and French culture.

At this time, she gave me the flute solo *Laconisme de l'aile*, a piece she had just written in Freiburg, for a Finnish flutist friend of hers, Anne Raitio (now Eirola). I had just been working intensively with Karlheinz Stockhausen on a piece he had revised for me—*Amour* for flute—and Kaija's score, by comparison, looked vague, and I remember asking her many questions about what this and that meant and how much time I should take here and there. Eventually, however, I not only played her piece, it became one of the most-performed solos of my repertoire. And I became her "muse" for all subsequent flute pieces!

But this happened gradually. After Darmstadt, we remained friends and in close contact, but it wasn't until 1992 that she surprised me with a new piece. One day she phoned me in Cologne and said something like "I am afraid I must write you a piece"—almost as if it were bad news! For her, in a way, it was bad news, since contemporary repertoire was already crowded with music for solo flute and she was hesitant about adding to it. On the other hand, she had these gestures of ascending scales "flying around in her head, haunting her," and she wanted to get rid of them, as it were, in order to be able to move into something else. Happily, her frustration with solo flute had already taken her into new territory for this piece, as she was determined to create a polyphony not only with extended techniques and added voice but also by using electronics in various ways. The result was *NoaNoa*, which also became a "classic" in the genre of flute/electronics.

The premiere in Darmstadt that year was definitely not a success. The signals from the flute to the computer didn't work (we were working with next and pitch-following), so what the audience heard was less "complex polyphony" and more "melody-with-reverberation"—not exactly in keeping with the prevalent Darmstadt Aesthetic. Although I had played my part well, we were shocked that no one came backstage to greet us after the concert. Later, a journalist friend took me aside and advised me to maybe think twice about continuing to work with this composer. Saariaho had had a great start with *Verblendungen* and other works, but now that she'd had a baby, she seemed to be getting too "soft," losing her cutting-edge aesthetic—not good for the career of an avant-garde flutist!

Not only did I not listen to that advice, but a few years later, I decided to include Saariaho's music in my doctoral project, "Twentieth-Century Classic and Exotic Music for Solo Flute," dedicating one recital exclusively to her music and that of Karlheinz Stockhausen.

The next flute solo was *Couleurs du vent* for alto flute. Because it was written for the birthday of our flutist friend Mikael Helasvuo, I had to wait forever to perform it. Mikael kept putting off the premiere and finally performed it in Finland—but on the C flute instead of on the alto. I then went ahead and premiered the original version for alto flute in Wisconsin in February of 1999, and in Paris later that year. The piece was long and difficult, however, and wasn't programmed by either of us much after that. Until one day...

One day I played *Couleurs du vent* and it was much shorter than usual. As I was nearing the end, I wondered what had happened to certain favorite passages of mine. It turns out that at some point I had turned two pages instead of one, thereby making a cut, apparently one which had been organic enough that I hadn't noticed it right then. Nor had Kaija, who was listening in the audience, although she wondered at how short the piece seemed. Since it actually worked in that version, she set out to officially revise the piece. This is now the published edition, and since this revision, the work has been programmed more frequently!

Later in 1998, Kaija wrote a flute solo as another birthday present, this time for her flute-playing godchild Liisa, who was turning ten. The Finnish title, chosen by Kaija's then nine-year-old son, is *Liisan taikahuilu*, or *Liisa's Magic Flute*. Twenty-six measures long and limited to four or five pitches hardly extending beyond the first octave, this "simple" piece nevertheless employs some of Kaija's favorite flute techniques such as air sounds, trills, and glissandi (and has proven to be a challenge even for some conservatory players).

Eventually, I also received a solo as a birthday present: the little piccolo piece, *Dolce Tormento*. About a month before my birthday I had been asked to introduce her orchestral piece *Orion* at the Beethovenfest in Bonn. Since the piccolo is quite prominent in one of the movements, I brought mine along and played excerpts for the audience. Certain gestures, especially the poignant "falling" pattern of the third octave Eb–D–B from the second movement "Winter Sky" then found their way into the piccolo solo.

Of course, Kaija added a text (Petrarch's Sonnet 132 from his *Il Canzoniere*), thereby presenting me with two new challenges: how to speak/whisper Petrarch's Italian, and how to somehow integrate the vocal sounds into the music without the help of a resonant flute. (The inside story of why she chose that particular text for me, well, that would be another one altogether!) In any case, I enjoyed premiering the piece at my "birthday concert" in the Finnish Institute in Paris, and continue to play it often.

Kaija Saariaho's major work for flute, however, is her flute concerto, *Aile du songe*. As with *NoaNoa*, this was also a surprise for me, but this time she built up the suspense about some "news" and waited for one of my visits to her family in Paris. Then she announced it with a flourish and we promptly celebrated with champagne. A concerto with strings, harp, celeste, and percussion, *Aile du songe* was a joint commission by the orchestras of the Flanders Festival, London Philharmonic, and the Finnish Radio, so the first performances were already set.

An interesting note: one of the original commissioners was to be a major American orchestra, but since the contract with their solo flutist didn't permit guest flutists, Kaija refused. In fact, most of the top American orchestras had (and still have) similar contracts with their wind soloists, making the scheduling of guest performers rather challenging. Apparently, I was finally allowed to make the U.S. premiere with the Chicago Symphony because it was "only" during their summer season at Ravinia, and they made special compensations for their own flutist as well. If only I played piano, violin, or cello, it would be a different story!

But no—I'm quite content playing the flute, I love this concerto, and, happily for me, I am still invited by dozens of orchestras to perform it with them!

Kaija Saariaho and Musical Research at IRCAM

Jean-Baptiste Barrière

ENTERING THE HIVE

In January 1982, Kaija Saariaho arrived at IRCAM (the Institute for Research and Coordination in Acoustics/Music) in Paris to participate in the Computer Music Session, a six-week workshop organized twice a year and mentored by the American psycho-acoustician David Wessel, Director of the Pedagogy Department. She was in the process of completing her studies with Klaus Huber and Brian Ferneyhough in Freiburg, Germany. Since the previous year, I myself had belonged both to the scientific team working on the CHANT synthesis program, and to the Pedagogy Department, where I delivered lectures and assisted composers in the realization of their works.[1]

Wessel's scientific orientation, which inclined toward musical speculation, was decisive for the workshop's conception. Rather than simply demonstrating software tools and how to use them, he would sketch a broader conceptual framework and in doing so would make use of the latest scientific knowledge—particularly in the areas of acoustics and psychoacoustics, which he considered essential for defining a field of musical exploration. He was keen to see technical innovations harnessed to support the development of musical ideas, as opposed to their advancement as ends in themselves.

At this time, the entire scientific team at IRCAM, still modest in number, took part in both the courses and practical applications. Works by all participants—musicians and scientists alike—were discussed regularly at presentations and seminars, which virtually everyone attended. Contact was therefore direct between composers, scientists, and researchers. The center's founder, Pierre Boulez, actively participated in the seminars on Artificial Intelligence researcher Patrick Greussay from 10 pm to midnight. Greussay taught AI concepts and the Lisp programming language to the IRCAM team. Discussions that followed these and other sessions extended well beyond scheduled hours, and often continued through the night. The in-depth exchanges encouraged by these circumstances—especially those with psycho-acoustician Stephen McAdams—were very important to Saariaho. They provided her with considerable knowledge about musical perception and cognition, and inspired further research. Saariaho returned to work at IRCAM on several occasions over the course of the spring of 1982. Upon completion of her studies in Freiburg the same year, she moved to Paris. There she continued to participate in various activities organized by IRCAM, among them research projects, commissions for musical realizations, courses, and lectures.

From her collaboration with McAdams between 1983 and 1985 emerged an innovative conception of timbre as a form-bearing musical element. Their development of these ideas was indebted to the study of speech, especially poetry, as a model of timbral hierarchies. Together they strove to combine psychoacoustic concepts, such as auditory image, with compositional ideas aided by computer music tools that were then becoming available.

Even before her first works at IRCAM, Saariaho had experimented with forms of instrumentation and orchestration by amplification: using the microphone as a microscope to search for new timbres; amplifying modes of playing whose intensity were too weak to be heard under normal concert conditions; and processing the hidden territories of instruments with the first digital reverberators and harmonizers (EMT, Publison, Eventide, Yamaha, etc.), as, for example, in *Sah den Vögeln*, her 1981 composition for small ensemble and electronics. The workshop in IRCAM thus presented Saariaho with confirmation—indeed, affirmation—of her musical intuitions. And she was soon able to realize ideas through computer music in ways that had, until then, not been possible: not with traditional instruments, nor with the analog electronics that she had previously come across in Helsinki (at the Sibelius Academy and the Finnish Radio studios) and Freiburg (at the studio associated with the Hochschule für Music, the famous experimental studio of SWR German radio).

With computer music, her aim was to continue this work by exploring musical materials through the analysis and synthesis of sounds deriving from instruments, voices, and nature (winds, birds, and so on). She then deduced organizational principles from her findings. These efforts were contemporaneous with spectral music, which she had discovered at the summer courses in Darmstadt in 1980 through presentations by Gérard Grisey and Tristan Murail. Her musical vision, however, remained decisively non-dogmatic. She would not limit it to the rigid constraints imposed by models of the spectrum and the harmonic series—systems central to spectral music.

Saariaho's interest in synthesis and filtering grew thanks to the CHANT program and to Formes, an aid for composition that was then in its infancy. The CHANT program, modeled after studies of the singing voice, had already been extended to sound synthesis in general. The research Xavier Rodet simulated several instrumental sounds approaching the vocal model (especially the nagaswaram, an Indian oboe), while I systematically simulated instruments from all families (woods, brasses, strings, percussions) to validate CHANT's domains of application and provide models that composers could adapt according to their needs.

To work on synthesis, you had to harness all of the available sound analysis tools (fast Fourier transformation, linear predictive coding, pitch estimation, etc.)—each of which was still heavy and clumsy, at least in terms of interface—in order to determine partials (harmonics and inharmonics), formants, and spectral envelope. More generally, these tools could also be applied to help understand the structure and behavior of individual instruments. The parameters drawn from these analyses had to be retrieved by hand on graphical outputs/prints, or directly from the data lists to select values for the parameters of (re)synthesis.

This was a tedious process, as were the consecutive computations for synthesis. It was by no means unusual for a few second-long sounds to require several days to compute. You often had to run calculations repeatedly in order to refine the settings by trial and error. This procedure would continue until you finally decided to accept the result—however distant it might prove from one's initial expectations. The control interface of CHANT, however, was easily accessible. You specified the values of sound parameters (fundamental frequency, formants) by constants and/or time functions (described by segments), directly in dialogue with the program (through a conversational interface) or through a file. Saariaho mastered CHANT quickly and soon conducted a series of radical experiments on sonic materials that interested her musically. During the workshop, she sketched and then realized her first piece with a computer (for tape only), *Vers le blanc*, which she presented in the fall of 1982 at the International Computer Music Conference at the Palazzo della Mostra in Venice. The piece was a process unfolding in a single "breath" of fifteen minutes, created by three virtual voices interpolating from one chord to another, their pitches crossing in an imperceptibly slow glissandi.

Later, Saariaho would depart from the original context of CHANT to elaborate more abstract models constructed with compositionally modified instrumental sound analysis. She conceptualized and realized a continuum between timbre and harmony, one that would prove fundamental for her musical aesthetics and contribute to the great originality of her music. She would then use CHANT, its principles and its extensions—in particular, models of resonance—transported and applied into various computer music environments, for most of her pieces with electronics.

Conceived in 1985, models of resonance was initially an application inspired by the vocal model as represented in CHANT: an excitation source (the glottis) coupled with a resonator (the vocal tract), simulated by a specific technique (formant wave functions). CHANT made it possible to superimpose processing with filters to synthesis with formants, which permitted treatments of all kinds of sound sources.

One could then easily take this model and transpose it to other instrumental references, for example, to a specific mode of playing wind instruments in which three types of sounds are layered: the playing of the instrument; the use of the instrumentalist's voice (whispering, speaking or singing) filtered by the resonator (the instrument's body); and a third layer that results from the amplitude modulation between the two previous sources.

Models of resonance, developed by Yves Potard, Pierre-François Baisnée and myself in the department of musical research, is a conceptual approach inspired by this instrumental model. It permits the researcher to automatically produce parameters for filters modeling instruments, which can be represented with the excitation/resonance model, especially impulse-like sounds (percussions, slaps with winds, pizzicati with strings).

Thanks to models of resonance, Saariaho could now imagine all sorts of metaphors for the cross-composition of instruments and electronics.

One such example would be *NoaNoa*, where the voice of the flutist, who utters fragments from Paul Gauguin's diary, is at some moments filtered acoustically by the flute, and at others the flute and/or voice are filtered by a series of models of resonance based on percussion instruments.

Already in *Io*, a work for ensemble, tape, and live electronics, she analyzed—among other sources—sounds from the double bass and bass flute to produce harmonic pre-compositional materials for the instrumental and electronics writing. She used models of resonance to realize the synthesis part. In doing so, she created a blend unique to music that mixed instruments with electronics—a combination that would soon become one of her trademarks.

From the moment of her arrival at IRCAM in 1982, Saariaho had always been interested in the use of computer as an aid to composition. She endeavored to elaborate musical structures by generation and/ or transformations, the results of which could then be used as pre-compositional materials for both instrumental writing and synthesis control. With the assistance of researcher Pierre Cointe, she conceived one of the very first applications of the Formes program in 1983. It calculated interpolations for all sorts of parameters. The scores devised by this method were printable, albeit in rudimentary form. Parameters could be applied directly to synthesis and processing to control CHANT and other programs.

Jardin Secret I (1985), for tape only, emerged from this research, and pushed musical reflection on timbral and rhythmical interpolations in abstract synthesis to its very limits. *Jardin Secret II* (1986), for harpsichord and tape, explored interpolations with treatments of voice and harpsichord sounds. She also used these interpolations for the instrumental writing of *Nymphéa*, a string quartet, and *Petals*, for cello—two works that also incorporate live electronics.

A SECOND WAVE OF MUSICAL RESEARCH

The second part of the eighties was particularly productive at IRCAM. In many respects, most of the important programs produced by the institute originated during that period.

In 1984, I succeeded American composer Tod Machover as director of the musical research department, which was distinct at that time from scientific research and musical production. Musical research created close partnerships between composers and scientists. It placed musical objectives rather than technological or scientific ones in the forefront, while not limiting them to the production of a specific work.

Musical research opened up to a new generation of composers, one more or less born with computer music. Transversal programmatic axes were introduced: interactions between materials and organizations, cognitive and perceptual processes, intelligent interactions with instrumentalists, personal systems and knowledge transfer, modes of playing and composition for instrumental research. The department became a forum where musical ideas and their technical realizations could be shared openly without an artificial need for consensus. Debates of all sorts—whether musical, artistic, technical, or even philosophical— were lively and frequent. Strong aesthetic oppositions clashed openly after concerts, especially premieres. The creative process and its multiple possibilities were endlessly theorized and discussed. Two collective projects organized in the framework of the musical research department serve as testimonies to the creative fertility and exchange of that period: the Seminar on Timbre (1985), which led to *Le timbre, métaphores pour la composition*, a book that I later compiled and edited (Christian Bourgois, 1991); and the Symposium on Personal Systems and Computer Music (1987) and its subsequent proceedings. A key reason for the advances that occurred during these years was the arrival of the Macintosh personal computer, which offered, amongst many novelties, the opportunity to work interactively on graphical representations directly on the screen. Beforehand, computer interfaces at IRCAM had been largely textual. On the rare occasions when graphical representations did exist, they were only printable. The Macintosh's introduction brought about a major technological revolution—and a democratic one, too, since from this point on anyone could work on their own computer instead. This liberated people from having to share the same equipment, and made it possible for composers, such as Saariaho, to work from home. Suddenly, one could represent and edit the musical notation as well as all sorts of graphics that emerged from data analysis. You could even program graphically. Relations between musicians and the institution were to henceforth evolve rapidly and deeply, as the composer became less dependent on the latter for approaches to musical research and production problems.

Thanks to the links established by Wessel with Apple, IRCAM was able to receive the first Macintosh computers in 1986 almost immediately after their release. This would soon lead to the conception of an entire series of new graphical applications for musical research and production. Around the same time, an industrial version of the 4X—a specialized computer for sound signal processing conceived by Giuseppe di Giugno at IRCAM— became available in the institute's studios. The 4X enabled the rise of real-time electronics, something that had been impossible with general-purpose computers.

Musical research welcomed Miller Puckette, the American mathematician from MIT who conceived PATCHER (renamed later MAX), a graphical programming software for Macintosh. PATCHER was initially used to pilot the 4X in MIDI, then eventually for many other kinds of musical tasks. The collaboration of Puckette with composer Philippe Manoury gave birth to a series of mixed pieces, including *Jupiter* for flute in 1987 and *Pluton* for piano in 1989. These works became milestones of real-time interaction, in particular for score following: a process where the computer analyzes and "follows" a musician's performance by playing the electronic part according to variations in the interpretation.

At the same time, Esquisse was the first "aid to composition" software environment to incorporate representations in traditional musical notation; it was developed in Lisp on the Macintosh by Jacques Duthen and Pierre-François Baisnée under my direction. Esquisse could generate, visualize and manipulate graphically structural operations and compositional calculations. Many composers participating in musical research contributed to the project: the class that had just graduated from Conservatoire National de Paris, including Marc-André Dalbavie, Philippe Hurel, Philippe Durville, and Frédéric Durieux; young international composers such as Saariaho, Magnus Lindberg, Marco Stroppa, Michael Jarrell; and individuals from previous generations, such as Murail, Brian Ferneyhough, and those who had worked in the production department for the realization of their pieces. Esquisse was later encapsulated in PatchWork, a collaboration between Mikael Laurson (at Sibelius Academy in 1985), Duthen, Gérard Assayag, and Camilo Rueda.

Projects were numerous, and their advances considerable. Assayag and composer Claudy Malherbe collaborated with acoustician Michèle Castallengo on the classification of multiphonics for wind instruments. Their work led to a number of concepts and tools for the analysis and musical organization of complex sounds, among them the program Iana. Iana used the algorithms of spectral masking created by German psychoacoustician Ernst Terhardt to determine the perceptible pitches and perceptual weights of the spectral components of complex sounds. Francis Courtot used the programming language by constraints Prolog to develop musical applications aimed at solving specific compositional problems for Hurel and Jarrell, while Rueda and Antoine Bonnet focused on musical constraints inside PatchWork (Situations library). Mosaic by Jean-Marie

Adrien and Joseph Morrison became the first physical modeling synthesis program. This made it possible to describe sounds through the physical equations of their production; later it was renamed Modalys. In the scientific research department, Philippe Depalle started to develop SVP, a software toolbox for analysis and processing which became AudioSculpt after the addition of a graphical interface. Meanwhile, Jean-Pascal Jullien, Olivier Warusfel, and Jean-Marc Jot conceived the Spat, a tool that allows to move around sound sources in the virtual acoustics simulation of any space.

Composers started to enrich working environments for "aid to composition" in PatchWork or for real-time in MAX by building their own libraries. They created functionalities as needed and shared their programs, experiences, and knowledge by making them accessible to others. This generosity no doubt helps account for the software's longevity—much of it has now existed for some thirty years! A real community of musical research emerged through the free circulation of tools, ideas, and knowledge.

Saariaho's interpolations were ported into Esquisse then PatchWork. They are today available in OpenMusic and PWGL. She used Iana to analyze complex instrumental sounds—modes of playing such as multiphonics and breath with winds, pressure variations of the bow with strings—in many of her own compositions, such as *Lichtbogen*, *Io*, and *Amers*. She has worked on synthesis with physical models since the genesis of Modalys, which she used for *Amers* and then *Solar* (1993). She was fascinated by its potential to manifest virtual instruments that are impossible in the real world—for example, a gong made in crystal or an infinite bow. She continues to use AudioSculpt today for analysis and treatments in electronics parts. And Spat plays a part in nearly all of her pieces with electronics. Spatialization has indeed always been of interest to Saariaho. For *Amers*, for instance, she collaborated with René Caussé, the head of the instrumental acoustics lab, to create a special microphone to capture separately each of the four strings of a cello and distribute their sounds in a quadriphonic space around the audience.

Saariaho was always critical about the sonic quality achievable in real-time with the 4X. She therefore elected to elaborate, in non real-time, sequences of synthesis and processing in order to achieve greater sonic quality and complexity. These sequences were triggered from a computer hard disk and synchronized with musicians during the concert. It was only with the IRCAM Signal Processing Workstation—a signal processing card inserted in the Next computer, developed in 1989 and accessible to composers in 1991—that she finally deemed the sonic quality attainable in real-time acceptable. She used the ISPW in 1992 to write *NoaNoa*, for flute, and *Près*, for cello. Both works were originally conceived within a pedagogical framework aimed at demonstrating the musical possibilities of real-time signal processing.

A LIVING LEGACY

During the second half of the nineties, real-time became increasingly available on personal computers. Since then, the electronics for all of Saariaho's works are played live with MAX while incorporating pre-calculated sounds either still too complex to be synthesized (or processed in real-time) or unrealizable by nature in concert.

Musical research at IRCAM during the eighties had been conceived to bring researchers and composers together. This model vanished over the course of the subsequent decade. In its place emerged an institutional model that separated functionally scientific research, software development and musical production—a shift initiated to improve the efficiency of each domain, yet in practice left less time and latitude to composers for musical research. Direct contact between researchers and composers became exceptional, even discouraged. The occasions when it occurred were largely thanks to the mediation of musical assistants, who acted as bridges between the scientific and musical worlds. But what had in many ways been a golden age of musical research gave way to another conception of technological and musical productivity.

Whether it actually proved more efficient in practice remains to be seen. One wonders whether the striking productivity of the eighties, which had no subsequent match, was achieved precisely through its close collaborations. It is unthinkable to imagine their existence apart from IRCAM's earlier concept of musical research, and its institutionalization in a department.

Saariaho also realized the electronics for *Lonh*, a work for soprano, as well as her operas *L'Amour de loin*, *Adriana Mater*, and the oratorio *La Passion de Simone*, at IRCAM. Like most composers, she today prepares the electronics for most pieces in her own studio, occasionally with the help of various collaborators (selected according to the specific conceptual and technical needs of each project). Perhaps the composer's workshop is now the space best equipped for musical research, and not institutions preoccupied by the administrative and commercial spirit that dominates the present cultural scene. In her music today, Kaija Saariaho still applies the concepts and tools that she discovered and developed—along with their extensions—through her participation in musical research, an experience that left an everlasting mark on her musical aesthetics.

Kaija Saariaho (above) and Jean-Baptiste Barrière (below) at
work at IRCAM in 1985.

The Blossom from the Darkness:
Reflections on Kaija Saariaho's *Nymphéa*

David Harrington

Kronos Quartet first met Kaija in the summer of 1984 at the Darmstadt Festival of New Music. I remember it was the same summer that we played Morton Feldman's big and beautiful String Quartet No. 2 there. And it was the same festival where we met Kevin Volans, the South African composer who would go on to write *White Man Sleeps* and *Hunting: Gathering* for Kronos—very important works in our repertoire, and among the first string quartets ever by an African-born composer. So in meeting both Kaija and Kevin, Kronos began two very important relationships that summer.

I heard a piece of Kaija's performed at Darmstadt. Afterward, she and I corresponded, and she sent me an LP of her music. The thing that was amazing to me about her music, from the very first time I heard it, was the sheer variety of sounds, and the way acoustic instruments and electronics felt so natural together. It also seemed natural to me that Kaija should write for Kronos, and so I asked her, and eventually *Nymphéa* arrived.

Nymphéa was perhaps the first—or at least, among the very first—pieces Kronos ever played that involved live electronics. This was long before the days of laptops, of course, and to perform the piece required a very particular form of machinery—something developed while Kaija was at IRCAM, I believe. It was so complex and so specific to Kaija that both she and her husband, Jean-Baptiste Barrière, had to be there in order for Kronos to perform the piece. We didn't have our own sound person at that time, so performing *Nymphéa* represented a big step in the evolution of our work, and of our team. It was also one of the first times in our history that a piece required a sound engineer be able to read a score—there were specific cues that had to come in at exact moments during the live performance. It was a direction we'd continue to explore with Steve Reich's *Different Trains* (1988) and many works since then. But it was really *Nymphéa* that prompted this growth of our work with technology in concert.

Initially, because of these technical requirements, we weren't able to play the piece that much. But when we did, it took our sound world into totally new places. We were able to transform a concert hall into a very different space. At various points in *Nymphéa*, we develop the sound further by adding in our voices, reciting a poem by Arseny Tarkovsky. We'd chanted and shouted before in George Crumb's *Black Angels*—the voices are counting in various languages, sometimes like drill sergeants. In *Nymphéa*, the voices are very internal, very sensitive, just like Kaija herself. That's something about Kaija in general: her music is so much like she is that for me, listening to her work is very much like talking with her, and vice versa. I think of her work and her personality as being almost the same.

In working with Kaija on *Nymphéa*, first in our rehearsals and then later in the recording, it was wonderful to experience how clear she was about the sound and feeling of the music. That was the most important aspect of the process to her: arriving at that particular sound and feeling. One thing I always sense about her is that she listens to the center of the music in a very beautiful way.

I was reading something once where Kaija was describing the *nymphéa*—the water lilies—how they grow out of mud and darkness, and out of that mud comes this unbelievably beautiful flower. Her comment made me think of all the lilies I've seen—and all the depictions of lilies in art throughout history. The *nymphéa* is the sacred lotus from ancient Egyptian art, and of course, closer to our own era, it's the water lily of Monet's famous series of paintings. The sound of Kaija's music definitely brings to my mind the look of Monet's coloring, from the panels of water lilies I've seen in Paris. When I step back and listen to Kaija's piece, I can feel what she was describing in that article I read: it's like the high frequencies of the violins blossom, but beneath it there's this earthy, or muddy quality. It captures my imagination and my feelings just as powerfully today as it did back in 1987, when Kronos first received Kaija's score. And *Nymphéa* has been a key part of Kronos' sound for all these years.

Kaija Saariaho with Gidon Kremer
at the Maison de la Radio, Paris.

Graal théâtres

Paul Griffiths

GALEHAUT: I am a character.

VIOLIN: Perhaps I am too. I have no physical existence. I am not an object, though I need a certain class of objects—wooden boxes with strings and a bow—to be heard in the real world. I am represented, bodied forth, by these objects, just as you are by a voice, even a silently reading voice. I am not to be identified with the object that renders me, nor with the musician, any more than you are with the voice relating your words, or the reader or actor whose voice this is.

When Kaija Saariaho describes her 1994 composition *Graal théâtre* as being "for violin and orchestra," or as a "violin concerto," we may imagine her to have had in mind a musical instrument in its actuality, including its tuning and its responses, and we may suppose her to have been considering also Gidon Kremer, her destined performer, but she will have been thinking not only of but through these manifest conditions of her work, to me, to an entity whose features are not materials and dimensions, not personality and technique, but sound, and a design for sound, and experiences of that sound through time.

The note she places in the score is almost explicit about this, where she remarks that "the title expresses the tension I feel between the efforts of the composer when writing music and the theatrical aspect of a performance, especially in the case of a concerto where the soloist is playing a major role, both physically and musically." On the one side, then, the *graal* of as-yet-unrealized music, where the action is that of the imagining mind and the traveling pen, moving in a world where instruments and performers are all still in the future; on the other, the *théâtre* of a concert hall, a show, a virtuoso converting difficulty into astonishment, an audience in attendance and attention. Tension, however, implies communication. I feel within me the stirrings of this imminent *théâtre*, even though I belong to the domain of the *graal*.

We are virtual beings, you and I, living out our lives in a world as impalpable—and as vivid—as that of dreams or memory. The analogy may be supported by how Saariaho, thinking back to the book by Florence

Delay and Jacques Roubaud from which she took her title, remembers an episode of dream interpretation.[1]

GALEHAUT: I dream, but even in dreaming I am dreamt.

VIOLIN: Exactly so.

GALEHAUT: Is that why my great love—not just the object of my love, but the feeling itself, in all its strength and multiplicity—remains out of my reach?[2]

VIOLIN: No. Our deeds and our hesitations, our enlightenments and our incomprehensions, are all written for us.

GALEHAUT: Not entirely. Galehaut cannot be forced by any poet or romance writer into the shape of Galahad or Gawain, of Merlin or of Morgan. Galehaut cannot be made twin to Lancelot. I know this.

VIOLIN: You are right. I cannot be Harp, cannot be Trombone, cannot be Cello. We are defined, and then redefined in each telling of our story.

GALEHAUT: What is your story?

VIOLIN: I have many, but one is perhaps not so unlike yours, of being placed with another, Orchestra, in a striving for union that can never be achieved. It is a story that has been told by Bach, by Mozart, by Beethoven and by Mendelssohn, by Tchaikovsky and Brahms and Sibelius and Elgar, by Berg and Bartók and Stravinsky and Schoenberg, and then by countless more in recent times. It is always the same story. It is always a different story.

Saariaho's telling, perhaps more than any other, has me aware of these predecessors, and even of concertos that were, twenty years ago, yet to come. Again, her note says something of this, when she speaks of how she wanted "to bring an idea of the violin concerto, a genre with so many moving and skillful examples, into my musical framework and language" and of how she was encouraged to achieve this by the example of "Roubaud's interpretation of the old legend."

So there is another union here, of a venerable story, authorless for having had so many authors, and a new redaction, personal for being the work of an individual. It is the same for my story as for yours.

GALEHAUT: It is, indeed, but let us be clear that for neither of us is there an original version. A child gathers dew-wetted spider webs in a looped twig, until eventually the layers of silk and water cohere into a mirror. Such is my story, and yours: an image created by many tellings, not to be found in any one of them. Once again we have a *graal*, unfindable, partially realized in so many *théâtres*, which together are responsible for the mysterious existence of the *graal*.

VIOLIN: I accept what you say. By the time my concerto story was being told by Antonio Vivaldi, by J.S. Bach, and by Giuseppe Tartini, it had already been circulating for two or more generations.

GALEHAUT: How does it begin, this story of yours?

VIOLIN: It begins when I speak. Or it begins when Orchestra is preparing for me to speak, inviting me to speak, waiting for me to speak. And, always, I speak. I have to do so. I want to do so. There can be no concerto story unless I take part in its telling.

GALEHAUT: You see, it is different for me. My story could be told without my participation—even, perhaps, in such a work as the Delay-Roubaud *Graal théâtre*, which has the form of a playscript, though these authors do indeed give me much to say (as well as much to hold in silence).

VIOLIN: It might be possible to imagine a violin concerto without me—or, rather, with me as an absent protagonist, evoked, gestured toward, even partly imitated by Orchestra. However, no such work yet exists. Always I am there. And in the Saariaho *Graal théâtre*, I am there from the start.

The work opens with one of my fundamental sounds, the A on the treble staff, the note to which my second string is tuned, and it is this string that produces the note, an "open string," unstopped by the violinist's left hand. This note oscillates with harmonics played on my next string down, tuned to D: the A an octave higher, and then the D a fourth above that. At this initiating moment, both strings are bowed close to the bridge, to produce a constricted tone—"nasal" is the word commonly used— suggestive of a coarser instrument: a folk fiddle or perhaps a medieval vielle. The whole sound—tremulous, emanating directly from my tuning, here in the present, but sounding out also from a distant past, with the A stationary and harmonics flickering above it, the sound level, having risen from inaudibility to modest volume—conveys a sense of "once upon a time."

GALEHAUT: Or of you becoming yourself, testing yourself, beginning to feel for the center and the limits of yourself. As we all do, when our stories begin.

VIOLIN: Indeed. Then I start to spin a fragment of melody—a scalewise ascent from A to B flat to C sharp—over and around a drone D, conforming to a scale remote from the concert hall in which this théâtre will be taking place: the "double harmonic scale," also known as the "Arabic scale."

This first step, from raw sound to incipient melody, is significant in its direction, for it may remind us that bowed string instruments probably entered European culture by way of the Islamic world. From telling of my sound, I have moved on to tell of my history. And as I develop this story, the story of my arrival from the East, I gain echo and encouragement from Orchestra. This, my companion, has been there from the beginning, but almost unnoticeable: a silver fizz of triangle when I started, an antique cymbal chiming with my A. Now Orchestra comes forward, its harp concurring with me, its drums pressing me on. At the same time, the exotic reference is dissolving. It will always be there, right to the end. This music remembers everything, and most certainly it remembers itself. But the quasi-oriental pattern becomes transformed, and extended into something larger, no longer a more or less specific cultural marker.

A tendency to rise, also there from the beginning, finds its endpoint in a high F sharp, a note that had been picked out by an antique cymbal within the music's first minute. On that note I am now joined by glockenspiel and piano, for still Orchestra is putting forward only resonant percussive instruments and drums, joined recently, and almost imperceptibly, by low strings. This F sharp is a point of brilliance to which I keep returning all through the piece, finding it in this register and also an octave higher, as a destination that can be only glimpsed, caught for a fleeting instant, not fully attained.

GALEHAUT: A desire that cannot properly be felt, so much the less consummated.

VIOLIN: It may be, but other metaphors are possible, or other understandings of the metaphor that is music. You encounter my story through the doorway of your own. Others will do so as well, but all of them differently. Music welcomes this, especially Saariaho's, rooted as it is in basic elements of sound quality, melodic motif, and regular pulse, and moving through a time whose depth is measured in centuries.

Rotation, from the first, has been crucial to how this music proceeds, repeating an idea with progressive change, and so moving from one harmony to another—from a pure octave at the beginning to an "Arabic" motif with four notes in play and now to a melody that, repeatedly touching on that high F sharp, is formed from a six-note scale that includes the notes of the F sharp major triad (F sharp—A sharp—C sharp) but has a minor sixth (D) as well as the appropriate second degree (G sharp) and fourth (B). This is a scale from no known location, and residual elements of the major-minor system are placed in question partly by the shape of the melody, holding the notional keynote high, and partly by the accompaniment, which, in reiterations that include an echo of the "Arabic" figment on glockenspiel, adds five more notes to the harmony. We are in Saariaholand, an iridescent world, where streaks of the familiar are destabilized in shimmer. I find myself unsettled here, and at home.

GALEHAUT: So it is with me, in my *Graal théâtre*, where the Age of Chivalry has all the conveniences of high-speed travel and psychoanalysis.

VIOLIN: And the resemblance is even stronger, for my *Graal théâtre*, while reverberating with the immemorial, profits from advances one might judge scientific. Saariaho moved from her native Helsinki to Paris in 1982, principally to work at the computer-music studio Pierre Boulez had set up shortly before, though the French capital was also alive at this time with the new scintillating sounds of spectral music, as it was being developed by Gérard Grisey (the original version of whose *Les Espaces acoustiques* was performed for the first time in 1981), Tristan Murail, Hugues Dufourt, and other composers just a few years older than the new arrival from Finland. Spectral music had to do with using the harmonic spectra of real sounds—the spectra of frequencies constituting those sounds—as models for harmonies, which, each related to one source, would have wholeness as well as complexity. For example, the many instruments of an orchestra could be given diverse frequencies across a range of six octaves or more, imitating a wide spectrum and so creating sounds of imposing singularity.

For Saariaho, as for the pioneer spectralists, this principle tied in with work in the studio. Computers provided means for analyzing sound spectra, and the analysis could then be adapted to compositional needs. Moreover, some of the basic techniques of electroacoustic music—notably ring modulation, which, from two frequencies x and y yields sum and difference tones (x + y, x - y, 2y + x, 2y - x, etc), often creating a clangorous result—could be imitated orchestrally by using the spectral method of assigning specified frequencies to instruments. Some approximation might be inevitable, but the use of quarter-tones, such as Saariaho occasionally introduces in her *Graal théâtre*, would reduce this.

One might say that spectral thinking, like so much else in this work, has been there from the beginning, where the harmonics on the D string reinforce harmonics naturally present in the sound of the open A string. However, adherence to spectral models has been limited up to this point by the music's relatively narrow range of just under three octaves, from the G of my fourth string to the F sharp so much mentioned, and by the restricted instrumentation. All this changes with the coming of the strings, followed soon, in the dissolving of the F-sharp passage, by the first woodwind instruments. Bell-like sounds are created a little later by a fusion of piano, tuned percussion, and high strings. Later still, when the brass section has finally been mobilized, after six minutes or so, strong spectral harmonies become possible. This late entry of the brass introduces another element: an unexpected alter ego for me in a solo trumpet with which I am in a dialogue of imitation and counter-imitation.

But we are not yet halfway through this sixteen-minute movement, and there is a second still to come, a finale that continues the story partly by contrast. Where the first movement drifts by way of allusion, around a solo line that is almost continuous, the second is at once more dynamic and more dramatic, often cutting between its two principals, Violin and Orchestra, in vigorous dialogue.

At the same time, however, this second movement is a reliving of the first. Its unaccompanied opening, which serves as the solo cadenza any concerto should have, is initiated by intensive repetitions of a four-note descending pattern, a kind of driving-rain music that has appeared in the first movement—except that here in the second the pattern is directly in keeping with the first movement's harmonic material, descending from F sharp through the "Arabic" motif reversed (C sharp—B flat—A). Later, among other cross-references, a decelerated cascade through the orchestral registers from the high treble to the far bass is repeated in varied form. The high F sharp remains a feature, too.

The two movements are like two tellings of the same story, or perhaps more like two stories in which some of the same characters and events appear. One may be indeed a story of unassuageable desire, the other a record of combat: a love song and a ballad of war.

GALEHAUT: These may not be such different categories.

VIOLIN: Indeed, they are not in this case. Both movements end with the kind of delicately excited tremolo from which the work was born. In doing so they bring forward different notes, the first movement closing into F sharp, the second into D, but the difference is also a sameness, for these notes join with the originating A to create the triad of D major, the key in which my concerto story was told by Beethoven, Brahms, and Tchaikovsky. The whole work is thus bordered by these wisps of great predecessors.

GALEHAUT: In my *Graal théâtre* it is as if modernity is a wisp, as if time were proceeding backwards, from an indistinctly defined contemporaneity toward the fullness of the epoch of legend.

VIOLIN: I might rather say that in my *Graal théâtre* time has no fixed direction, but rather wavers in an abundance of presence. However, perhaps we could continue our conversation in the language I know as my own.

An Excerpt from *Graal théâtre*

Jacques Roubaud and Florence Delay

Translated from the French by Jan Steyn

The following excerpt from Graal théâtre, *appearing here for the first time in English, was selected by Kaija Saariaho as representative of passages that inspired her violin concerto, which shares the book's name. The concerto was written for and debuted by Gidon Kremer.*

ALENTIVE: Master Petronius from Oxford Master Helius from Toulouse and Master Blaise from Northumberland have arrived. King Arthur sent them in response to your letter.

GALEHAUT: Masters I am embarrassed to have had to drag you away from your work and bring you all the way here. I know I should have undertaken the journey myself but the recent disasters at Sorclois prevented me from doing so.

BLAISE: You have no blame in this. we have travelled most excellently well and these days it is easy to work even while on the road thanks to the wonders of modern locomotion.

PETRONIUS: But have you ever managed to write while at sea?

HELIUS: We are here to listen sir.

GALEHAUT: Masters King Arthur has summoned each three of you to aid me. I am consequently as thankful to him as I am to you. I have need of your good counsel for while I am big and strong and in good health as is evident from my thin and healthy limbs yet a faintness has entered my heart that has troubled me so much that I have lost the power to eat and drink and have long gone sleepless. I don't see any cause for this illness that has taken hold of me other than a great and sudden fear though I cannot say whether it is the cause or the result of my ailment.

HELIUS: you were right sir to come to us. and I will answer on behalf of my colleagues as well as myself as precisely as recent advances in medical science allows me. you said it was an illness that entered the heart. illnesses of the heart are different from all others because the heart is the most candid and distinct part of man and takes upon itself all the body's shame and evil. the body is but the heart's shelter and when it is battered or damaged it is repaired and soon forgets its wounds. but the heart forgets nothing and that is why illnesses of the heart are so different from those of the body. and know that there are three illnesses of the heart. the first stems from sins and evil deeds for which there is but one cure that of our Lord which is to say charity fasting tears prayers and the counsel of hermits. the second stems from poisons released by the body's infirmities for which one ought to take doctors' medicine which is to say potions herbs and infusions. but the third illness is far more serious it is the illness of love the illness of heroes. love is a thing that enters the heart through the gateway of the eyes or that of the ears and when the heart is under siege from one of these entry points and succumbs and becomes a prisoner in love's dungeon it is very difficult to mount an escape because once the heart falls through those gates it keeps falling deeper and deeper like Daedalus in his tower. unfortunately we cannot right now determine with certainty that it is this third kind of illness that afflicts you. for that you shall have to agree to answer some questions.

BLAISE: My dear Dean these questions are at times delicate and the subject might feel more at ease if we ask some of them indirectly.

HELIUS: Hmm how would you like to go about it?

BLAISE: We could for example give the clinical table of symptoms for the third illness.

HELIUS: I see what you mean. you are correct.

BLAISE: The signa or signs are according to Bernardus Gordonius and his liber medicinae capitulum 20 de amore qui heroes dicitur chapter which agrees with Arnaldus de Villanova and Geoffrey Chaucer. the signs thus that follow the causae are the following. Loss of sleep lack of appetite acedia. the body is...

PETRONIUS: Allow me to however briefly recall the causes. the patient has conceived the form and figure of a being or object that he believes and argues to be the most beautiful the most desirable by far the best endowed with natural virtue and morals of all objects or beings. and he desires it and wishes to possess it so ardently that he believes all happiness would be barred him should he fail to bring it under his power. a patient loving a frog would claim that frog to be Diana herself. quisquis amabat ranam ranam putabat esse Dianam.

BLAISE: And so the signs that follow the causes are the following. the patient falls into a meditative state called melancholy solicitude. he runs day and night along pathways and off pathways scorning heat and cold. he loses sleep he has no thirst he is no longer hungry. his body grows stiff maceratus totum corpus and dry as is a shaft. his cogitations are deep and obscure and accompanied by heavy sighs. if the patient hears songs of lovers separated he cries. he laughs when he hears songs of lovers reunited. his pulse is irregular and often inordinately fast and changes when the loved object is named or in sight. the last is a certain way to know the malady as was demonstrated by Galen. these are the signs of the so-called hero's disease.

PETRONIUS: It is now time to ask the decisive question. have you not recently had one or several dreams?

GALEHAUT: How did you know? a month ago I had two dreams and since then every night I've again dreamt one or the other. in the first I was taken back to there the place where I was lost in a crowd.

PETRONIUS: There?

GALEHAUT: In Arthur's house. a serpent left a bedroom and made his way…

PETRONIUS: Which bedroom?

GALEHAUT: I don't know. the snake was yellow and blue and made its way to me everything moved away but I was fixed to the spot. it covered me in flames I lost half of my limbs.

PETRONIUS: Which ones?

GALEHAUT: That's all. in my second dream I have two hearts. I look at them in my belly and I am astonished at how similar they are when suddenly one is lost. next I see a leopard a herd of wild animals and among them a leopard. by the time I stop watching them I no longer even have a single heart. and as far as I can make out after that I die.

HELIUS: We now have all the elements at hand. we thank you for your assistance. is there somewhere we can retire to consult among ourselves?

ALENTIVE: Come with me.

GALEHAUT: I expect from you the whole truth. promise me you will not hide anything.

PETRONIUS: We promise not to hide anything from you about what we are able to discern. I will speak first. I'll be followed by Master Helius and Master Blaise of Northumberland will conclude. we follow the signs that are our guides. in the logic of your bestiary sir the serpent and the leopard are your enemies. one devours half your limbs and the other runs off into the forest carrying off a heart which happens to belong to you. while this is taking place your other heart fails. you are a double prince and your illness is well known by those acquainted with psychiatric medicine. you are sir a hypochondriac hysteric and suffer from split personalities. your nerves are unstable. neither man nor woman you are Adam experiencing the charms of the leopard's fur but you are also Eve yielding to the serpent's virile force. you are seduced by feline femininity. you are struck down by the lizard's erectile powers. and your fragile personality forever marked through your education by a mother whose nickname the Beautiful Giantess no doubt had an excessive influence on your childhood does not know to whom to give your heart. to a lover who would prefer a queen or to a king who would make you his vassal. the illness of love eats away at you because it is said that in the beginning all beings were double and that each half will endlessly approach the other without ever actually succeeding in finding unity. the serpent is simultaneously the king and your mother. the leopard simultaneously the queen and your male lover. for woman leads the world on the path of sexual illnesses. you are touched by the poison of Delilah who under the unctuous charms of a pelt hides a flamethrower that destroys your body. the symptoms are all there. I recommend some sessions of hypnosis which thanks to modern techniques will give you back your lost unity. Such is my counsel.

HELIUS: Our esteemed colleague whose work is rightly renowned remains a follower of the old neurology. he ought to keep himself up to date with current research. your illness is an imaginary illness and your nervous fever is a doctor's illness. Galehaut is not an ordinary patient. he is not a modern neurotic sick of civilization but a knight from the Matter of Britain. a hero made of adventures and prosody. he expresses his dreams as a dramatization. the destroyed limbs the suddenly-removed heart the flamethrower serpent symbolize an Oedipus complex neatly arranged in this naïve fable. the hero represents his family members disguised as childhood toys. A cardboard cut-out serpent with painted flames a red crepe paper heart a stuffed toy leopard such were the favorite playthings of a little man who too soon became a knight. he dreams of dominating kings but the kings in his dreams dominate him. Arthur is a crowned dragon or a serpent. Lancelot is a leopard and knightly combat becomes preying on wild beasts. the set is as dangerous as he could wish. the locations are mysterious filled with animal sounds that seem to come from a zoo or a natural history museum. the dream expresses the mute desires of childhood loves which bring together the prince and the gangster dressed in armor and pelts. the talking cure is to be recommended for this hero who likes to make up stories.

BLAISE: I am in wholehearted agreement with the wisdom of my friends from Oxford and Toulouse to whom I give homage but I would like to take some distance from their oracular knowledge and science of dreams in order to provide a new version of the Prince's lovesickness. once upon a time there were two crowned dragons. the first came from the west. the other from the east. the first was a good king yet often sad. the second was aggressive and ambitious. from his mother a giantess and eater of men who was beautiful but also as large as an ogre he lost all taste for simple loves. having become an adult this dragon prince dreamed of conquering kings and kingdoms collecting the crowns if not the heads of his enemies. destiny called on him to take marvelous Logres and keep it in his proud grip. while invincible in battle the dragon prince soon had his heart conquered when he met the leopard also known as the knight armed in black and white then armed in white. this knight without knowing robbed the giantess of her place and her influence. the dragon prince suffered in half of his heart half of his body and half of his lands. this conqueror was taken with lovesickness and transformed into the most faithful of lovers. the leopard however had a liege in the first crowned dragon and a Lady in the wife of that sovereign. the son of the Beautiful Giantess gave up his arms despite having conquered the territory in order to ask for the leopard's love. the lands of the realm from east to west were pacified since war is simply politics in another guise and politics is but another face of war. the dragon prince found a lover in his own image and a sovereign to match but the peace that reigns over empires and households is not the same peace that reigns over the heart and the prince of the Distant Isles whose destiny was marked by conquest and division found no happiness in trading part of his lands for a half-portion of love. the half-body of a knight. for the heart and the body of the leopard like his own heart and body had become perpetually shared and always divided. it spent two seasons close to its Lady and its sovereign the crowned dragon. the other two seasons it spent in proximity to the pacified dragon. the leopard of the Lake and of the Cart was in the image of the one dreaming it a fragmented body. its heart was enchanted by a queen a lady whose realm is a Lake which she herself stole from another queen her mother. my teacher Merlin the great doctor of sexual illnesses gave me the following details during a conversation. he spoke as is his wont of the future or perhaps of the past. the lion is superior to the leopard he told me and only the first among the knights of the realm can achieve the Grail. the quest is an act of sublimation and the hero who directs towards it his flames while renouncing the flames of sex – the serpent – the flames of mothers ladies dragons and leopards can find this new path to ascendancy. my teacher suggests no treatment. he does not want to interrupt this story's flow for he prefers poetry to science and every day follows the adventures of his favorite knights with ardor.

GALEHAUT: But do you then know how long I have to live?

Kaija Saariaho with Amin Maalouf.

The Making of *Adriana Mater*

Kaija Saariaho and Amin Maalouf

Translated from the French by Daniel Levin Becker

After the premiere of L'Amour de loin *at the Salzburg Festival in July 2000, Kaija Saariaho and her librettist, Amin Maalouf, began planning the composition of a second opera, a work they initially referred to as "Number Two." They discussed various elements of the new opera during meetings in Paris or over lengthy telephone conversations, but a significant part of their collaboration took place over email between December 2001 and April 2003.*

20 December 2001

Dear Amin,

After our discussion… From "Katia Kabanova" to "Anna Karenina," I've leaned toward "Belle de Jour," thinking that in Finnish there are lots of first names that come from nature (Jour, Étoile, Nuage, Mer, Neige, etc.) Then I thought of those jellyfish that Peter mentioned, which have a special name; is there a bird or another animal that could have some of the characteristics of this woman, like "Merle Noir"?

Otherwise it's difficult to find a name without connotations.

Love,
Kaija

*

20 December 2001

My dear Kaija,

True, it's hard to find a proper name with no ethnic connotation. A challenge, but not an insurmountable one. That said, a name in the style of "Belle de Jour," "Merle Noir," could be nice too. (The kind of jellyfish Peter mentioned is called the "Portuguese Man-of-War.")

At this point, any idea we bat around moves us forward. The aforementioned names have in common that they exist in the real world, whereas *L'Amour de loin* needed to remain an abstraction.

I suggest we collect some names that you find harmonious or evocative, taking into account only their sonority; we'll find a way to deal with their origins…

Love,
Amin

*

20 December 2001

Dear Kaija,

I've just had an idea for a *provisional* title: "Adriana Mater"

What do you think?
Amin

*

20 December 2001

Excellent!

Shall we say "Adriana Mater" for the time being!?

Very good, very good!
K

*

22 December 2001

Dear Amin,

Thanks for yesterday.

I thought this morning about the distribution of voices: that Adriana's voice should be a dramatic soprano (like Karita) or mezzo (like Lorraine Hunt), and the sister a lyric soprano (like Dawn).

I had a fundamental question about the men's voices: I'd like the father to have a deep (low) voice in Scene VI. Do you think the man in Scenes I and II can be the same person (baritone) as the son afterward? That way the appearance of the father and his encounter with the son would be musically rather striking.

This morning we saw a screening of the film about me and *L'Amour de loin* by Anne Grange and Serge Steyer. Very good, really. There are clips from the opera, especially lovely. Your commentary and Peter's and Kent's are also terrific.

Talk soon,
Kaija

*

22 December 2001

My dear Kaija,

Peter told me again how delighted he is with what we told him; I think this is the beginning of a new adventure together. Personally I'm always hesitant to speak of projects before they're completely finished, but I've forced myself, because it's good for each of us to plant the idea in our heads and let it begin to ripen and spread.

Regarding your indications about the female voices, I will add them carefully to my notes; you were right to give me concrete examples, which will help me imagine the voices while choosing the words.

As for the men, yours is an audacious idea. I'm sure Peter will love it. It's tempting to me also, but I need to mull it over a bit. The appearance, in the fourth scene, of a character we've seen in the second scene in a totally different light could have quite a powerful effect. It will also be a bit disconcerting, naturally, a bit "confusing"; there's also a risk of "overstressing"... But that's only a first reaction, and I'll think about it some more—and, again, I find it fairly tempting. Stay tuned...

I'm glad the Salzburg film is good; for various reasons, particularly because it will allow us to keep the traces of what was not otherwise filmed. Perhaps we should ask Anne and Serge for copies of the dailies they didn't use; I imagine there will be several, which also deserve to wind up in the *L'Amour de loin* archives.

Andrée joins me in sending love to you and Jean-Baptiste, as well as the children, and in looking forward to seeing you soon,

Amin

*

23 December 2001

Dear Amin,

Thank you for your message. We're not in a hurry to make decisions— but, as you know, the brain works even when we don't want it to. So let me know if your thoughts about the voices evolve more.

Now we're in Finland. Very dark, with just a bit of snow.

With best wishes for Andrée, you and your family.

Talk soon,
Kaija & co

*

24 December 2001

Dear Kaija,

You're right to say the brain works even when we don't want it to. And also when we don't know it's doing so—during sleep, for instance. This morning I sat down, notebook in hand, and took a few notes. Nothing conclusive yet, but it seems to me that there are two possible options.
—The first is for the father from the beginning (Scenes I and II) and the son (Scenes IV to VII) to be identical, and for this to already be *indicated in the text*; they would then have to be played by the same baritone while another singer, a bass, played the father in Scene VI.
—The second is for the voices to be similar but not necessarily identical,

and for this to not necessarily be indicated in the text, in which case *the director could choose* to have the roles played by two different singers or by just one. In either case, someone else would need to be cast as the aging and grizzled father in Scene VI.

I don't know which solution you prefer, nor do I know how much the composition of the music would differ from one hypothesis to the other.

Merry Christmas to Jean-Baptiste, you, and the merry little pranksters.

Talk soon,
Amin

*

26 December 2001

Dear Amin,

I tried to call you to clarify the character question further.

I talked this morning with Peter, who does NOT want the father and the son to be the same person; he says he thinks it would be good to have a new character in Scene IV. Maybe. I'm not convinced yet. I have faith in his dramatic sensibility, of course, but when it comes to writing a story my faith is in you.

In any case, regarding your e-mail:

To your first point, regarding the text, I think you should follow your instinct. Think about it as the father of three sons.

As for the second, this is the most important point for me; musically, it's essential. Peter didn't seem convinced by this either (although he understood its musical importance)… As you can see, I can always find a reason to be anxious! I'd like to talk about this further; I'll try to call you tomorrow if I haven't heard from you.

Talk soon,
Kaija

*

Dear Kaija,

I thought a bit more about everything we discussed, and things seem clearer now—I don't think they'll cause any real problems anymore.

Essentially, for the beginning, it seems logical to me that the young father and the son have the same kind of voice; they could be played by the same person, or by two different people (preferably not too dissimilar), but that should be left to the director. That gives us more flexibility, more freedom and scenic richness. For the moment that solution seems preferable to me, since it won't do any good to impose a single vision once and for all. There could also be subtle references in the text to the resemblance between father and son, whether they're played by one person or by two.

Regarding Scene VI, your desire to give the aging father a low voice is fair, and important. So we'll need a different singer for that scene, but he should be clearly identified with the character from the first two scenes, by a physical or costume similarity, such that there's no ambiguity about his identity. The question of whether there will be two singers (one baritone for the two young men and one bass for Scene VI) or three (two baritones, one bass) will be decided by the direction and the production, but, it seems to me, doesn't affect my work or yours at all.

For these reasons I now think there's no real problem and no difficult choice for us to make at this point. You and I can follow our idea without concern. Everything else will follow. Am I being too optimistic? I don't think so. I really think this is a realistic assessment of the eventualities at play.

Yours,
Amin

*

26 December 2001

Amin,

I received your last email only after having sent you mine about the women.

Essentially, for the beginning, it seems logical to me that the young father and the son have the same kind of voice; they could be played by the same person, or by two different people. **This works for me.**

Regarding Scene VI: *we'll need a different singer for that scene, but he should be clearly identified with the character from the first two scenes, by a physical or costume similarity, such that there's no ambiguity about his identity.* **There will be a musical identity as well, clearly recognizable even if it's transformed from the first two scenes.**

I now think there's no real problem and no difficult choice for us to make at this point. You and I can follow our idea without concern. **You're right.** *Am I being too optimistic?*

No Amin, you're *comme il faut*!

Love,
Kaija

*

27 December 2001

Dear Amin,

I had a rather horrible day today.

Maybe to escape my reality, I thought a lot about Adriana and her sister during the day: that the sister is not just "le common sense" like the chorus in *L'Amour*, but a real person; is she single (I think so), why, does she have children (I think not), why, a little sister, a big sister? A real bond between sisters who come from the same parents but who are so different—(the same idea of blood that emerges later on with the son).

Again, this idea of simultaneous and independent realities, which in my mind manifests itself as superposed sung lines... If this aspect seems worth developing to you, it could be good, and unusual too.

Talk soon,
Kaija

*

Dear Kaija,

I thought a bit today about the two female characters, and I think you're right, it would be a bit of a shame for the sister to be nothing but a "sounding chamber" for the ambient sensibility of the opera. I think she should be the more "cerebral" of the two, maybe even the more intelligent one, and in any case the more driven, the one who wants to live her life her own way, while Adriana is intuitive, "passionate"; it's the sister who wants Adriana to renounce the child and put the incident behind her, and it's Adriana who resigns herself to destiny (even if she does so by a sort of intuitive faith in humanity, which gives us the grandeur of her "wager," and of her character... and of her maternity)... I don't know if all of this is clear, because I'm trying to summarize several hours of "cogitation" in a few lines... In any case, we'll discuss it further.

Also, I thought the name of the sister, now that she's been "rethought," could be Elsa, unless you've thought of using that name for another character...

The provisional name I'm using for the father is Sarko; for the son, Yannis.

Talk very soon,
Amin

*

An amusing incident ensued. In December 2000, Amin Maalouf chose the name "Sarko" for one of the main characters of the new opera, not realizing this was also the common nickname of the politician Nicolas Sarkozy, who would become president of the French Republic in 2007. In the mind of the librettist, whose concept for the story was inspired indirectly by events in the former Yugoslavia, the sound of the name—which recalls Radko, or Mladko—was meaningful. Not until 2002 did he realize that the name absolutely had to be changed.

*

My dear Kaija,

I'm delighted that everything is going well, and that *L'Amour de loin* was so well received. I hope you'll also find time to relax…

I printed out the text of your message to add it to the *Adriana* file. Everything you send me will be extremely useful for the final draft. I haven't worked on it much since April, but it's never far from my mind. I'm sure now of the name Revka (in addition to Jonas and Adriana, obviously); on the other hand, I'm hesitant about Sarko. I still like the sound of the name, but I'd like to find a variation on the same model, maybe just Arko, or Harko. If you have any thoughts, they're most welcome…

Love,
Amin

*

Dear Amin,

Everything continues to go well here, but I'm glad for you that you don't have to attend all these social occasions, which have already proven a bit exhausting. *L'Amour de loin* really has been successful in all respects.

I saw Peter for a few hours today to talk about *Adriana*. We tried to call you, but his phone won't call international numbers, even though he tried several things. He has your numbers now and may call you.

The most important thing for me was to talk about the singers, and to hear Peter say he understands that I need new voices… He thinks *L'Amour* will go on living its life and that we need to do something very different.

Here are a few aspects I described today. For me, the voices are now: Adriana/mezzo, Jonas/tenor, Revka/lyric soprano, Sarko/bass baritone.

The music for each is beginning to have colors; Adriana's music is mysterious and intense, her sister's very clear and luminous. I don't know why, but I imagine Revka having a bit of the personality of Simone Weil, intelligent and deep. What do you think? I want these two sisters to have a real dialogue, and for Revka to be a complete person.

For Sarko's music, I hear it fast and energetic initially, but becoming increasingly heavy and tragic for Scene VI.

Jonas's music has the energy of his father's, but with a lighter and more joyous character.

Each music changes differently for "20 years later": Sarko's music slows down and gets heavier, Adriana's changes color but the tempo remains the same.

I also see these characters as different speeds that could be superimposed in variable ways for the sung ensembles.

The "two hearts" begin in Scene III, which is the birth of Jonas's music. "The hearts" are still there when Adriana and Jonas are together.

The dreams have a musical logic that is different from the other scenes.

Love,
Kaija

*

6 August 2002

Dear Amin,

About the third scene: could we conclude it with a song (a "lullaby") that Adriana sings for her future child at the end of this scene? A mysterious and sensual song.

As for the man's name: if nothing else, I don't want Adriana and Arko, because both begin with A. Harko in French also sounds like "Arko." I do like Sarko because of the S, but if you want to change it let's do so. In general I like all the names you've given, because they have very distinct characters and sonorities.

Love,
Kaija

*

My dear Kaija,

About Sarko, the truth is quite silly. I liked the name, and I still like it. Except that I recently found out that it's a common nickname for Sarkozy, and I don't want us to find ourselves at the Bastille opera in the spring of 2006 with a big misunderstanding on our hands…

Thus it has to be changed, just a little, to avoid this headache, without departing too much from the sounds it includes or the consonances it suggests…

Noted, for the third scene. It will be a peculiar kind of "lullaby," naturally, because it's marked by questioning: What will my son be? What blood will course through him, the victim's or the torturer's? Will he be a Cain or an Abel?

In any case, it would be very useful for me if you could develop the idea of the lullaby as you wish, so I can integrate its tonality, its sensibility, fully in the final composition…

Love,
Amin

*

2 December 2002

My dear Kaija,

I'll be happy to come to the meeting tomorrow. I like these "all-hands" meetings very much, rare as they are… Afterwards, if you have a few moments, let's have a coffee and talk a bit about all of this *viva voce*…

Everything will be fine.

Lots of love,
Amin

*

3 December 2002

Dear Amin,

Here's the website of D…, whom Peter is considering for Adriana. She's very good but I wonder whether she'll be ready for all this work…

Kaija

*

4 December 2002

Dear Kaija,

She's certainly quite… American!

I wasn't expecting that the question of selecting singers yesterday would be centered on "Black" or "White." That would call for another meeting when all of this has come into focus. For Peter it seems important. For Gerard, I don't know if the reticence he expressed on the spot will be a lasting reaction…

True, for Peter, the themes in question, especially the violence, immediately evoked the world of the black community. Me, I don't have a strict preference in the matter. Even though the setting where I was imagining the events was Bosnia in the 1990s, I wanted it to be detached from time and place, so that the universality of the passions in question could remain limitless… and the adaptability could too. The names, for that matter, don't come from any particular society. It's also true that for the character of elderly Tsargo, in scene six, I had the silhouette of Willard White in mind, maybe because when we discussed the possibility of having two different people with different voices play the role you said that the older of the two would have a voice like W.W.'s… On the other hand, the image in my mind of Adriana, Refka, Yonas, and even the young Tsargo, has never been of black characters...

The more I think about it, the more I feel that several interpretations, and thus several adaptations, several productions, are possible, "in white," "in black," "in Latino," etc. The only thing to forbid completely is a "mixed bag" distribution. It's essential, vital, that all of the characters belong clearly, without any possible ambiguity, to the same ethnic environment; in other words, that aggressor and victim be the same color; otherwise, the message could be corrupted. Tsargo isn't the external enemy, not "the other"; he's the abusive protector.

In any case, I'm not concerned; we'll figure it out. And I think the debate, in a way, is bringing us closer to the work...

I also spoke with Peter about Simone Weil at length yesterday afternoon. I'll tell you about it later. I'm increasingly convinced that, after *Adriana*, it will be our common opus. And that it will be, for the three of us, an essential work, one that matters. I want to dive in at the beginning of next year, while you're deep into *Adriana*...

Andrée was very happy to hear about the Grawemeyer Award. She sends her congratulations and hugs and kisses. As do I...

Give me a call when you have a moment.

Yours,
Amin

*

5 December 2002

My dear Kaija,

Speaking to you yesterday, I felt your haste to dive into *Adriana*. I just wanted to say, on the eve of your departure, that I've already dove back into it myself, and that it seems to me that by the time you get back, and certainly before Christmas, we could have a new reading session, after which I will leave you at least part of the text so you can begin to work (one or two scenes, one or two dreams...). If we feel, you and I, that some passages still need to be "fine-tuned," I'll make sure you have a complete text, final or almost, mid-January or at the latest for your return from America. (Then I'll dive back into my "whale-novel," but not without the occasional quick, tender glance toward "our" *Simone*...)

Do you think that's a good "schedule"?

Love,
Amin

*

15 December 2002

My dear Kaija,

I'm happy you liked these scenes, and that they inspire you. I'm sure the new opera will be even finer, even more ample.

I haven't reprinted the pages I gave you yet, so I don't have them in front of me. But I have them in my head, and it seems, at first glance, that we could get rid of *"impatient mais digne"* without disturbing the balance of the text.

Regarding the two hearts beating in the same chest, I know it's an important theme for you, perhaps even the nodal point of this opera, and I'll add some lines in the direction you suggested. Starting tomorrow I'll reread that passage calmly.

As for the word *"corsage,"* I do indeed like that word—I find it very subtle because it evokes desire even as the sound of it contains something mischievous... Let's wait a bit to see how you feel about it upon later readings. For the moment I'm going to leave it; we'll have time to discuss it again...

See you very soon, then!

Love,
Amin

*

16 December 2002

My dear Kaija,

This morning, before diving back into the fourth scene, I looked a bit at the passages you had pointed out...

On page 8, I confirm that *"impatient mais digne"* can go without leaving a hole...

On page 29, I thought Adriana's monologue could be changed as follows:

Non, Refka, je ne suis sûre de rien.
Je sens seulement, je sens un cœur,
Un deuxième cœur qui bat tout près du mien.
Qui est cet étranger qui m'habite?...

Let me know if that addresses your concern.

Also, I thought a bit about the "dream" sequences for the scenes in the second act...but I'd rather we discuss them over the phone; it's easier that way. I'll try to call you...

Love,
Amin

*

30 March 2003
(To : Evamaria Wieser)

Dear Evamaria,

The preliminary version of the libretto for *Adriana Mater* is ready and Amin would like to send it for Gerard.

Where should I advice him to send it, to Paris Opera or Ruhr?

Regards,
Kaija

*

Having received the libretto in early April 2003, Saariaho could now devote her full energy to composing the music of **Adriana Mater**. *The work would be performed in Paris, at the Opéra Bastille, three years later, in early April 2006. The entire process of its creation—initial reflections, conception, exchanges, writing of the text, and then of the music—took four and a half years.*

A Conversation with Aleksi Barrière

Daniel Medin

Transcribed by Chloe Elder

DANIEL MEDIN: *I'm curious about the challenges of producing this adaption of* La Passion de Simone *for chamber orchestra. Were there structural elements in Saariaho's score or in Maalouf's libretto that helped guide your interpretive choices?*

ALEKSI BARRIÈRE: Well, *La Passion de Simone* doesn't have stage directions. It's just words and music, there's no hint whatsoever as to how it should be staged, whereas Maalouf's libretti for both *L'Amour de loin* and *Adriana Mater*—and, to some extent, *Émilie*—describe the setting of each scene and contain explicit instructions pertaining to the characters' movement. These are interesting in that they help us understand some of Kaija's musical choices (for example, the scene from *Adriana Mater* that is set in the countryside at noon, for which Kaija stylized the sound of crickets, or the bits of orchestral music written expressly to permit entrances and exits onstage). Nowadays, it is common to consider such indications as mere guidelines, and no production so far has taken all of Maalouf's notes literally. Sellars himself [who has staged most of those works] has generally held to his policy of "staging the music": seeking clues and cues directly in the score, as opposed to in stage directions, which often reflect theatrical conventions that have dated in practice. In any case, I can understand the disinterest of other directors vis-à-vis *La Passion de Simone*, since the work is so resolutely undramatic. We had to deal with these questions constantly: How are you going to stage this? To what extent can we interpret what is written? Production involves adding a new layer to the work, but in a different sense of "new" since additions should draw from elements already present in the score. For example, the chorus Kaija created for the chamber orchestra version of *Simone* contains the four typical voice types. There's only a single singer for each, so the relationship's meaningful when the women, one soprano and one mezzo, sing together. The same is true of parts sung by men (a baritone and a tenor), or by the higher or lower voices: topics of gender and generation, that are definitely relevant to the piece, emerge. These musical meanings may be absent from the libretto, but they're audible in performance. You become conscious of their effects once you start to examine the work closely.

It's difficult enough to stage a work of music, but La Passion de Simone *seems to pose an even greater challenge: that of staging ideas, or an entire philosophy. Maalouf seems to encourage this by incorporating aphoristic passages by Simone Weil into the work. How did you approach this aspect of the libretto?*

Everyone loves puzzles. It's fun to take a score, especially when it's well-crafted, and to look for the meanings inside of it. The structuring elements in *Simone* are not indicated explicitly, but they're extremely strong... especially through the interactions between the speaker, this "direct" voice of Simone Weil and the solo soprano, a contemporary figure (the evangelist of this passion play) who reflects on Weil's life and work. It's worth mentioning that the passages of Weil selected by Maalouf, which are recited by the speaker, do not come from any of her published articles. They're all fragments that appeared in posthumously published notebooks where Weil recorded her responses to anything and everything. So what we're dealing with in *La Passion de Simone* is really the movement of a mind—her mind—at the moment of writing. This process was critical to Simone Weil, for whom the conversion of thought into action was of principal importance. Another structuring element is that of history. It's helpful to remember that historical novels are Maalouf's specialty. Part of what makes Maalouf a master biographer is his ability to reconstruct characters from history within a broader context. There's no such thing as an isolated individual. This is true of even the most independent thinkers, such as Simone Weil: they remain part of a larger society and history and ideas.

Your La Passion de Simone *reinforces precisely this, namely that the work is not exclusively concerned with mysteries evoked by the life and death of Simone Weil, but with history itself—the tragic history of Europe's twentieth century. You take this up in the black-and-white video feed assembled for this production, which incorporates documentary footage from the thirties and forties and screens them alongside more recent instances of political turbulence.*

Interpretation is constantly underestimated as a factor in operatic productions. It's not uncommon for operagoers to assess performances as either "authentic" or "subversive," while failing to understand the extent to which any reading of a work results in interpretation. What you're initially dealing with is just notes on a score, or words on paper: the decisions concerning how they're to be played constitutes the interpretation. That's really important, because once you begin to stage music there are a whole range of decisions that can influence the atmosphere. One example of this would be the first production *Adriana Mater* by Peter Sellars in 2006, the ending of which was extremely problematic. The scenes concern a young man who learns that he was conceived during an act of wartime rape. He seeks out his father with murderous intent but realizes, when they finally meet, that the man is now blind and aged and cannot defend himself. Unable to kill, he returns to his mother and apologizes for his failure. To which the mother expresses tremendous relief, since this reluctance to shed blood reveals the son's difference from his father. The end of Maalouf's libretto offers a glimmer of hope, though it's largely dark. Little is said about how people will deal with this terrible situation. We don't know anything about what will happen to the father either; presumably he dies somewhere offstage. But musically, the scene concludes with a bit of pure orchestra, which is extremely lush and full of light and hope. James Ingalls illuminated the set from below, using transparent plastic to make the stage glow. The atmosphere was dreamlike and poetic. Anyhow, for Peter it was clear that the story could not end where the libretto stopped—so he staged a new ending to take the music into account. The father returned to the stage and the son just opened his arms to his father, suggesting…

…a reconciliation?

Right. Which is not in the libretto, where there's no hint that this horrible monster could ever be redeemed.

Which just goes to prove that Peter Sellars is an incorrigible optimist!

[*Laughs.*] Exactly! Of course, Maalouf had a huge problem with this. It's interesting because this could be a textbook case of a producer staging the music rather than the libretto. It's problematic because once you make such a huge call about the ending, you've clearly changed the plot. What was interesting was that the journalists who covered *Adriana Mater*'s premiere claimed that the once-controversial Sellars had now relaxed into something approaching kitsch. They didn't realize that his optimistic interpretation had actually made the production genuinely controversial! It generated debate about the work. He couldn't keep it as such, because Maalouf objected. But this issue was fascinating to me, especially at Santa Fe when I worked with Peter on a revival of his production of *Adriana Mater*. A lot of thought went into the consideration of how to rework these things. He ultimately managed to include what he wanted to say elsewhere in the opera. It was a terrific lesson in how to build a global vision, how to make one's interpretation coherent.

The basilica Saint-Denis, where this latest adaption of La Passion de Simone *was produced, is a unique space, and I'm curious about your efforts to incorporate—or exclude—elements of this particular environment.*

The challenge of working in such a location is huge, obviously. Our productions always involve incorporating the actual space—making the setting a meaningful one for whatever music is being staged. Hence the differences in lighting from one venue to the next, and a long, ever-evolving work with scenographer Pauline Squelbut and lighting designer Étienne Exbrayat. But it's hard to compete with that architecture. Saint-Denis is a gothic cathedral, and as such already functions as one giant lighting construction. We had to take into account the fading of natural light in that space, since the concert began in the evening. This involved measuring the light, and finding a solution for its dimming slowly on one side of the cathedral. By placing a wall of projectors on the other side, we managed to balance it out, taming the elements rather than going against them.

The usual procedure in theater is to disguise things, to hide them. If natural light's a problem, then put up a curtain. If someone has a pimple, then just make them up. This only adds layers of fakeness, which I find contrary to the spirit of performance. I'm interested in productions that reveal, that make things naked. Some spectators would no doubt consider this approach horribly limiting. They're not accustomed to seeing the orchestra on stage during an opera, or to the lack of an elaborate set. But I'm drawn to limiting oneself to the actual location and the participants— to retaining what's essential in the natural setting, to finding nuance there instead of within the layers of illusion more commonly associated with the theater. The search for ways to make the environment work, such as the lighting in this production, is really interesting. I don't at all view it as restrictive.

Things are similar when dealing with the cast and staging. Working with singers has contained psychological challenges for every opera production I've ever witnessed. And these challenges can be even greater when you try to address something extremely fragile within each performer, and make that their subject matter in place of the usual disguises and tricks. But it's a collaborative process: you work together toward the essence of your material, and that is something Clément Mao-Takacs is very good at (which is why we have strongly relied on each other during the two-year process of putting this production together with the company we created). I think it's also an important process for Kaija. She's not the type of composer who writes her soprano part in a certain way and then obliges singers to provide the appropriate voice and technique. She's willing to tailor or modify bits and pieces—to create an alternative version—in order to better adapt the music to the performer's range. And this is, of course, also her approach when collaborating with instrumentalists. Her lack of rigidity and willingness to take life as it comes into the artistic process, that's been extremely present in her creations—especially within the framework of her theatrical collaborations.

An Introduction to *Tsunemasa*

In a 2012 "Noh Project Description," theatre director Peter Sellars proposes the creation of "an evening of chamber opera, based on the texts of two Noh plays translated as fragments into English by Ezra Pound in 1914." This proposal has since been realized as *Only the Sound Remains*—a chamber opera that comprises two works, each based on a Noh text and scored by Kaija Saariaho, with staging by Sellars. In the spirit of literary reinvention, we are proud to present the first of those two Noh plays, *Tsunemasa*, in Paul Griffiths's interpretation. Sellars describes this particular drama as "speaking from the darkness," and perfectly suited for Saariaho's compositional touch, since her music has "always located its luminosity in deep darkness [and] opened into unimaginable inner space." Saariaho began composing these two pieces for a small ensemble of seven instruments: string quartet, flute, kantele, and percussion. Small chamber choirs and a dancer also feature in the opera. The second Noh text, *Hagoromo*, appears in Griffiths's rendering in the January 2014 online edition of *The White Review* and is searchable in its website archive.

Tsunemasa

Paul Griffiths

And then there was Tajima-no-kami Tsunemasa—Tsunemasa who was the boy favorite of a prince, learning the arts of war, love, and music, Tsunemasa who has died on the same red shore as his younger brother Atsumori and many more of their clan, Tsunemasa who has left his lute to be picked up from the battlefield, with the other relics.

In grief his prince has ordered a memorial to be built for him, in a temple within the palace compound. Now Gyōkei, an officer of the prince, is bringing the rescued lute to be placed with prayers on this memorial, where it will lie silent forever.

He enters the temple, does as he has been bidden, and takes a step back.

Rippling upwards on the walls are shadows of candlesmoke, which can easily be mistaken for a moment as forming the outline of a young warrior, and perhaps in the chanting and the somber instruments and the shuffle of steps there may be heard a voice, or colloquy of voices, sounding together, like the strings of a lute.

> The wind blowing through withered trees…
> …sound like a rain in sunshine…
> Yet again I appear in the world of the living…
> …the tie of a blind passion…

Who are you? says Gyōkei.

The answer comes that this is the ghost of Tsunemasa, but when Gyōkei looks in the direction of the voice or voices he sees nothing. The shape, if shape it was, has dissolved.

The words trouble Gyōkei all the more for having no visible attachment, for coming out of the air, out of the darkness. But he finds an answer to his anxiety in pride—pride that his prayers have been so steadfast as to call up this spirit and make it speak.

It speaks. It tells of coming to the palace as a boy, of singing and dancing, of playing this lute, the gift of a prince.

Let the lute sound again, one last time.

No fingers touch it, but gentle music begins to arise.

Along with that music comes the sound of the rain, but this is not rain, rather the showering of pine needles brought down by the wind onto the temple roof.

The sounds of the lute fold into those of the wind and the falling pine needles, the instrument's four strings opening like a hand to receive these shivers from the natural world and embrace them in the one harmony.

> Le premier son de la flûte du phénix
> Ein Ton der Phönixflöte
> The voice of *shō*
> One note of the phoenix-flute

Gyōkei knows how the poem continues; it continues thus: draws the clouds down from the autumn mountains. This lute will do the same.

Still the spirit cannot be seen, only heard singing and playing, and yet there is the impression also that it is dancing. There is a sense in the air of a whirling, a spiraling perturbation beyond the reach of feeling. No stirring, no draft, but movement, silent movement.

Then what had never been there was no longer there.

The Complete Works of Stig Sæterbakken

Flytende Paraplyer (1984) / *Floating Umbrellas*

23 dikt (1985) / *23 Poems*

Sverdet ble til et barn (1986) / *The Sword Became a Child*

Vandrebok (1988) / *Wanderbook*

Incubus (1991) / *Incubus*

Det nye testamentet (1993) / *The New Testament*

Estetisk salighet (1994) / *Aesthetic Bliss*

Siamesisk (1997) / *Siamese* (2010)

Selvbeherskelse (1998) / *Self-Control* (2012)

Sauermugg (1999) / *Sauermugg*

Det onde øye (2001) / *The Evil Eye*

Kapital (2003) / *Capital*

Besøket (2006) / *The Visit*

Usynlige hender (2007) / *Invisible Hands*

Sauermugg Redux (2007) / *Sauermugg Redux*

Ikke forlat meg (2009) / *Don't Leave Me*

Ja. Nei. Ja. (pamphlet, 2009) / *Yes. No. Yes.*

Dirty Things (2010) / *Dirty Things*

Umuligheten av å leve (pamphlet, 2010) / *The Impossibility of Living* (2014)

Gjennom natten (2011) / *Through the Night* (2013)

Det fryktinngytende (pamphlet, 2011) / *The Terrifying* (2014)

Block to Block (2011) / *Block to Block*

Essays i utvalg (2012) / *Selected Essays*

Der jeg tenker er det alltid mørkt (2012) / *Where I Think, It Is Always Dark*

A Tribute to Stig Sæterbakken

Karl Ove Knausgaard

Translated from the Norwegian by Benjamin Mier-Cruz

The following is an excerpt from a speech given during a ceremony in memory of Stig Sæterbakken at the Norwegian Festival of Literature in Lillehammer on January 30, 2012.

Everything Stig Sæterbakken did was charged with an immense belief in the power of literature, as well as a virtually limitless curiosity in the human condition and its countless expressions. He conveyed this belief and curiosity in all of his writing and various appointments—whether as an editor, teacher, or as the artistic director of the Norwegian Festival of Literature. All of this, which was so easy to take for granted, became strikingly apparent when he died. Norway is a small country, and Norwegian represents only a small linguistic area. And what we call a literary generation doesn't add up to a lot of people. Stig Sæterbakken was one of the most important authors of our generation, particularly because he defended and attempted to grasp that which takes place beyond the center, in the marginal spaces of human experience where nothing is given yet everything can be taken away. His essays explore what this sort of freedom and abandon might afford us, yet this process is clearly a form of escape as well, since the essays work to provide us insight into nothingness, nihilism, and death, which awaits us all. The very makeup of his essays is an escape in itself: the writing on the page, the energy it generates, the pleasure it arouses, and the solace it may provide. For instance, in the last compilation of his essays, the final text, "Sacred Tears"—on Emmanuel Vigeland's mausoleum, a dark, eerie, catacomb-like building in Oslo whose walls are covered by grotesque frescos where sex and death coalesce into one—suddenly and unexpectedly confronts us with the line: "In the end, crying is all that matters." And then there is the very last sentence: "It's the prayer we direct toward any great work of art: God, take this pain away, which is me." With this final piece of insight, it's as though a new level of truth supplants all the others that came before it. We are no longer in the realm of analysis and criticism, rather we have taken a step into the wordless body, the emotionally wrought self that can be free or shackled, isolated or in the heart of the community; in any case, it's a step into something we all know, what [Gunnar] Ekelöf referred to as "the same," something that perhaps only art can approach and, as a result, manage to lift us out of our selves. In his final novel, *Through the Night*, Stig Sæterbakken moves into that place, is there himself, his prose permeated with darkness; the novel explores not what freedom wins us, but what it loses us.

Through the Night is about an all-around average man, a married dentist and father of two, who after twenty years of marriage falls in love with someone new. He is plagued by a deep doubt about what to do. Should he honor his responsibilities and stay with his family, or give in to his desires, put himself first, and have an affair? He chooses the latter.

But it doesn't work out, so he goes back to his family. Yet everything has changed. There is now a rift between the man and his family, or rather the affair has made the rift more tangible. His son will no longer speak to him, and the father feels like a complete outsider. Then one evening his son commits suicide. *Through the Night* is a novel about endless pain, endless guilt, and endless alienation. It concludes in a kind of nightmarish bliss: at an earlier point in time, the son had written down what his ideal world would be like, and in this world Christmas Eve would come around every four weeks. This idyll is then precisely what we are left with in the final pages of the book: the small family is celebrating Christmas with their special traditions, everything is peaceful between them, and no one and nothing else can ever threaten them, and so it repeats over and over and over again. The ambivalence in this is abysmal; happiness is just as desirable and fundamental as it is nauseating and impossible. These components, freedom and isolation, the creative and the destructive, happiness and hell, life and death, are firmly embedded throughout all of Stig Sæterbakken's writings, though it never is as harsh and brutal or as tender and sorrowful as it is here. That which is lost is forever lost. Night disappears into night.

Sacred Tears

Stig Sæterbakken

I

QUICQUID DEUS CREAVIT PURUM EST, it reads above the entrance to Tomba Emmanuelle, EVERYTHING CREATED BY GOD IS PURE, in what seems to be the perfect antithesis to the dark inferno of sex and death one enters seconds later. But only seems. For what, if not purity, is the very essence of *Vita*, with its never-ending cycle of birth, growth, and death, purity of vision, and purity of form, all of mankind's vitality and anxieties and unspeakable fears frozen in almost ornamental patterns of naked figures?[The scenes are those of both productive and counterproductive human activity, men and women engaged in Kama-Sutra-like lovemaking side by side with skulls and bones and decomposing corpses, with the ultimate synthesis of life and death conjured up in what is perhaps the most extreme image of them all, that of two skeletons copulating at the base of a monolith of levitating infants.]

It wouldn't be far-fetched to call it a marriage between Heaven and Hell, the heavy lumps of struggling bodies on each wall transforming into lighter elusive shapes as they hit the ceiling, evaporating into some unknown realm. Yes, Emanuel Vigeland's *Vita* is Inferno and Paradiso combined, depicting raw nature with a sort of sublime dignity, the latter underlined by the fact that one has to lower one's head when entering, bowing for what is slowly to become extinguishable in the semi-darkness of the crypt, placed in a small niche just above the entrance door, still, even after a while, only barely perceptible against the dark brown wall: a hollow stone—an urn—holding the artist's ashes. It is as concrete— and as abstract—as it gets. And what a great metamorphosis as well: the artist's studio turned into the artist's tomb, the spirit of Vigeland forever contained within the walls of the magnificent brick building at Slemdal, with its legendary acoustics, creating droning dreamlike soundscapes out of the lightest footsteps, the slightest cough, a sigh, or even a single breath (the reverb lasting up to twenty seconds, I've been told). Why the hell isn't every artist buried where he or she worked?

II

Inspired, possibly, by the shape of the room, I always think of Jonah and the whale whenever I visit Tomba Emmanuelle, the ceiling curving like gigantic ribs above me. And given the two representations of the artist himself, both in the right corner of the entrance wall, one—alive, brush and palette in hand, in the act of painting (*Vita*)—above the other—dead, with the palette and brushes scattered on the ground, as if the work itself has first exhausted him, then killed him—I can't help thinking that there is a third representation as well, which is the crypt itself, and that while Dante and Virgil had to climb over Satan's hairy body to get to Purgatorio, the dead Vigeland has left his mouth open, in rigor mortis, for us to climb in, down the throat and into the holy chambers of his chest and stomach, the naked bodies crawling all around us playing the role of the mental intestines, so to speak, of his—literally—inner world.

In that respect, Tomba Emmanuelle is as close a relative to Per Inge Bjørlo's *Inner Rooms* (1984-1990) as it is to Michelangelo's *Last Judgment* (1537-1541).

III

A wonderful sense of being consumed, this is what the Vigeland mausoleum offers its unprepared first-time visitor. But the feeling does not fade through repetition. On the contrary, I'd say. As if the knowledge of what awaits you heightens rather than diminishes this overwhelming sensation. And I guess that's why so many visitors keep coming back: they want to be devoured again. And again. And again. And isn't that what drives us, repeatedly, toward art in any form, the dream—however often it leads to disappointment—of being overpowered, shocked, overcome by horror and joy, the stubborn dream of becoming one with the object in question, melting into it, rather than standing at a distance watching it, analyzing it, evaluating it, in other words: the dream of being swallowed, digested, and spat out again, presumably dizzy, definitely shaken, thoroughly and utterly confused, as we re-enter the so-called real world?

IV

I don't know any work of art that incorporates such a multitude of grand-scale elements—architecture, ornament, sculpture, painting, illumination—and, at the same time, deals with emotional conflicts on such an intimate level. Mere speculation, of course, but I'm convinced that *Vita* reflects a variety of inner Vigelandian demons. Lust, envy, pain, pride, sorrow, remorse, joy, jealousy, ecstasy, horror, it's all there, as one troubled man's innermost dreams and nightmares take the form of a grandiose *Gesamtkunstwerk*.

The huge investment of personal anxiety into his work is what suggests, I think, the most plausible explanation for the radicalism of Vigeland's imagery. I mean, newborns resting on a pile of skulls—or erect penises for that matter—must have been pretty out of the ordinary, to say the least, as subject matter for a fresco in the 1920s, '30s, and '40s, when it was made. At the same time, with regard to extenuating circumstances, Vigeland was obviously loyal to a solid tradition of monumental art, enough to be forgiven his excesses to a certain extent. In any case, this is what keeps his masterpiece fresh, rendering it no less beautiful and powerful in 2010 than it was by the time it was finished, Vigeland's ability to cut to the bone of human behavior, regardless of time and place, the fight of—or for—our lives, so to speak, and thus unveil, through ruthless tableaus of existential extremes, the roots of both our deepest desires and our deepest fears.

V

"The violence of spasmodic joy lies deep in my heart," Georges Bataille writes in *The Tears of Eros*, in what could have been an outline for the overall concept of Vigeland's *Vita*:

> This violence, at the same time, and I tremble as I say it, is the heart of death: it opens itself up in me! The ambiguity of this human life is really that of mad laughter and of sobbing tears. It comes from the difficulty of harmonizing reason's calculations with these tears... With this horrible laugh...

As a visionary, Vigeland saw what Bataille saw, that the things which threaten our very existence and the things which keep us striving for more, are often one and the same thing. Where would we be, as sexual beings, without the knowledge of death? How strong would our passions be, separated from our fear of dying? We want to live, sure. But we want to die as well. We want to be torn apart. We want to drown in the wonders of ecstasy. And what work of art could possibly be worth studying that doesn't, like Vigeland's *Vita*—by evoking these antagonisms of life—bring us to the brink of tears?

Bataille:

> In the violence of the overcoming [of reason], in the disorder of my laughter and my sobbing, in the excess of raptures that shatter me, I seize on the similarity between a horror and a voluptuousness that goes beyond me, between an ultimate pain and an unbearable joy!

Yes, I think it's the intimacy of the *Vita* that both disturbs me and pleases me the most.

Bataille, had he seen it, would have been flabbergasted.

VI

As if a sort of visual excavation is taking place, the way the fresco gradually emerges as our eyes get used to the dark. And as the outside world disappears, like some already-forgotten fairytale, an inner world comes to life, constituting—from the moment of its revelation until the time we finally exit—our sole view of reality. While inside, we're entombed, as is the painter. No escape, as day turns to night. And utterly astonished, as the fresco reveals, little by little, its myriad details, we accept our imprisonment with delight, lost in self-effacing contemplation, our eyes digging deeper and deeper into Vigeland's visionary remains. For just as we lose sight of the outside world, we lose our grip on ourselves as well, forgetting who we are, in a perishing moment's blissful infinity, as if absorbed by this wailing wall, becoming, willingly and reluctantly, participants in its orgy of eternal struggle.

VII

"I is an other," Rimbaud wrote in triumph to a former teacher of his upon discovering, at the age of sixteen, that he was a poet, launching the concept of a chaotic multitude of personalities, rather than a solid and stable I, as the foundation—or absence of foundation—essential to any poetic creativity. And if we imagine these principals of creativity in reverse, the same rules applying to the experience of art as to the making of it, we would see that in order to fully appreciate the work at hand, we have to let go of ourselves as individual beings, thereby, at least for a short while, allowing a stranger's paradise—or hell, if you like—to possess us, to become us, fully and completely.

Art teaches people to become someone else. Or at least, at its most powerful, it opens an abyss in people's notion of who they are. It brings out the otherness in us, simply by preparing us to share, as we say, somebody else's fate, to the point of taking on their identity as our own.

Eventually, all of us is an other. Or we possess the ability to be so, if pushed far enough. It's a lovely and frightening idea, the dissolution of the I as its ultimate fulfilment. We are rent asunder, we lose ourselves, and then regain ourselves, for the sake of losing ourselves once again.

VIII

In the end, crying is all that matters.

Tears flowing, that's the only worthwhile state in which to finish a book, or watch the end credits of a movie, or reach out for the repeat button on the CD player. Through this salty liquid, produced by our own bodies, we dissolve as individual beings and make contact with something greater than ourselves. It is one of our deepest needs, to be lifted above ourselves and thrown, by force, into a limitless, and therefore self-destructive, communion with something that exists as much within us as outside of us, unattainable save for in certain extremely emotional moments.

It's what one might call a sacred experience.

Be it through art or sex or drugs, it's the closest we get to Heaven.

It's when the dam within us bursts.

It's everything we dreaded and hoped for.

It's nothing, really.

And nothing is why we came here.

And nothing is what we so awkwardly strive and fight for.

It's the goal of all achievements, though we hardly ever dare pursue it.

It's the prayer we direct toward any great work of art: God, take this pain away, which is me.

Stig Sæterbakken, circa 1971.
Courtesy of Elizabeth Sunde.

The Impossibility of Living

Stig Sæterbakken

Translated from the Norwegian by Stokes Schwartz

There is something childish within me that endures and refuses to go away, as if there is still a boy inside who gets in the way of my various attempts to become an adult. To put it another way, I've always been childish for my age, and I'll probably stay that way, no matter how old I get. All it takes is a glance around me: everyone else seems so sensible. So wise. So calm. So serious. So thoughtful. So well-adjusted in their lives, so adept in their dealings with others, so sure of themselves, regardless of the challenges they face. No matter what, they're routine and set in their ways, while inside my own head the most ridiculous urges are cooking away, idiotic fears, detailed suicide schemes, filthy sex fantasies, and totally disrespectful notions about the so-called important things in life. It's a veritable witches' brew of puerile garbage, more or less constantly at the boiling point, an unending torrent of nonsense that, if anyone else ever heard it, any of it, I wouldn't be able to avoid biting my tongue off in shame.

*

Will it ever go away? Will it really follow me until the end of my days? So when I'm lying there on my deathbed with my nearest and dearest around me, will this grotesque callowness still be stuck in my mind? a feeling that has rotted instead of ripened, and now dissolves, as if in an acid bath of perennial infantilism?

*

If we accept the term *undeveloped country*, meaning an underdeveloped country, I am an *undeveloped person*. And above all as a writer. It's incomprehensible, all things considered, how anyone has taken me seriously. After countless pathetic excuses, there are no other conclusions to draw but this: that it is the child in me who writes; no matter how much the rest of me tries to hide it (or not), the overgrown child wins every time I pick up the pen, my invincible childishness shines through every sentence, every written word, like playthings between the sausage fingers of a feeble little brat. (A glance at *Sauermugg* is recommended for any of those who are in doubt.)

*

Believe me, I have no greater wish than to be in a class with my highly respected colleagues. I dream of managing my literary talents as well as they do, reaping the same bountiful harvests, playing an equally inspiring public role, saying intelligent things during interviews, imparting pearls of wisdom with as much ease, speaking in the same steady voice, writing the same crisp sentences and in the same characteristic dialect, giving the same distinct speeches (full of witticisms and the nonsense that makes people laugh), appearing as absent-minded and self-assured through it all; to carry myself like them, to be like them in every respect, the sacred figures of literature—Espedal, Enquist, Trotzig, Müller, Cărtărescu, Swift—authors who are accomplished in their maturity, so confident in their responsibilities and commitments, *so level with themselves and with the world*, presenting literature as something positive, something enriching, something stimulating, something that all people grow to engage in, all while I constantly try, as Carl-Michael [Edenborg] said, to pretend that my own motives are respectable, presumably driven by the pleasure of pestering, of tormenting, of tearing apart, of—what did he call it?— "annihilating the cosmos."

*

Hello? A forty-four-year-old man, with a wife and children, with a house and state support for his writing, trying to wipe out the cosmos?

*

I find myself in a totally hopeless situation. For how can a human being— can you explain this to me, you grownups?—how can a human being reach maturity, when there is no way to attain this maturity without accepting the fact that we remain perpetually childlike?

Not that I haven't tried countless times to pull myself together. Just to end up with the same scornful taunt from my inner hairy barbarian. *Nanny nanny boo-boo!*

*

For a long time I believed that, after having been a child for a while, one beautiful day someone would switch on a light in my head, and everything would change. For a long time I waited for exactly that. I convinced myself that this was exactly what had happened to all the men and women I knew, and that the same thing would eventually happen to me. Just as Lars Jakobson describes it in *Hemsökelsen* [*The Haunting*], "I would wake up in the morning to a world of reason and meaning, I would leave home, I would go to work and buy things and rush around and drive my car. In the evenings, I would come home worn out and plop down in front of the TV." Exactly like that. "I would have breath like rotten meat," and "my eyes would roll around in my head and sometimes it would even feel as if a needle were stuck in my pupils." But it never happened. Or, it hasn't happened yet. I'm still waiting. My body is losing its muscle, my features have grown gaunt, my face is hollowed out, but I'm still here waiting. Or, I was, until recently, when I was forced to accept that I'll never experience this. So, goodbye decent life. Adieu, respectable existence. It's a relief, to be honest: no more pointless experiments in front of the mirror in which I push my face into serious expressions and loudly pronounce, "We are facing a global catastrophe!" or "Boycott Israel!" or "Get Norway out of Afghanistan!" or "We must acknowledge the worth of Others!" Just keep steering down this absurd road, the road that ends in Suicide. Let disorder rule. Let Parnassus crumble. Let the cosmos collapse. Let ambition dissolve. Let time regress. Let the petals fold together, the flower buds implode and become seeds once again.

*

"It's important to remember that these are stories written by a child for his fellow children."[1] Ha ha! Is it such a surprise that I love Teratologen?

*

And isn't it odd that I have my greatest moments when I'm drunk?

*

It's as if there is something about life itself that I struggle to take seriously. As if I am still just pretending to be an adult when I am out in the world.

*

To such a degree that I sometimes think that I don't count for anything, even in my role as a father; maybe if I were to sit in a wing-backed armchair with an unlit pipe between my teeth and an old copy of *Aftenposten*[2] outstretched in front of me and grumble in a serious, sober voice, "Well, well... Hmm... I say! No, is that true?!..."

*

While others remain glued to live broadcasts of the tsunami and pray to higher powers for the best possible outcome, I find it fun and hope for the worst. Waves as high as mountains! All of the buildings smashed to pieces! Mounds of corpses! Bruegel & Bosch! Dürer & Dix! Goya & Masereel!

*

And yet, I have, at times, tried in earnest to develop a concern for the environment. Not a chance! It doesn't work, doesn't take root in my mind.

*

But when someone hiccups at the wrong moment, well then, I laugh until I cry.* Let's call this impulse by its proper name: an inferiority complex.

* One of the most embarrassing incidents occurred while I was in Kotenget, Bjugn, on the farm of my grandmother's nieces, Johanna and Astri, both spinsters, and when Johanna sat down and told, crying all the while, about the sister with whom she had lived all of her life and who had just died, and about how she had sat next to Astri's bed and held onto her hand as she died, and Uncle Albrigt, who also sat nearby and listened solemnly, suddenly began to hiccup, and not the quiet kind either, but of the most powerful sort, which with some dreadful burps shook all of that corpulent, tobacco-chewing military policeman who looked like an Italian mafia boss at least half a meter up into the air from the seat of his chair each time,

The Other is hardly a guarantor of brotherly cooperation and tolerance, but on the contrary is the main threat to the existence of the Same. Maurice Blanchot states in *The Writing of the Disaster* that

> in the relation of myself to the Other, the Other exceeds my grasp. The Other: the Separate, the Most-High which escapes my power—the powerless, therefore; the stranger, dispossessed. But, in the relation of the Other to me, everything seems to reverse itself: the distant becomes the close-by, this proximity becomes the obsession that afflicts me, that weighs down upon me, that separates me from myself—as if separation (which measured the transcendence from me to the Other) did its work within me, dis-identifying me, abandoning me to passivity, leaving me without an initiate and bereft of present.

*

Inferiority, not human worth, is the gift I receive from the Other. He presents my shortcomings to me neatly wrapped with a bow on top. (*To: Stig. From: Everyone. Merry Christmas!*) My neurosis is the offspring of His paternal sternness and maternal care; my anxiety is a direct result of His profound tranquility.

*

I have so much anxiety at times that I often wonder if there's nothing else I consist of.

---

and then smacked him down again, and the awful expression on his face, like a Bugs Bunny trap had just snapped shut on him, and the unbearable waiting time in between, and all that while the tears ran in torrents onto the deceased, but who I always—when I was a child, something that I still am—thought of as Aunt Johanna, the only thing I, in my state of hilarity, was mature enough to do with trembling lips was to wait for the next personality-changing monster hiccup that would soon lift my uncle to new heights, something that left me with no choice but to get up and move from this death- and sorrow-filled room, for as soon as I stood there by myself in the courtyard and let myself get carried away completely, then felled flat by the spastic who rummaged around inside of me: I was lying in the grass like a snake, bulging with suppressed laughter, just a few meters away from my inconsolable Aunt Johanna Mikkelhaug.

Comfort is not easily found on occasions when there is genuine need for it. But one who has never betrayed me when it matters most is Gombrowicz, the foremost apologist for immaturity, who said, during one of his many conversations with Dominique de Roux, "Even into my forties I acted young and felt that way too. I am the kind of person who has never experienced middle age; as soon as I said farewell to youth, I felt the twinge of old age." Gombrowicz achieved youth, to the extent that we can take his word for it, before he aged, that is to say: he attained a higher level before becoming bent and crooked. In any case, youth is just a slightly finer name for childhood. And the inverted education he describes is, in reality, a direct link between childhood and old age, where a person virtually flies from one kind of senility to the other, without any layovers or stops along the way—if there is a pre-senility, it is indeed childhood!— or, as in one of Jakobson's fantasies, Confirmation in its literal meaning: you are a child one moment, then you are middle-aged, and nothing exists in between. One of Gombrowicz's great achievements, I believe, is found in the way that he takes the infantile and transforms it into a form of erotic worship, and thereby, to a large, albeit limited, extent, cleanses it of that layer of shame and disrepute under which it, quite naturally, has been hidden. I think that it is this point that moved me so deeply when I devoured his peculiar novels, one after another, I, completely seduced by the playful chaos within them, in glimpses, at least, was put in touch with the possibility of a sort of satisfaction not to have become any more mature than I had, since there was clearly one other person, at least, who was as immature. As if immunity had been offered, precisely when mastery of the adult world's unbelievably dull challenge started to become a serious problem for me, a temporary immunity that sadly ended the moment I finished reading the book and reality once again drew itself tightly around me like a net.

*

As Sauermugg says, "I'd prefer to float within a clear, gelatinous mass, doing nothing."

*

Or, as Bartleby says, "I would prefer not to."

*

Of course, I hear it so well, my outside voice, when everything about a situation calls for an inside voice. For some reason, I struggle while others can be content with simply being. All of my speech wracked with pain, every strained witticism just a link in an unbroken chain of attempts to avoid revealing my crippling anxiety, every word I utter articulated with the intention of drawing attention away from my actual paranoia, yes, everything that I have ever said and done, everything that I have undertaken throughout my life, has, in reality, been an attempt to cover things up! It is a barricade of courtesies and boasting that I hide behind, like a shivering child. A Babylonian wall between the boy and the world.

*

Let me state this categorically: These lips have never tasted the flavor of a natural remark, this tongue doesn't know how to form an earnest word.

*

For a short time, by the way, the working title of *The Visit* was *Slowly, Slowly, My Voice Is Giving Out.* (This is something that characterizes all children: they are pathetic.) Later, in yet another exhausting effort to step into the ranks of adulthood, I tried the title *The Silence of the Attorney* (but either Øystein Lønn or Lars Saabye Christiansen are welcome to use those titles). At the other end of the refinement scale—or, of the body, you could almost say—I had, in the early stages of the book that became *Dirty Things*, a desire to call it *Piss and Shit.* Just to have done it. But the worst part is that this title would have been accurate.

*

Blanchot quotes Bonaventura: "Many times over I was driven from churches because I laughed there, and from brothels because there I wanted to pray."

*

It's remarkable how closely connected our voice is to our concept of maturity. To voice your opinion through voting, for instance, is an essential part of the ritual of turning eighteen, a right for which, if one does not exercise it, one is judged as a nobody by the enlightened middle class. Similarly, raising one's writing to the status of "literature" is a kind of milestone, the very stamp of approval for mature authorship. *Is he ours now? Yes, now we've got him! For now we recognize his voice!* On the whole, when something sounds "right," it is in its proper place, which is the eternal goal of everything; all that doesn't sound "right," that is, what doesn't make sense, is thrown into the bottom drawer, labeled as rubbish. Why is it like this? When we know that everything is just crap anyway, all of it? Perhaps this is, in fact, why?

*

I remember the meters-tall Lego towers that William Maxwell Le-Normand[3]—a candidate for Confirmation this year!—used to build when he was a boy; fantastic, painstakingly made constructions that he might take an entire day to build, and, after admiring his creation for a mere minute or two, would then reduce with a joyful backhand to a pile of rubble. Equally disappointed and astonished every time by his son's meaningless game of destruction, Robin's question of why on earth did he do that? was always met with a defiant: "*I must!*"

*

And this explanation stands, I think, for most of what we do.

*

"*I must!*"

*

But this explanation does not suffice as I.D. that one can throw down on the table out there in so-called "society."

This is how I read Kafka's famous parable "Before the Law": that "the Law" means society, and that the "gatekeeper" is the gatekeeper at an entrance to the tavern called Manhood, or Mankind, it could be said. This is what I think of as Kafka's greatest problem, that he was and remained a child. A child with ears that were far too big ("Sæterbakken ears," as I often heard them called back when my internal and external ages were still more or less in equilibrium) but that were able to detect every last flea in the fur collar of the gatekeeper, yet he remains shut out from the adult world, as much now as he was before he came to the unhappy idea of wanting to take part in it. Yes, I don't think there can be any doubt about this: "*Er wird kindisch*," Kafka writes of the man from the countryside: like a child, he asks the fleas to help him persuade the gatekeeper to change his mind. He is, in other words, not mature enough to push past the guard himself, but still childish enough to lose himself in impossible dreams and fantasies, wrapping everything that encourages development and progress into a soundproof covering of sweet stagnation. A womb of contentment. *Wrapped up in fucking eternity.*

*

Kierkegaard is absolute in his judgment of these matters:

> He who wills repetition is a man, and the more emphatically he is able to realize it, the more profound a human being he is. But he who does not grasp that life is a repetition and that this is the beauty of life has pronounced his own verdict and deserves nothing better than what will happen to him anyway—he will perish.[4]

Or, to put it another way: *See you later, you damned childish aesthete.*

*

When we get right down to it, the question is, Does anyone actually wish to mature? This is one of the best things about being an author, when I think about it, that you are able to get away with a great deal that you would, in a different line of work, be judged mercilessly for. As if literature shelters me, at least temporarily, and that I, *as an asylum seeker*, know that a resident permit will never be granted, but neither will I be kicked out nor will I return to the kingdom of the childhood I escaped from—not because I wanted to, but because I had to.

*

This is why both the Church and the State fear intoxication, because it dissolves the veneer of decency and the upstanding citizen regresses to the simple-minded idiot. Intoxication separates the individual from the crowd and tears his clothes off for all the world to see, it destroys focus and makes people behave as though they are thirty, forty, fifty years younger than they are; any interest in the important things vanishes with just a wave of the magic wand, replaced by the most useless and meaningless crap. The mass infantilization is the subject's retaliation against those in power, or it has the potential to be; it is revenge for years of conformity and submission, or is, at least, an unpleasant reminder of what really exists within them and which, at a certain point—unlikely as this may be—might predominate. What worries the State is the idle person without a wage. The person who abstains from drinking, therefore, is the ideal citizen of the Church State, because one can always predict how he will behave, unlike the drunk, whose life consists of abrupt, unforeseeable transitions, from one existence to another to yet another.

*

Not that I don't understand the authorities. What state consisting solely of drunks and children would last long?

*

The need to drink oneself into intoxication is closely related to the drive toward death, which in turn is related to an incurable deficiency, or *Unfähigkeit*, as it is known in German, vis-a-vis the realities of adult life. For who else, if not the child within me, would constantly be reminding me that suicide is a possible way out, if it should get too bad?

*

"Why?" I ask, just to test him. "Why should I kill myself, when I have everything I need and more?" *"You must!"* he replies.

*

To live like this, with death so near at all times, is like never losing sight of—regardless of which room I am in, and regardless of how much I want to be able to say to myself that I'm okay there—the door which is slightly ajar at the end of the room. Sometimes the sight of it is unbelievably burdensome. But also reassuring.

*

Suicide is childishness taken to its most extreme consequence.

*

Most nerve-wracking of all is that the boy looks so anxious where he is standing, as if he's looking directly at something frightening, so frightening that he can't turn away. Is it his own future he stares into? Everything that lies ahead of him, literally speaking, the unbearable effect of continued existence, the inedible banquet of life, with its exuberance of overcooked vegetables, bits of charred sausage, pigs with brown apples in their mouths, baskets of intestines, nuts and fruit, urine in the glasses, chopped tumors on a dish, a soup tureen full of vomit, cakes containing layers of shit, candelabras, place cards, pretty floral centerpieces, and knives to slice open your belly in case you eat too much…

*

Or is it, in reality, an old man who stands there? A person who looks, not ahead, but back, a person who realizes that his life is already finished, that everything that could happen has happened, that what happened wasn't great, and that all that is left is to live through all of it one more time? And that the only thought buzzing around in his head is, *This won't do. This won't bloody do!*

*

No, actually, I think it's me he is looking at. Scared to death of what I might do in his name.

*

All of those bright, sparkling expectations we imagine we see in children's eyes are, in reality, the first stars in a night sky of terror.

*

There is something infinitely sad about all children, happy and carefree as they are, yet destined to be called too soon by distant sorrow. Where does it come from, if not from everything that awaits them? To have been a child is our great sorrow in life. We walk around carrying a dead child inside ourselves right up until the moment we die. In that sense, it's already too late to kill oneself, because a person, as soon as it occurs to him to take his own life, is already dead. It is terribly gruesome to have to admit that, but life always gets in the way of the person who commits suicide, by already having killed in him or her the very thing that could have saved them. Viewed in this way, suicide is, by definition, a futile act, cheating one out of everything except the futility that motivates the act, the romantic notion of the final remaining possibility to *do something about it*, that is, to throw away the assumption of doing anything at all with it, that is, with oneself and one's own life. The truth is that there is nothing to take from life. Just like there is nothing to live for. Nothing left—neither life, nor death.

*

If there is a task left for literature—something it alone can achieve—it is to take this sorrow—this impossibility of living, which is at the same time the impossibility of dying—as fully into oneself as possible, and attempt to give shape to it, to reflect on it, with empathy that is free of restrictions of any kind.

The Terrifying

Stig Sæterbakken

Translated from the Norwegian by Gry Bakken
Drawings by Sverre Malling

Sooner or later, we all reach that point in life when something terrifying dawns on us, something terrifying concerning ourselves, our person, our reputation, *the very way in which we present ourselves to the world*, no less terrifying in the light of our previous ignorance, something which infects the experience with a kind of *retrospective shame*, if I may use such an expression. As if a curtain is lifted. As if your diary is made public. As if a mirror image comes flying toward you. As if you suddenly see yourself as somebody else, in front of yourself. And just as suddenly you understand what a fool you have been, or have been perceived as, all these years. And at the exact same moment you are shaken by a limitless sense of shame, exactly as when, in a dream, you discover that you are naked from the waist down. A sense of shame that, even though its prominence might vary, will never again leave you, so that, from this day forward, no matter how well dressed you are for any gathering you imagine it important to attend, you will not be able to escape the fact that you are naked from the waist down.

*

Especially the fact that you have not realized it before! Not until now, when it is too late to do anything about it! I can imagine that it would be like the experience of a person who routinely goes to confession, and if the priest, who for years has listened with endless patience to all of this person's dubious escapades and each time has sent him home with a few Ave Marias as punishment, suddenly, one day, in the middle of confession, opened the confessional door with a bang, bore his eyes into the pathetic sod, and hissed: "You know what, pull your fucking act together, you bloody bastard!"

*

As if your days as an unsuspecting idiot are suddenly over. *Self-awareness* is, perhaps, the word that would normally be used. A self-awareness not achieved over time, but which occurs instantly, like lightning from a clear, blue sky, and which instead of strengthening, does the opposite, tears the ground away from under your feet, scatters your well-being in bits and pieces, strips you of the last remnants of inner peace, cuts the mooring line between you and everything that may be called *integrity*, dissolves your potential right then and there, shatters your determination once and for all, throws your desires onto the trash heap of life's possibilities. A shocking fall from the heavens of respectability. A kind of miscarriage of self-confidence.

*

I myself reached the terrifying point early on. Stated differently, it is a long time since I wore trousers when among other people.

*

But still there are those who, luckily or unluckily, I don't know which, are unable to see that the emperor stands naked.

*

Yet not an hour passes when I do not clench my muscles, or nerves, it would be more accurate to say, in expectation of the first who cries, "Wow! Look!"

*

It's like having the shakes when sober. It's like a shadow—your own shadow!—that you cannot escape. As always, I can only speak for myself, but this is the ghost in my life, an everlasting expectation of being caught up, if not by my disgraceful mistakes of today, then by my foolish indiscretions of yesterday, those that, time and again, in this, the most trouser-ripping of spins, strip me in front of myself and the rest of the world. But could it be exactly this we were made for, to sit around and wait? Wait for exposure? Wait for someone to start lecturing us, plainly

Lion of St. Mark, 2013

and simply? Well aware that all those who nod their heads and smile could, in reality, if they wanted, finish us as easily as if cracking open a nut.

*

By the way, I withdraw what I said at the beginning ("...we all reach..."). It's not true. This does not happen to everybody. Quite the opposite. This is self-evident, since the realization of the terrifying after all presupposes a minimum of sensitivity and/or nervousness. (If you are daft as a brush, you are in this respect lucky, since consequently you are not intelligent enough to understand how stupid you are.) To a certain extent we are talking about an elite phenomenon. As if the Devil, who keeps an eye on us, chose a few He particularly likes to dance with. In my case, He can help himself from an enormous memory bank of putting-one's-foot-in-it, each withdrawal causing a tiny scream to emanate, bird-like, secretly, as a primitive expression of the psychic blow then and there, triggered by a particularly vile memory, so immediate and so brutal that I have already released my piercing little bird cry before I am completely aware of what is going on. Thirty times a day, if not more, such a mnemonic ambush occurs—*bang!*—blowing to pieces my occasional contentment with the fragile flesh I was dealt, as if there are no limits to how many times I will be caught in the trap and no limits to how often my satanic memory sees fit to rip it open.

*

Memories as comforting to dwell on as having barbed wire pulled through your small intestines.

*

"Oh, God!" "Oh, God!" "Oh, God!" "Oh, God!" "Oh, God!" "Oh, God!" "Oh, God!" "Oh, God!" "Oh, God!" "Oh, God!" "Oh, God!" "Oh, God!" And so I go through my days twittering like a brain-damaged thrush.

*

This will be, when I can finally muster the courage to commit it, the main reason for my suicide.

*

I mean, to pass judgement on yourself is wearisome enough without having it thrown back in your face thirty times a day or more.

*

The correct term, to the extent one can trust Freud, is *repetition compulsion*. Driven by an uncontrollable inner force, it is as if I can never get enough of throwing the most agonizing things in my own face. Like a child enjoying torturing an insect. Only that, in this case, the insect and the child are one and the same. Cognitive self-mutilation, if I may introduce that term. A form of reverse exorcism. Instead of driving the scary things away, I nurture them and kindle them and pamper and spoil them as if they were my sweetest of sweethearts.

*

Man must be the only animal capable of wishing misfortune on himself.

*

What type of insufferable embarrassments are we talking about? OK, some examples: ██
██
██
██
██
██
██
██
██
██
██
████████████████████████████

Randomly chosen. Because it is not important what these are. The point is. That it appears. The terrifying. Oh, yes. Just wait. It will appear. Sooner or later, it will appear. And then you are there, Hopalong Cassidy, with your bottom bare. From then on and for the rest of your life. Having made an ass of yourself once and for all.

*

Oh, to be given a day or two to clean up everything in the past!

*

Or even better: To have an on/off button at the back of one's neck!

*

But truly we would appear grotesque if given the opportunity to go back in time and redo the less fortunate results of bygone enterprises, or, stated differently, if we, with years acquired in the meantime, had the opportunity, with a retrospective eye, to perfect our earthly labors so far (out with that, and out with this, and out with that…).

Yes, we would most likely appear quite disgusting as we staggered around our own pasts trying to hinder our worst blunders, like overgrown insects, our heads too large, swaying, tottering, limping, like old men, all the while trying to reach the finely tuned wheels of time with our greasy fingers, looking like lost monstrosities, restlessly walking around the places we are usually, and by necessity, barred from entering, pouring our troubles onto a one hundred percent indifferent moon, simultaneously cut off from any tangible result, since our hands will almost certainly be solely occupied with holding in place giant heads, dangling like those of babies, yes, it is doubtful whether we would be able to hold them up at all…

*

All night long
you wash the moon from your face,
you do not wash it away, alas

With my face I am the moon,
I draw up water in the wells,

nothing, not even darkness, can help me.

*

Oh, God!

*

How I wish that the relative strength of memory/oblivion was reversely distributed!

*

It must be due to some fundamental distortion of my system that this unreasonable imbalance is allowed to continue. Whereas my lucky chances are thrown out with the bathwater, my blunders are stored in a fireproof vault. My finest hours are trampled lustfully to pieces by the march of time, while the mouthfuls of defeat remain whole and undigested, so that I have to attempt to swallow them again and again.

*

We have, I believe, reached the source of melancholy itself, which may best be described as a disagreement—a disagreement between two elements that, in reality, is a disagreement between four, since there is also a disagreement within the two; primarily, it is a disagreement between yourself and the world, but this is twice doubled because, on the one side, there is also a disagreement within yourself, since, sooner or later, via the terrifying, you-as-you-are is forced to confront you-as-you-would-wish-to-be, and, on the other side, yet another disagreement between the world that you, not without regret, are obliged to conclude is the real one and the world as you would wish it to be: a quadrupled imbalance, in other words, just as humoralism once explained it, precisely as an imbalance between four bodily and, in an ideal world, balanced elements—or, more precisely, fluids—an equilibrium you cannot reach, since it only exists as

Forest/Dead Bird, 2013

an idea, like a withered ideality, exiled to a stooped, hollow existence in the shadow of the forever blooming imbalance taking its place.

*

Strindberg wrote: "The peace of oblivion upon my dust!" But what does it really mean to forget? Do you pile on so many new memories that they grow into a heap that buries the old? Or should you, on the contrary, ponder and dwell so intently on what has happened that it changes and becomes something else, remember it so well that, in the end, you do not know it for what it was, but for what it has become, a story of a stupid and malcontent person who wasted happiness on his path through life? Perhaps it actually helps to think about it, think about it so much that you, in the end, do not know what you are thinking? Perhaps it helps to go through it all again, down to the most minute and startling detail? With the effect that the recollection squeezes the juice out of the agony, so to speak, leaving only a shrivelled fruit, some dried skin to write your story on so that you do not forget it, so that you remember what happened but no longer remember how you felt when it happened, so that you can describe it later, to others, but without pain, without sorrow, you can tell the story without having to relive it, can be the one to tell the story of time spent in hell, because you managed to save yourself?

*

Not that I believe in salvation. More in the hope of having my head securely placed in the noose. People who aim for salvation invest their money in what is called *unethical trade*. God is a pedophile sadist, and we are all lonely in His countenance.

*

Oh, God!

*

(Blanchot quotes) Nietzsche (from *The Dawn of Day*): "That oblivion exists: that remains to be demonstrated."

*

Oh, God!

*

Passion, in the short bursts that it deems appropriate to conquer us, is our only salvation from all of this. We lose our heads, as it is said, and with that, everything that torments and haunts us. Saved by drowning. Set free by decapitation. And isn't that what we do when we do not love, look for things that nevertheless, via something else, can put us in touch with it? That which we really, in our innermost being, want to do all the time, that which we want all the time, but which, for various reasons, it is impossible for us to hang on to, that which is fated to be broken into pieces by interruptions? Is this not why we get lost in books, films, paintings, music, in short all types of art, to nurture the longing while we languish?

*

In the meantime, more and more of what we need least is piling up, and less and less of what we need most.

*

"I do not accept any evidence that a passion is great other than the ridiculous ways in which it manifests itself," wrote Stendhal. And so it is: anything that means something is that which, in retrospect, in the bright light of day, seems completely idiotic. Because what makes a person happier than seeing the most well-known of faces, but distorted, unrecognizable, in a mixture of rage and angst and perhaps most of all despair, seeing these intently staring eyes, with an expression that is at once pleading and vicious, and that keeps you hanging on until, until... until the world is yet again shattered, together with the dividing line that normally splits one into two?

*

But love speaks incomprehensible languages. This is why we laugh at he who tries, that is why we call him inflated and pompous. Not because his words are inflated and pompous, but because we do not understand them, because we are excluded from the absolute seriousness of them, because we stand on the outside looking upon something that we, for the time being, are not included in. If we were involved, tears would flow, no matter what he said. Then everything would be true, no matter how pompous and inflated it was.

*

Oh, God!

*

I do not know what makes you best suited to describe a storm: having experienced howling wind and beating rain, or nice weather and a warm breeze. I believe that it is the latter. You ought to have some distance when performing heart surgery. Medical science has always, as such, led by example. A doctor is a person who heals, or tries as best he can to heal, be it the heart, the rectum, or the molar. And perhaps we are doing the same, we who write? Trying to heal the world? Trying to make it a little bit better, a bit more reasonable, a bit more sensible, a bit more orderly, harmonic, and meaningful than it actually is, through simplification and stylizing, changing it into a comprehensible whole, and thereby a tolerable place to be?

*

You write, therefore you beautify. You comfort yourself, and maybe, while you are at it, if you are lucky, someone else. You agree on a healthy and uplifting view of the world. You say to yourself, and to it: You are in good health!

*

Cripple writing. Freak words. You would think that to write was to release something, something that has been locked up but that regains its freedom. More often it appears to be quite the opposite: that by writing, you lock something up that used to be free, coil a rope around something that could previously walk wherever it wished. Were words invented for the purpose of reflecting our thoughts unfavorably? What is really going on? These strange whirls that never stop so we can study them properly. These strange whirls that are us. Is it at all possible to trust a person who talks about himself?

*

To write, in contrast to what I believed at the beginning, does not help against anything, does not break anything open, does not relieve me. To write does the opposite: it only fills me with even more that I should have told, even more that I should have written, even more that I fear might remain forever locked up inside of me. Actually, nobody should write. You should never start, because once you have started, it is impossible to stop.

*

Writing is what you do when you do not love.

Some Autobiographical Notes

Stig Sæterbakken

Translated from the Norwegian by Stokes Schwartz

My mother always nagged me about why I didn't go out more with others, "out with people," why I didn't go visit anyone in my class, why I didn't think of something to do, occupy my time with something, participate in something, like Boy Scouts, soccer, ice hockey, whatever—volleyball, which they just had started at school. She never left me alone, I couldn't sit by myself for more than a couple of minutes before she turned up and started all over again; shouldn't I go out for a while? look, all the others are already outside. Was I planning to isolate myself completely? Was my mission to spend the rest of my life in my own company? Shouldn't I try to find some interests, "like the other normal boys"?

Finally, the mere sight of my contemporaries was enough to give me a twinge of guilt. And when I was alone in my room, I always sat listening, on guard for sounds from outside. Shouts, screams, laughter, sounds from the real world, where I ought to be, in the cheerful company of my playmates, instead of languishing inside, in the dark, in my own corrupted and destructive company.

As if, with every hour apart from the company of the other boys, from the community of others, from their world, I could feel the advance of decomposition.

Slowly, but surely, I was destroyed. Gradually everything inside me broke down, as I was sitting there, in my room, afternoon after afternoon, all by myself. It was like I could feel it, how it worked inside my body and up in my head, how it rotted away inside me, the foundations upon which my adult existence was supposed to be built. I remember thinking: Maybe it has advanced so far already that it is only a matter of time before I fall apart, before I disintegrate completely, before my mind succumbs to decay? Maybe madness is already on its way? Maybe soon there will be nothing but a musty lump left of my brain? Maybe I've long since thrown away my chances for being a normal person? I read in a magazine about a man from the United States who dug up bodies from the church yard, skinned them, and used their skin as clothes, and I thought: *That's me in a couple of years.*

I tormented myself; I always felt that there was something else I ought to be doing and never managed to calm down or to find peace in my own seclusion; yet, every time an opportunity arrived, I made up all kinds of excuses. If the doorbell rang, I scrambled for a good reason not to go out, in case one of my "friends" stood there with a valid suggestion. I always tangled myself up in long and unrealistic excuses. I never said just yes or no. I always needed time to think, I always tried to play for more time while I frantically searched for excuses to get back inside. And no matter the outcome of these tiresome activities, the day was destroyed. If I let myself be persuaded to go along, I cursed those who had removed me from my solitude. If I stood firm, or if a plausible excuse came to my assistance, it was with a thick lump in my throat that I shut the door behind me, so overwhelmed that I barely managed to concentrate on what I had been doing prior to the interruption. With a heavy heart I returned to the Indians and cowboys, my pleasure diminished to a pathetic remnant of what it had been mere minutes earlier. More than once I just sat by my desk, inert, almost paralyzed, looking out the window, watching the others who ran around happily. Just as difficult as it was for me to continue playing in my own, happy prairie world, it was just as inconceivable for me to retreat and join the others outside.

The world was split in two. And I didn't thrive in either, not in the world outside, with the others, where the only thing I could think of was all that I would miss out on—everything I should have done, the figures I should have painted, the fortresses I should have finished, the armies I should have amassed, the battles I should have fought—and not in my inner world, with myself, clouded as it was by my awareness of everything I didn't participate in, everything I was not a part of, the whole of humanity from which I shut myself away.

Twice a year, course and activity catalogs were dumped in the mailbox, and I always dreaded the evening, because I knew that she would turn up sooner or later, that she would knock on my door, enter with one of the catalogs in hand, opened to a particular page, and launch into a well-founded argument in favor of a course I could enroll in, an activity I could become involved in, a hobby I could take up, and hopefully, if I understood her correctly, become absorbed in. Each time I managed to wriggle free. And each time a dark shadow slid across her face. I hated it when she got that way, how her face changed, as if the tendons beneath her skin had been cut: everything hung slack. One evening, I couldn't take it anymore, couldn't stand watching her like this for days, so I stopped her in the doorway and said it was all right, that I had changed my mind, that I could try the rowing club for half a year as she had suggested, and the following Monday, the first in an endless number, I stood in the boathouse, and wished that the world would go under, or that a war would break out. The lump in my throat grew and grew, and when the instructors showed up with life vests and oars, it felt like a dry tennis ball was stuck just beneath my larynx. I swallowed and swallowed, unable to respond to any of their questions. I just nodded and smiled, following the instructor's directions, mimicking everything demonstrated to me in the most conscientious way, rowing back and forth and diagonally with stiff, perfect movements, all of it staged so as not to draw any attention, everything aimed at making direct communication, a sudden question or correction, unnecessary.

Where does it come from, our deep-rooted obsession with "gaining experience"? All empirical knowledge tells us the opposite, that it is not we who go through experiences, but experiences that go through us. Not we who gain them, but they that gain us. They, experiences, cut us down with electric knives, pull us up by the roots, tear us apart, grind and thresh us into a gray, unrecognizable mass, tie and bind us until we all become some hard, dry bale of hay, difficult to distinguish from one another. We desperately try to stake out a course. But it doesn't work. There is only one way: into the jaws of the thresher and out the other end. This is how we all end up, no matter what we use to divert our attention, whether we indulge in religious speculation, sexual excess, altruistic charity work, a capitalist rat race, or—we believe—an absorbing artistic endeavor. Strong and beautiful and malleable we come into the world; brittle, impotent, and anonymous, we take our leave, every one of us.

*

An autumn storm that ravaged Denmark had moved over southern Sweden, howling and bringing down the power lines on Bishop Arnø's Island in the middle of my presentation on *Sauermugg*. The evening ended with two candles flickering on the desk in front of me and an enormous, constantly shifting shadow, shrinking and growing on the wall behind me, which the students saw but I could not. It was still pitch dark on the island when Mara Lee, Arne Sundelin, and I headed to the hut to polish off what I had gotten from the duty-free shop, we sat talking for three hours unable to see our hands in front of us, we had met for the first time only a few hours ago and had been reduced to three disembodied voices in the blackness, the world an eternal night, we sat in a grave, we became intimates without seeing each other. We were shocked as the electricity suddenly came back, Arne's instinctive reaction, as quickly as possible, was to scramble toward the switch and turn off the light, restoring the darkness.

*

"You make far too many demands on people, yourself included," Elizabeth has said to me many times. And presumably this is not only true, but also an explanation for nearly everything.

*

"What you, and what you write, is worth nothing, because you are addressing your own people, not the unknown, and not yourself."[1]

*

When I think of friendships I have had, which are now in the past, it is readily apparent to me that none of them could have lasted indefinitely, as if they had only enough life to last a certain number of months and years, and then it would be over, then the box would be empty and there would be nothing more to gain. But isn't friendship, anyhow, at its best in the beginning, in the attentive uneasiness of uncertainty, when nothing yet is definite, nothing yet has found its form, when the roles have yet to be determined, when we are still getting to know each other, sounding each other out, challenging each other about our views on this or that, still not sure of how long we can go in one direction or another, cautious of any signs of disapproval, or provocation, instinctively emphasizing and giving prominence to everything we suspect is to our liking, discretely downplaying everything we feel is not? I believe that I have always preferred becoming acquainted with people to actually knowing them. When I think of myself and R., for example, that first time at the Norwegian Printmakers Gallery, so carefully tentative we were, so polite in our cross-examination, challenging each other in our opinions, both of us, mutually paying attention to every little detail, each equally important parts of the picture that was taking shape; the happy beginning, striving to win each other's approval and convince each other of it, inviting only the best from ourselves and seeking only the best from the other: What if we could have continued like this, held on to this, an everlasting introductory phase, with its careful and slightly nervous attention to everything that is good in oneself and in someone else...the same uncertainty and respect that later will turn into nothing but recognition and a mild annoyance at the familiar, the typical, what's been repeated for the hundredth time? Friendships last for a while, then they end. They move upward toward a peak, and then slide down again.

*

I can scarcely read a page of Gombrowicz's diaries without starting to make my own notes; there is something tremendously beneficial about the man's thoughts, even where his frustration at others' stupidity is at its most annoying. The diaries, in the three-volume Swedish edition, are a little over nine hundred pages, which in theory should produce approximately nine hundred notes. And if we consider that each of these notes produces approximately half a page of text (not all of them do, of course, some are less, some more, some nothing, in any case, it won't be too far from the truth to suggest an average of approximately half a page per note), means that I am soon sitting here with 450 pages myself. Gombrowicz spent fifteen years writing his diaries, I spent fifteen days reading them the first time. What in the meantime became of the book of 450 pages, I don't know. No, I really don't know.

*

Sentences of luck: this is what I, during my many attempts to explain to my students, have come to call them, and I recognize them as easily in others' as in my own writings, these radiant, stand-alone, and even illuminating sentences in a text, often found at the end of a paragraph or some longer passage, and which are sheer excess, created in the aftermath of an intense period of work, and which have their own distinct clarity, their own unique and almost careless precision, in such a way that their reflection, or description, strictly spoken, is unnecessary, but precisely in their power of being superfluous, convey a crucial meaning for the text's, or part of the text's, completeness. Indeed, when it appears, the sentence of luck, it seems incontrovertible, as if the whole chapter would collapse if one were to take it away. Still, it does nothing else but take out a little bit extra from the preceding or surrounding text, as if the preceding or surrounding text would have managed just fine without it—but once it, the sentence, is there, the chapter seems unimaginable without it.

Because the writer was doing well in his work, something superfluous came out. Because he let himself be absorbed and carried away, he reached new heights. The sentences of luck are surplus. They come into being in the final moments, created by the whirlpool of an intense period of work. These are the moments when the writer exceeds himself. They are irrefutable, irreversible. They crown the text, or part of the text, by tossing out, in a somewhat coarse way, what the text fundamentally is about.

These sentences lighten their surroundings, that's what they do, and as such, they are the core assumption for a text, as a whole, to function, or to be able to appear as a whole at all, even though they are, as I said, something it could manage without, because if one were to talk about necessity in connection with the sentences of luck, they are a result of an external, not internal, development. They are ornamental etchings that become the very framework of the piece.

*

Few things impress me more than people who are good at telling jokes.

*

I look at the cover of the new edition of Current 93's *Earth Covers Earth* from 1988, a pioneering work; it singlehandedly set a precedent, becoming the template for the style of music known today as neo-folk. I glance at the hippy-ish group photograph, a play on the cover of The Incredible String Band's 1968 album *The Hangman's Beautiful Daughter*, I look at all of these things that have held so much meaning for me over the years, arranged like one enormous family: David Tibet, Douglas P., John Balanance, Tony Wakeford, Steven Stapleton, Rose McDowall, Ian Read, and I wonder what has become of them. Today, three are bitter enemies and one is dead from alcoholism. I cannot come to any conclusions about what this inevitable, unavoidable drive toward change, breakup, destruction, and at the same time, renewal, development, and sharpened creative abilities, actually implies, whether it is for the better or for the worse what happens, and has happened, as if getting better and better as composers and better and better as musicians paralleled their having become worse and worse as caretakers of one another, and of what they shared together, and of what once formed the foundation for everything they have done since—but at the same time I find a kind of comfort in this inevitability, this unavoidable process, and I think that it is neither for the better nor the worse what has happened: it is just what happened, it is just how things turned out.

*

As I head in from the flagstones in front of the cabin (Old Smokey), where I had sat reading four of the essays in *There Where We Are Happy*,[2] it is like walking into a different house: the kettle, which I forgot I had put on the stove, has boiled furiously for a long time over the propane flame. The steam sputters out of the spout and seems to have no end, like it is trying to consume the entire cabin and suppress the peace that usually dominates the place. Will the rage, I thought, at last overcome the damned silence? And I remember that I thought, after drinking the small portion of coffee that was possible to make of what was left in the kettle and having then finished reading "To a Picture of Harriet Backer," where Ole Robert, alluding to Montaigne, writes about being disturbed, when one is thinking about something, by the thought of something else, how it is still possible to hold two thoughts at the same time, the one you had, and the new one you got or that unexpectedly came up, or as it is written: "What if they could be your own half-thoughts, if not on the way of being half of it, so that you, totally engrossed and focused, started thinking," that couldn't the same thing be said about oblivion, that it also operates polyphonically, so to speak, that in the same way that you can have several thoughts in your mind at the same time, it is also possible to have several oblivions in your mind at the same time? Several. Hordes. Multitudes. Legions of forgotten things, which are simultaneously there, and yet not there because the one is fastened onto the other, and in this way they are dependent upon each other for preserving their prominent place in a person's memory, like the one thing drags the other along, like an inverted version of association, a negatively defined line of connection, where one thing after the other is erased, until one wonderful day we rediscover them, some or all of them at the same time. So that things constantly pop up, and things disappear within the remarkable attic space that exists just underneath our hair. And where a ceaseless undertaking takes place, a feverish activity, an archival work of cosmic dimensions, with the goal of preserving the most possible and, at the same time, recording as many of the bits as possible that we remember from every event in a well-ordered and meaningful whole, and which makes it so difficult for us to experience something, let alone remember something, or even conceive of something without simultaneously thinking, in a split second, about this experience's or memory's or thought's place in the larger scheme of things, that our staff of many millions of workers are piecing together into a whole the great contexts which are our lives, pure and simple, as they, in bits and pieces, unfold themselves, as we, in bits and pieces, remember them, and as they often appear to us, imperfect as an incomplete whole, which they are, and always will be... And furthermore, that the problem, to speak for myself, is the same for Konrad Ofting,[3] that there are those things I really would have liked to remember but that I have mostly forgotten, while those memories I could have managed without, I cannot get out of my head!

Georges Simenon often comments on this in his dictated memoirs, how key events seem to be erased from his mind, or they remain fragile remnants of something vague, while many disconnected and apparently random details are etched into his memory with "stereoscopic" — the word he uses several times — clarity, which only confirms what I have suspected for a long time, that it is high time to reevaluate our memories' conception of the essential and non-essential in our lives as far as we, at any given time, have experienced our life.

For a long time I believed that there was something wrong with me, some kind of perverse suffering or a serious lack of feeling, this thing that has consequently left me unmoved by the so-called great moments or dramatic events in life. Yet, at the same time, those things that most people are inclined to characterize as inconsequential whip me up into a state unimaginable agitation, desperation, insane joy, etc. And the worst part of it is that I am still this way. While the most crucial events don't make the slightest impression on me, there doesn't seem to be a trifle too small to get me worked up (I can't offer any specific examples without wounding certain individuals, so I won't). The difference is that now I know better, now I realize that it is the fundamental reassessment of the essential and non-essential that I just called for, and that it is this complete overturning of all emotional values, which have found a place in me and left their mark on me for many years, maybe most of them, when I think of it, if not all of them, or said in other words, my whole life, and which, throughout the years, I have tried to adjust, this means to turn back to what I considered the normal assessment of life, based on the response patterns I, from childhood, had observed in those around me and which I, from then on, naturally took for granted was proper, or in other and simpler words, the most normal. For the first time, I understand that I was right all along. I, who, without realizing it, had taken the right attitude for a long time. What I, in my ignorance, had mistaken for a sickness or a defect, one so strong that I, ignorant of my privilege, of my huge advantage, saw a curse when in reality I was in possession of a gift. And thus, time and again, I managed to convince myself that the problem was here, within me, not there, in others.

The memory is always wiser than the person who remembers it, which is underscored by the fact that it refuses to let itself be directed. Garbage can be meticulously sorted according to municipal waste procedures, but it ultimately forms its own path anyway. Our classification of memories as "important," "less important," and so on, is only a convention, a form of systematic organization. No wonder: we would rather associate our past with scenarios with an extra flair to them. That's how it is: we use all our strength to hold large and dramatic images in front of ourselves, and in front of others, only to, in the next moment, while we are standing there, shivering, with a far too heavy picture in our arms, fall victim to a minor embarrassment's cruel ambush from behind. The more tedious and less grand the event was, the more clearly it stood out. Yes, I venture to claim: those things that shape a person are often far, far less significant than we think. Therefore, among other things, Simenon has difficulties recalling the appearance of a woman he almost married, while the face of a girl who had to jump out the window when his wife suddenly came home one evening (this was when they lived in Tahiti) remains fixed in his memory like a photograph, fifty years later.

Ineluctable Catharsis

Scott Esposito

I

Sooner or later, we all reach that point in life when something terrifying dawns on us, something terrifying concerning ourselves...
—Stig Sæterbakken, "The Terrifying"

We are stuck with the idea that we are damaged, like a ripe tomato whose scarlet flesh hides a center overgrown with mold. We will never be free of our rot—our original sin, our childhood trauma, our regrets, our mortal bodies, our monthly bills, our failures, our unquenchable desires—our humanity. A melancholy fate, we're told...but is it? Wouldn't we find perfection dull? And, more to the point, what would we then have to aspire to?

Or better yet, how much can we desire a thing that we know nothing of? We use the word *perfection* constantly, but instead of filling it with meaning we only describe the area around it: perfection is without defect, free from blemishes, complete, whole—in other words, an idea that's empty inside. We obviously need something to oppose to our fallen state, but that is all this word can be for us. I say perfection as naïvely and as fluidly as anybody, even though all I really know of it are those instants in a warm, bubbling spring, when my muscles unclench, my vision blurs behind the heavy steam, and my mind finds a moment of eternity.

Art loves our fallen state because we can talk about it endlessly and never come close to exhausting it, whereas perfection leaves us cold. The rot seduces us, and we sanctify it. Freud was among our first fathers in this respect. His key insight was that we must root around for our trauma so that we may stare into it, and once we free ourselves from this repression we experience catharsis. This is the goal of our difficult psychological excursions, a thing we are made to applaud almost reflexively, and yet, it is a victory of dubious benefit: once we unearth our trauma it begins to exert a mysterious force on us until, our eyes locked upon this grotesque discovery, we become it. It is now the central fact of our identity. I'm the way I am because I was molested as a child. That relationship really fucked me up, and now I'm trying to move on. I just realized this morning that the thing that's holding me back is my fear of failure.

Freud unleashed the monstrous possibility that our rot could define us, and moreover, this was a good thing. It meant that at last we were beginning to see the truth about ourselves. The truth, our disease, us. I think this accounts for very much of the appeal of those authors who fetishize the rot. Truth. With them we learn to see ourselves with the utmost clarity allowed by the prosthetics that augment our senses. Is this not what art is for?

Now to complicate a simple story: things happen differently in the work of Stig Sæterbakken. He is suspicious of the Viennese doctor, cautioning in one essay "to the extent one can trust Freud." His characters are not good Freudians. They tend to live in terror of unearthing their trauma, and repression is their only hope of maintaining balance. It is a very different world than you and I live in: what sort of truth exists when getting to the heart of the matter is almost guaranteed to undo you?

We see the dangers of upsetting repression constantly in Sæterbakken's novel *Through the Night*, his last and quite possibly his best. Here are but three instances: the first comes when the protagonist, Karl Meyer, faces his doubts about his marriage and leaves his wife for a younger woman; this begins Meyer's descent into the depths of self-loathing and unanswerable regret, from which he never escapes. The second time is when Meyer's affair ends and he attempts to reconcile with his wife, leading his despairing son, Ole-Jacob, to commit suicide after comprehending the falsity of his parents' marriage. And the third and worst: Meyer, attempting to find some way to endure the unbearable pain of his loss, ventures to a haunted house said to bring you face-to-face with that one thing you fear the most. Far from the catharsis he seeks, his experiences in the house produce either madness or death. In this novel, seeing one's trauma only ever brings negative feelings; once brought to the light it becomes like an indefatigable boogeyman always ready to smite down any hint of happiness.

The case is much the same in Sæterbakken's early novel *Siamese*, about a husband whose decaying body and mind leave him living in a chair in his bathroom, and the wife who chooses to serve him because she cannot bring herself to confront any other life. Both find the cruelties they regularly visit upon one another preferable to a confrontation with that terrifying realization locked upon the deep.

I do not mean to say that I find Sæterbakken's novels lacking in effect or honesty; quite the opposite, though his protagonists are almost purely manifestations of their trauma, they are very nuanced, sympathetic, and fascinating. They are lifelike. And I find it significant that he troubles the popular picture of catharsis. For him, psychological excavations do not move you toward greater health; it is more like a pit that grows deeper and darker with each discovery, his suffering characters fighting ever harder to breathe amid the dust of their revelations. How different this is from what we've been taught, not just by Freud but by contemporary culture in a million different guises, from the uplifting sit-com to the Hollywood movie, reality TV, advertisements, the personal essays in the latest magazines, superhero comics, cartoons, and even most novels.

Can the concept of truth in Sæterbakken's worlds be said to be the same as the truth in our Freudian one? Can we say that Sæterbakken understood himself in the same way we understand ourselves? These are difficult questions. One thing is clear: his unrelenting honesty. I am convinced that his portrayal of catharsis as a dangerous and forbidden thing is no pose or aesthetic contrivance; it is an authentic exploration of his own experience of life. Why did he see the world this way, and why have so many people become entranced by his vision?

II

In the end, crying is all that matters.

—Stig Sæterbakken, "Sacred Tears"

It is not that the rot fails to exist for Sæterbakken, or that he doesn't confront it. The problem is that this is always an extremely dangerous moment for him, and the pain required to even glance at it is immense. In his essay "The Terrifying," Sæterbakken talks about "memories as comforting to dwell on as having barbed wire pulled through your small intestines." This is not a matter of a quiet afternoon on an analyst's couch. In another essay he claims that "the things which threaten our very existence and the things which keep us striving for more, are often one and the same thing." Later in that same essay he says that the only "work of art [that] could possibly be worth studying" must "bring us to the brink of tears." More: he goes on to explain how they must dissolve us, they must make us forget that we ever existed. These are the stakes in Sæterbakken's world.

And this is what Sæterbakken does. His literature has brought me to tears—many times in fact. I have cried more tears over his pages than almost any other writer I can think of. His books have an uncanny capacity to make you see the fragility of everything you hold dear, and to make you feel utter shame and regret for each one of your transgressions against them. No matter that I am nothing like the chair-ridden man who loves the wife who torments him—their story broke me again and again. As to *Through the Night*...I would regularly pause and look up from it, full of self-loathing.

I have cried as Sæterbakken intended me to and still I do not know to what good.

In his essay on the sublime mausoleum of Norwegian artist Emanuel Vigeland, our author tells us that "when the dam within us bursts" we come face to face with nothing, and "nothing is why we came here." He links this idea to Rimbaud's famous declaration "I is an other." He loves this notion that in becoming something else, we might dissolve ourselves.

He says dissolve ourselves, but he does not say absolve. In fact, I do not know that I see absolution anywhere in Sæterbakken's writing. His vision does not admit the possibility of therapy, and he seems to find redemption dubious. Catharsis is for those saps who get their orders from Vienna. In Sæterbakken's world we receive the blandishment of tears, and those tears become the draught that dissolves; then the moment ends and we are just as much in the shit as ever. It is a compelling, rigorous vision that must be accorded respect, but I find it deeply troubling.

III

Why the hell isn't every artist buried where he or she worked?
                              —Stig Sæterbakken, "Sacred Tears"

What does it feel like to confront the trauma that does not release you? I return to "The Terrifying": "memories as comforting to dwell on as having barbed wire pulled through your small intestines." Do you remember the last time you vomited? The way your stomach gripped itself like a swollen fist for perhaps an hour, the pain that made you beg to kneel before your toilet and regurgitate. Now what is that to barbed wire tearing out your innards? Sæterbakken goes on to say that these memories "will be, when I can finally muster the courage to commit it, the main reason for my suicide." He tells us that he cannot stop torturing himself. This compulsion to continually revisit agonizing memories of humiliation is "cognitive self-mutilation...a form of reverse exorcism."

A year after publishing these words Sæterbakken did indeed kill himself. Shortly after his death, this essay was translated and published in English beside lavish drawings by Sverre Malling in the Norwegian magazine *Smug*. Gry Bakken's translation is excellent, but I cannot help feeling that it is a little like polishing a corpse. I wonder how Bakken and her editor felt as they worked on this piece. For that matter, I wonder how Sæterbakken's editors at the essay's Norwegian-language publisher, Flamme Forlag, regarded these words, and whether they felt any right, or responsibility, to counsel him against death.

And I wonder about myself, trying to not sound like an imbecile while handling the afflictions of a suicide.

This was far from the only time Sæterbakken prophesied that he would kill himself. He does it again and again in the essay "The Impossibility of Living," so much that it grows grotesque: "While inside my own head the most ridiculous urges are cooking away, idiotic fears, detailed suicide schemes, filthy sex fantasies, and totally disrespectful notions about the so-called important things in life"; "Just keep steering down this absurd road, the road that ends in Suicide"; "For who else, if not the child within me, would constantly be reminding me that suicide is a possible way out, if it should get too bad?"; "Suicide is childishness taken to its most extreme consequence"; "Suicide is, by definition, a futile act, cheating one out of everything except the futility that motivates the act, the romantic notion of the final remaining possibility to *do something about it...*"

I do not mean to moralize or to preach—I myself am titillated as much as I am disturbed by Sæterbakken's demented prose. I ask these questions because I am sincerely interested in the duties such work places into our hands. And I want to know what it means that this writing at times feels so true to me, even if I cannot accept Sæterbakken's vision of trauma, repression, and catharsis. These essays, terrible as they are, are outstanding, surging with vitality and resonance. The novels, too: I could not stop reading *Through the Night*, dispatching its final one hundred pages in a frenzied hour-and-a-half on Christmas Eve, of all nights. Even if that novel seemed incapable of believing in catharsis, it nonetheless wanted more than anything to go to the place where catharsis resides. It pleaded for an absolution that it felt was a childish fantasy. There is something irresistible about a mind fighting so hard to satisfy itself. "The Terrifying" shows two fierce, incompatible drives—that desperate lunge toward the cathartic moment, and that equally desperate recoil from what is found there. Such self-consuming work loses the transcendental qualities we want writing to have, and it instead becomes a tense portrayal of one's futile present. Because it is never satisfied with merely finding trauma, it goes to deeper and more perverse places. Sæterbakken says, "to write, in contrast to what I believed at the beginning, does not help against anything, does not break anything open, does not relieve me. To write does the opposite: it only fills me with even more that I should have told, even more that I should have written, even more that I fear might remain forever locked up inside of me."

Such tragic words for a writer. Why continue with this agonizing work? Sæterbakken's confessional, deeply personal essays provide one answer, for they always feel as though they begin in compulsion: the inkling that will not leave your head, and so you write it out, but then, once it's down on paper, out comes a sister inkling, and then another, and another. One also senses a feeling of freedom in writing such excruciating prose, to be able to get that rot out of you and play with it as one plays with the letters of the alphabet. Aestheticization is a powerful way of making dangerous thoughts impotent, if only while you are immersed in the act of creation. And then, lastly, I imagine fascination comes into play; a fascination much like when you lift the bandage from a purple gash running down your forearm and stare into the necrotic muscle.

A fascination with what should not be seen. These explanations, satisfying in some ways and unsatisfying in others, all clearly related but still inchoate in my mind, began to orbit around a primordial insight as I watched Pier Palo Pasolini's film adaptation of *Oedipus Rex*. It is one of the oldest tragedies in the world, certainly a foundational story in the harsh and unforgiving genre in which Sæterbakken wrote. Could there be a crueler tale? A baby is fated to kill his father and fornicate with his mother, so his father instructs a servant to throw him from a cliff. Instead, he is adopted by the ruler of a neighboring city, and as a young man discovers his fate. To circumvent his destiny he flees his foster home, unwittingly walking right toward his true parents and the culmination of his life's tragedy.

As I watched, I wanted to understand why Pasolini chose to tell this story, which he did in 1967, and why this legend had fascinated storytellers for nearly three thousand years. He made such re-tellings the centerpiece of his cinema, refashioning age-old dramas into his own narratives: Matthew's gospel was the first, in 1964, and then *Oedipus* in 1967, and *Medea* in 1969. Following that were stories from *The Decameron* (1971), *The Canterbury Tales* (1972), and *The Arabian Nights* (1974), and then finally de Sade's *120 Days of Sodom*. It is a very strange collection: the story of Jesus is one of the greatest stories of triumph in the whole Western canon. *The Decameron*, *The Canterbury Tales*, and *The Arabian Nights* are like life's pageant, at once whimsical and dark, ultimately re-affirming of life as an absurd but miraculous spectacle. *Medea*, *Oedipus*, and *120 Days of Sodom* are pure visions of hell.

Pasolini changes things most dramatically from Sophocles's *Oedipus Rex*, narrating scenes that the ancient playwright only recounts as memories: the future-king's discovery as a foundling, his departure from his adoptive parents, his encounter with the oracle who reveals his fate, the murder of his father, the lust that seizes him as he meets his mother as a grown man. Those terrible few days when Oedipus's world comes undone, which for Sophocles are the whole of his story, are for Pasolini but the necessary culmination to a very different tale: the existential confusion that consumes Oedipus as he flails beneath the wheel of fate. As with Sæterbakken, it is not the crowning agony that interests him but the cursed life that severs each possibility one by one, until all that is left is the most terrible. He will show us the untenable contradictions: the thoughts one fights, and fails, to repress, the slow realization that they will come to the fore no matter what, the many small mechanisms by which a human attempts to cope with this fact of life. His is the philosophy of one who realizes that all of life—and I mean to include here happiness, joy, fulfillment, love—requires one to live amid intolerable thoughts.

Pasolini's Oedipus is a man who similarly cannot soften the severity of his gaze. And what does his gaze return to, unerringly, no matter which way he stares? Why, himself. He has it all—a strong body, a kingdom, a beautiful, seductive, powerful wife—but he cannot escape discovering that they are all fundamentally poisoned. This Oedipus reverses Freud's, who symbolized not an obsessive search for the truth but the repression of things our conscious mind could not tolerate. Pasolini's imbricates every moment of pleasure with a suspicion that all is false, so he seeks out every last piece of hidden information about himself, and when he finds that there is nothing left to uncover, feeling the horror of complete self-knowledge, he stabs out his eyes. This *inability to repress*, even at the insistence of those around him, is Oedipus's tragic flaw. Again and again, right to the bitter end, even when there is still but one tiny veil between him and full knowledge, a veil held in place by the lowly servant who witnessed Oedipus murder his father and fled the scene in terror. This man begs Oedipus the king to simply let things be, but he will not rest: at length, hounded and threatened, the servant delivers the final, crucial proof. And then, two terrible lacerations. All is calm and quiet. Is he now at peace? Has he lost this demented compulsion to gaze into himself?

I would like to imagine Sæterbakken as Pasolini's Oedipus, the things he writes as the servant that runs cowering and later delivers the crucial, damning proof. As Oedipus's father, King Laius, I would like to designate this thing that compels Sæterbakken. And as to you and I? We, as always, are the voyeurs who seem to never drink our fill of this putrid spectacle.

In the pivotal scene when son kills father, Oedipus displays a bravado that is foolhardy, even by his overzealous standards. He has been wandering for days throughout the scorching countryside, picking paths at random, eager to have the vast land swallow him up for good. At a crossroads he is approached by a magnificent wagon bearing King Laius, escorted by four armed and armored men. Laius demands that Oedipus step aside, but the son insolently refuses. Once again the king demands, and once again the son shakes his head with a haughty stare. He is if anything more truculent for this bloody confrontation. Could this be but a challenge to his fate? For if he is condemned no matter his choices, then why not feel the divine presence in his muscles as he hacks through a king's guard? Why not push for every last thrill on the path to oblivion? And of course, Oedipus gets just what he wants: the elation of killing four superior men, the mad rapture of jamming his sword down a patriarch's throat.

Moments before Oedipus ends Laius's life, the king's servant escapes from the wagon and runs off into the badlands. As he trains his eyes upon his father and leaps into the wagon with sword drawn, the cursed orphan barely even notices this eyewitness who will become his ultimate undoing. If he had just tracked him down and murdered him too…But now nothing will keep him from the king, this instant where he at once creates his life and bows to fate. In Laius's final moments, watching this freakish demon he has enraged savagely cut down four men, understanding that now his turn has come, among these penultimate thoughts did Laius remember back to the years-old prophesy, did he see a tiny glimmer of familial resemblance and think that this was his son, unwittingly, now murdering the man who had brought him to Earth? And as we watch this anguished genius tear through his memory to write words that only clamp tighter upon him, as we watch his rare gift delineate the most excruciating pain, do we glimpse within these jagged words ourselves, and understand how weak and yielding is the flesh that covers our bones?

IV

It's incomprehensible, all things considered, how anyone has taken me seriously.
—Stig Sæterbakken, "The Impossibility of Living"

What if I told you right now that I hoped to kill myself? Anybody who writes a thing like that cannot claim that they give no thought to their audience. Although there are writers so empathetically atrophied as to really not care what their readers would think of such a declaration, its very utterance creates a responsibility. So let me say, quite clearly, that at this point in my life I have no plans to kill myself.

I do not count Sæterbakken among the empathetically atrophied; to the contrary, I believe he gave far greater thought to his audience than most writers. For two years he was the artistic director of The Norwegian Festival of Literature, an event whose purpose, of course, is to bring authors and their readers face to face. In addition, as director of the festival he was known for challenging his audiences: he was in fact ousted from the directorship when he invited the Holocaust denier—the anti-Semite, racist, neo-Nazi, and apologist for Hitler—David Irving to speak in 2009. Sæterbakken's intention was to provoke: his audience must understand that these words they held sacred could also be most profane; recall what he writes in "Sacred Tears": "what work of art could possibly be worth studying that doesn't...by evoking these antagonisms of life...bring us to the brink of tears?" So we can understand why, as one sponsor after another condemned him and pulled out, Saeterbekken launched what Benjamin Eastham called in the *Times Literary Supplement*, a "withering attack on the moral and intellectual 'cowardice' of those who pay lip service to free expression but are not prepared to recognize the ugliness of what might be expressed."

We can applaud Sæterbakken's honesty while still being shocked at its extent: to invite a man who makes one of the bloodiest statements possible today in Europe, purely so that he may inflict upon his audience the worst rot of which words are capable. Imagine: it is quite possible there would be people who endured Nazi atrocities in the audience, or their children, their dear friends. Sæterbakken does not seem to mind the potential for mayhem, he is so deeply invested in language's power to afflict. This is one of his primary goals. Many writers aim toward language's limits, but almost none choose these limits: to discharge linguistic sputum in a forum whose audience expects milk and honey. The impact must be as devastating as possible: to put this devil among people who use words to push civilization toward the utmost beauty and knowledge. You cannot glory in the light without withstanding the dark. This is what we see in Seaterbakken's literature. The two are bound together inseparably, and the honest literature all but tears itself apart with their tidal forces. He wanted this revelation enough to risk imperiling his position as director of the literary festival.

I regard Sæterbakken's repeated declarations of suicide in the same way: if you expect an author to give you manna, then you must also permit him to feed you shit. "Love speaks incomprehensible languages," he writes in "The Terrifying," and he indeed longs to hone his language to the point at which he can enter that divine space: "we stand on the outside looking upon something that we, for the time being, are not included in. If we were involved, tears would flow." His language does try to go there. But at the same time, he will also bring language to the most abominable places. This is an authentic response to Adorno's challenging statement that writing poetry after Auschwitz is barbaric. This oft-misquoted dictum is not the blanket condemnation that it is generally taken to be; rather, it tells us that it is barbaric to write just any poetry. Adorno's paragraph concludes with the admonition that "critical intelligence cannot be equal to this challenge as long as it confines itself to self-satisfied contemplation." The poetry of this new age must speak with sincerity about these new abominations that have been let loose into the world. It is barbaric to do otherwise.

But it is also barbaric to bring a Holocaust denier to a nation occupied by the Nazis, or to litter your essays with declarations of your own suicide. For words can do things to people: "I thee wed," or "the jury finds the defendant guilty," or "you are fired." Who among us doubts the impact of the statement, "I'm no longer in love with you"? These words change reality, as much as when I smack someone in the face, sign my name on a contract, or turn my key in the ignition. It is not as we learn to say as children, "sticks and stones may break my bones, but words can never hurt me." To the contrary, words can break you. They stick in your mind and haunt you. They infect your thoughts.

Sæterbakken forces us to confront the choice: which barbarism? The one that speaks as though the abomination does not exist, or the one that shoves it in our face? He makes this choice between barbarisms utterly personal: confronting his humiliations is pure agony, but he cannot imagine a life where he does otherwise. And as we watch Sæterbakken try to solve this impossible equation, it is as though we are the audience that David Irving never got to confront. For whatever else his novels and essays are, they are most definitely provocations. He tells us that he longs for the courage to kill himself—if any of us were to hear these words in person, our responsibility would be beyond doubt. More: writing for him is an essential link in this chain of humiliation and self-mutilation that will eventually ensure death's victory. These words so clearly implicate anyone who reads them.

There is a long history of writers fascinated by language's cruel potential. If Nietzsche is correct, such fascination stretches back to the Ancient Greeks, who celebrated Sophocles for helping them reach catharsis through tragedy. More recently we have the Marquis de Sade and Antonin Artaud, foundational writers in the modern vein of wisdom through suffering. We could count Adorno among them. But I do not find their hope for transcendence in Sæterbakken. What I seem to feel in his literature is the bare necessity of suffering. I think of the husband and wife in *Siamese*: how much they denigrate one another, the cowardice of their mutual dependency, the suspicions and lies they endure together daily, and yet, most miraculously, how much they love one another. This is their method for bestowing the gifts of compassion. It is chilling. Their love and their agony, bound up like the particles in an atomic nucleus. Such suffering is not a passage to greater wisdom; it is simply the boundary of existence on this planet. It is not meant to educate us; it has no value, no pit of enlightenment deep down, no hidden revelation. It is just there, a fact of life. And this is what I feel in Sæterbakken's essays: the presence of one who does not believe in transcendence, but who cannot undo the screws that drill down through his flesh, riveting his hands to the world's horrors and joys. This is a part of his truth.

V

If there is a task left for literature—something it alone can achieve—it is to take this sorrow—this impossibility of living, which is at the same time the impossibility of dying—as fully into oneself as possible, and attempt to give shape to it, to reflect on it, with empathy free of restrictions of any kind.

—Stig Sæterbakken, "The Impossibility of Living"

The terrible force of words is a thing we also see in Pasolini's *Oedipus*. Words initiate the tragedy: those which make Oedipus doubt what he believes about himself. More words perpetuate it: a prophesy that sends him back toward Thebes. Words seal it: the eye-witness's condemnation that breaks King Oedipus for good. Could we imagine that Irving's Holocaust-denying words do any less damage?

But whereas words and their dreadful consequences imprison Oedipus, the oracle at Delphi cannot be harmed. She is beyond the reach of anything her audience might say, and her own locutions only ever fly forth to encircle their hearers in a miasma. How different from Oedipus, whose speech arcs back to smack him every time.

Pasolini shows two prophets: the oracle at Delphi and the blind Tiresias. When we first see Tiresias he is alone, the only person for miles to sit calmly while the Sphinx ravages Thebes with its pestilence. Like the oracle he is unbothered by the sagas encumbering his fellow humans. He is aware that it is his gift to author the reality in which ordinary humans live; indeed, when next we see Tiresias he is telling the unbelieving Oedipus that he has killed his father. Can there be any doubt that this is the beginning of the rupture that ultimately brings the house down? Perhaps this is why Oedipus puts out his own eyes at story's end and, like Tiresias, begins to play the flute—he aspires to become like the prophet, author of the prison built by words.

It is a theme of the *Oedipus* tale and Greek myth more generally: one may only gain the gift of prophesy through great suffering. Tiresias is blinded by the gods, and as recompense he is allowed to speak of things that other men cannot. The oracle must endure the poison vapors at the Earth's navel in order to have her second sight. Oedipus must dishonor his parents in the worst of all ways and bloody his eyes in order to gain his greater wisdom.

Though prophesy is nothing but words, it is a uniquely powerful thing, and even though we use words every day, prophesy is never within our capacity. Nor was it within Sæterbakken's. It is a sort of perfection of language that only ever exists in a world ruled by the logic of fiction, yet it is a thing that we nonetheless want to believe exists in our world too. Great authors have become among the quasi-prophets of a secular age, but they remain more Oedipus than oracle: even their most prophetic statements always arc back to afflict them the worst. Sæterbakken seems to know this, and to fetishize it: we find him glorying in the cruelties that his words can lash against himself like no other thing. "Memories as comforting to dwell on as having barbed wire pulled through your small intestines"— there is an enchantment in being able to name one's torment with such beauty. This is what Sæterbakken aims toward, not the sort of asymptotic mysticism beloved by many of literature's prophets. Sæterbakken is not an asymptote man. His goal is too often reached: that golden bludgeon he swings to smack his neck, smacking ours too—he makes us feel as though this is a spectacle exhibited for our delectation, like those people made to eat worms and be buried alive on TV. His inner torment becomes essays and fictions that we might consume and glamorize in fine literary journals. We may opt to turn away, to not spend any time with Sæterbakken's work: an honorable exit. But if we do choose to read Sæterbakken, we cannot permit ourselves to be mere spectators.

VI

And furthermore…that there are those things I really would have liked to remember but that I have mostly forgotten, while those memories I could have managed without, I cannot get out of my head!
—Stig Sæterbakken, "Some Autobiographical Notes"

I've dwelled on the lacerations meted out by Sæterbakken's prose because they form the nine out of every ten parts, but there is that other tenth, a most significant portion. An aspiration toward the heavens.

"The Terrifying" intersperses its ugliness with words that whisper of a beauty beyond their ken. Even if Sæterbakken's skepticism is palpable, he still fights for it. The same man whose memories are like barbed wire pulled through his guts asks if we do not have memory so that "you can describe it later, to others, but without pain, without sorrow, you can tell the story without having to relive it, can be the one to tell the story of time spent in hell, because you managed to save yourself?" Further on he declares that we always struggle to find love:

> And isn't that what we do when we do not love, look for things that nevertheless, via something else, can put us in touch with it? That which we really, in our innermost being, want to do all the time, that which we want all the time, but which for various reasons it is impossible for us to hang on to, that which is fated to be broken into pieces by interruptions? Is this not why we get lost in books, films, paintings, music, in short all types of art, to nurture the longing while we languish?

Do we not pursue art to save ourselves from our anguish? asks Sæterbakken, and one might reply, Does that go for your books as well? Is the story of the man who is so guilt-ridden over his son's suicide that he eventually goes mad; is this also part of the art that "nurture[s] the longing while we languish"?

I think the answer is yes. True, *Through the Night* is a most sombering work, but for Sæterbakken there is always some good bound up in any awfulness. Even the most terrible memory will give birth to an unforeseeable surplus:

> Sentences of luck: this is what I, during my many attempts to explain to my students, have come to call them, and I recognize them as easily in others' as in my own writings, these radiant, stand-alone, and even illuminating sentences in a text, often found at the end of a paragraph or some longer passage, and which are sheer excess, created in the aftermath of an intense period of work, and which have their own distinct clarity, their own unique and almost careless precision, in such a way that their reflection, or description, strictly spoken, is unnecessary, but precisely in their power of being superfluous, convey a crucial meaning for the text's, or part of the text's, completeness. Indeed, when it appears, the sentence of luck, it seems incontrovertible, as if the whole chapter would collapse if one were to take it away. Still, it does nothing else but take out a little bit extra from the

preceding or surrounding text, as if the preceding or surrounding text would have managed just fine without it—but once it, the sentence, is there, the chapter seems unimaginable without it.

"The Terrifying" concludes with Sæterbakken renouncing writing as that which "does not help against anything," but the tension between positive and negative is unmistakable. It ceaselessly alternates between words that elevate writing to our best possible balm, and the painstaking prose that describes his most excruciating torments. Just moments before he renounces writing, he says that, "you write, therefore you beautify. You comfort yourself, and maybe, while you are at it, if you are lucky, someone else. You agree on a healthy and uplifting view of the world. You say to yourself, and to it: You are in good health!" As though using gold gilt to write a bitter excoriation of all things gold, the very form of Saaterbakken's writing rages against the things he uses it to say about words. It is an essay that does not want to believe what it is saying.

In "The Terrifying's" passion to become another, then a return to one's humiliating self, then further passion, then return, the incessant wrestling back and forth to the point of departure—in this...we come right back to the contradictions in Sæterbakken's description of the mausoleum Vigeland designed as his eternal resting place. In this bizarre tomb we may view statues of "newborns resting on a pile of skulls—or erect penises for that matter." Birth and death existing contiguously, purity and corruption as one. Are we at all surprised by Sæterbakken's immense pleasure over Vigeland's Tomba? He adores every last one of the contradictions he finds here: "A marriage between Heaven and Hell," he calls it, "Inferno and Paradiso combined," "as concrete—and as abstract—as it gets." The building's inscription, "QUICQUID DEUS CREAVIT PURUM EST" ("EVERYTHING CREATED BY GOD IS PURE"), prefigures your entry into the worst defilement. Death holds a screaming newborn. Two skeletons fuck with all the energy of spring. Bodies entwine equally in mourning and ecstasy, at once screaming in pleasure and bemoaning the greatest loss. Even the structure's acoustics are perfected so as to drown your breath. Voice and silence, the holy and the erotic, damnation and bliss, obliteration and reproduction. In the coinage of one onlooker, "a Sistine Chapel of eroticism."

Sæterbakken says he loves that Tomba for the raw feeling of being consumed:

I guess that's why so many visitors keep coming back: they want to be devoured again. And again. And again. And isn't that what drives us, repeatedly, towards art in any form, the dream—however often it leads to disappointment—of being overpowered, shocked, overcome by horror and joy, the stubborn dream of becoming one with the object in question, melting into it, rather than standing at a distance watching it, analyzing it, evaluating it, in other words: the dream of being swallowed, digested and spat out again, presumably dizzy, definitely shaken, thoroughly and utterly confused, as we reenter the so-called real world?

Not catharsis, not revelation, not prophesy. None of these. Not conclusion, not liberation, absolution, or justification. None at all. Only to be consumed. Consummation. The closest to death we can get while still being alive. To be overcome with tears and weep tempestuously with no sense at all in his head. Sacred oblivion. The oppositions that devour. This is what Sæterbakken wants. This too is the truth that he finds in his writing.

VII

Perennial suffering has as much right to expression as a tortured man has to scream.
                                                              —Theodor W. Adorno

Perhaps I am compelled by Sæterbakken's writing because of its ceaseless churn, that scab of revelation that cannot be scratched off the text's surface no matter how hard he tries. For this is what fascinates me most about literature, its unique capacity to describe a struggle, and Sæterbakken's struggle is one of the most formidable. In likewise fashion, I hope I have communicated to you my own churn over the dire fact that I do not know how to be a spectator of Sæterbakken's work. His pain seems so much larger than anything I am capable of. "Memories as comforting to dwell on as having barbed wire pulled through your small intestines." I have never felt this. I have tried to write about my own humiliations, the secrets that are covered over with shame, but suffering like this…who can relate? And Sæterbakken is dead, a suicide. All the compassion and moral rectitude with which I try to visit his work cannot do a thing for him. Is it possible to do anything but trivialize such writing?

Let me try yet again, one last time: I would like to turn to the moral philosopher of pain Simone Weil, whose searing essays certainly inform Sæterbakken's. In attempting to define *malheur* (which a translator's note tells me is not nearly equivalent to *affliction*, but which nevertheless must suffice), Weil explains that suffering cannot exist without a physical component: "A sorrow that is not centered around an irreducible core of such a nature [i.e. physical suffering] is mere romanticism or literature." Some sentences later, she continues: "Affliction is an uprooting of life, a more or less attenuated equivalent of death, made irresistibly present to the soul by the attack or immediate apprehension of physical pain." But this need not be a pain in the sense of a toothache; it can also be mental agony, for instance that caused by acute anxiety: "fear of physical pain is a notable example." Weil says that affliction must have the somatic component because without this threat of such suffering to chain the mind to one's mental agony, "thought flies from affliction as promptly and irresistibly as an animal flies from death."

I recall one morning on a packed commuter train. Not too long after we had transited from the light of day into the dark tunnels between stations, the whole thing ground to a halt. It was a common enough occurrence, the sort of thing that might happen a handful of times in any given week, but for some reason, still incomprehensible to me, I began to feel the stirrings of anxiety in my body. My brain felt like one of those thick steel cables used to hold up bridges. As my eyes locked onto the blackness outside the window, this sense of foreboding grew, that cable snapped. The whole physical state of my body altered. An uncanny apprehension was suddenly at the center of my mental and physical existence. My throat closed. I was certain that at any moment I might lose all control and faint.

I had once seen a woman swoon right down to the ground beside me, a whole commuter train reconfiguring itself to make her the center of its gaze, and I dreaded the shame I would feel in her place, coming to as the subject of spectacle. Somehow I remained still and upright as we rumbled toward my station, but as I climbed into the soft morning sun and began walking to work, I knew things were not right. A fuzziness had annexed a significant portion of my head, and I was in a life-and-death struggle to do whatever I could to prevent it from taking the whole thing. I continued to exist in this state for approximately two hours. At points within that span

I questioned if I was going mad. As I wandered around the city trying to set my mind to rights, I was brought back to feelings of helplessness that I could not remember experiencing since childhood. This is what it is to lose control of one's mind, I thought, and have no power to bring it back to heel. For perhaps two weeks thereafter I lived in fear that I might again trigger this state by some unknown and seemingly innocent action.

I bring this all up because I think this is in the range of what Weil means when she says "affliction," and I think it must have been a prolonged susceptibility to something along these lines that characterized Sæterbakken's agony.

Perhaps the most terrible case of affliction that I can imagine was described by Adorno, who hypothesized an individual that escaped the Nazi ovens:

> But it is not wrong to raise the less cultural question whether after Auschwitz you can go on living—especially whether one who escaped by accident, one who by rights should have been killed, may go on living. His mere survival calls for the coldness, the basic principle of bourgeois subjectivity, without which there could have been no Auschwitz; this is the drastic guilt of him who was spared. By way of atonement he will be plagued by dreams such as that he is no longer living at all, that he was sent to the ovens in 1944 and his whole existence since has been imaginary, an emanation of the insane wish of a man killed twenty years earlier.

Years before her mysterious death in 1943, Weil described in her essay on affliction a person who sounds much the same:

> Human beings can live for twenty or fifty years in this acute state [of affliction]. We pass quite close to them without realizing it. What man is capable of discerning such souls unless Christ himself looks through his eyes? We only notice that they have a rather strange way of behaving and we censure this behavior.

What can be done for such an individual? We are habituated to expect that words, those tiny cogs of psychotherapy, will prove our best and most trustworthy tool. But Adorno and Weil found otherwise. Likewise

Sæterbakken, who finds that language is no help:

> Cripple writing. Freak words. You would think that to write was to release something, something that has been locked up but that regains its freedom. More often it appears to be quite the opposite: that by writing, you lock something up that used to be free, coil a rope around something that could previously walk wherever it wished. Were words invented for the purpose of reflecting our thoughts unfavorably? What is really going on? These strange whirls that never stop so we can study them properly. These strange whirls that are us. Is it at all possible to trust a person who talks about himself?

I think this must be where this essay ends: Sæterbakken's unflaggable doubt that the finest thoughts at his disposal are cursed, admixed with his seemingly inextinguishable passion for the good that they might do. Such affliction should never be celebrated, nor is it the pre-requisite for making good art. These are notions we toss away with the romantic nonsense of late adolescence. In the great majority of humanity such a fate would foster an enervating malaise, and, somehow, in the case of Sæterbakken it led to a body of work that I find impossible to adequately respond to. This may in fact be my preferred definition of excellent writing: that which frustrates response. And yet, much as it scintillates on the page, I cannot stand how it confines me to serve as a witness to another man's affliction.

Finally, it is all beginning to make sense: you write in order to release, which brings further dread, which inspires more writing to release that dread, which brings more dread, more writing. Passion to become another, then a return to one's humiliating self, then passion...Sæterbakken's essays underscore literature's capacity to harm, that tightrope we walk when we try to figure out what we have to say. Must it be that, like Oedipus, I live within these terrible words until, at long last, I (figuratively) stab out my eyes? For even though we are all human, though we are all in the business of cruelty, either perpetuating it toward others or having it perpetrated upon us, despite that intimacy with abhorrence there are nonetheless limits—limits to what we will experience, limits to what we can explain. With these essays I approach them. And there, off in the distance...I see Apollo's statue, I see Tiresias's grave beard and his unobservant eyes. Beside them Sæterbakken. Not the one who wrote the words, no, not him, but rather he who rises from the words that were written.

The Wind from Outside[1]

Audun Lindholm

Translated from the Norwegian by Benjamin Mier-Cruz

Upon opening any one of Stig Sæterbakken's books, we find opposing principles in conflict: good and evil, subtlety and vulgarity, rage and resignation. The perfectionist and the derelict take turns guiding his pen; Logos and Chaos vie for the title of Principle of the Cosmos. As if Sæterbakken's writing was a product of the ceaseless struggle between a positive and a negative writer-demiurge, equal yet alternating, never in balance—the dream of a world at peace quickly martyred by an urge toward the dissolution of it all.

Sæterbakken matured as a writer during a transitional period between the 1980s and 90s that saw Scandinavian literary culture rediscover a Nietzschean impulse to radically question all assumed values and derive from this a critique of language. Instead of the conceptual gymnastics practiced by academic deconstructionists of the time, he took to exploring oppositional pairs from within; he struck out on an existential journey into the plethora of contrasting extremes within our consciousness—"a harrowing internal opposition released by the fist of constructive self-contradiction," as he described the band Joy Division's brief journey to the end of the night in his essay "Gray Was the Hour that Came and Went" (2009).

In 1988, the literary journal *Vagant* featured an interview with a twenty-two-year-old Sæterbakken, who had already written a trio of poetry collections, *Floating Umbrellas*, *23 Poems*, and *The Sword Became a Child* (the second of which was published by his own small press, Media-Apoteket, and is therefore not included in most official lists of his works). Interviewers Cecilie Schram Hoel and Nina Aspen noted that the young writer had also made his mark as a critic, pointing out that "in the paper *Morgenbladet*, he is often crass and outspoken in his poetry reviews. The result: outrage, bickering, debates. A counterpoint article in defense of Sæterbakken was quoted in the newspaper column *Dusteforbundet* (*Society of Fools*)." Sæterbakken's fearless attitude and high expectations for literature were made clear the following year in "The Element of Poetry," an essay where the middle portion consisted of finely-crafted critiques of the latest poetry collections by the most established and distinguished Norwegian poets, including Ellen Einan, Stein Mehren, and Jan Erik Vold. Only one, Tor Ulven, received an exclusively positive review.

Next came *Wanderbook*, a collection of short prose narratives, all of which are variations upon Norwegian rural tales, followed by a novelistic meditation on death, *Incubus*, and the 450-page novel *The New Testament*, which tells the story of one Lukas Landberg's hunt for Hitler's secret diaries. The novel was described by critics as a "postmodern pastiche," a "stamping mill," and "artistically unfulfilled," but also as an ambitious plunge, especially given the author's then-mere twenty-seven years on the planet, into the history of destruction in twentieth-century Europe. This was followed by *Aesthetic Bliss*, a collection of essays on a vast array of artists, writers, and filmmakers, including Per Inge Bjørlo, Julio Cortázar, Jeff Koons, and Lars von Trier. All of this before he wrote *Siamese*, the opening book in what would later become known as the S Trilogy (on account of the shared leading letter of the novels' titles), and his first work to showcase the style that readers now recognize as unmistakably Sæterbakken's: monologues by individuals in distressful situations that form Strindbergian stories, often about married couples, in which the laboriously built-up structure of the everyday is at stake and the slightest incident can lead to an abyss of utter ruin.

Even early in his career, Sæterbakken seems to have adopted the position that innocence is more dangerous than experience. Perhaps one could say that he wanted to rid his readers—to borrow a phrase from the Swedish writer Carl-Henning Wijkmark—of "the security that dulls the mind." His novels attempt to give palpable expression to our anxious response to fundamental conditions of existence, and thus they indirectly become, for the reader, a helping hand: you aren't alone in feeling that melancholia is never-ending, that the crisis is constant. In several essays, he offers ruminations in the tradition of Tor Ulven's maxim that literature soothes by confronting suffering in a refined artistic form.

Sæterbakken's varied conceptions of the writer's task all share a desire to expose internal conflicts that are invisible to others; as he wrote in a 1996 essay, "We are here to tarnish the glossy exterior that gives the impression that all the fractures are either healed or have never been."[2] Sæterbakken refuses to smooth over the contradictions and dualities inherent in our understanding; rather, he amplifies them into stark opposites. Nor does he seem to aim at providing clarification or harmonization, but rather intensity—the opposing poles spark electric discharges that coalesce (in the novels) into fictitious characters and (in the essays) into works of art.

Does it sometimes become monotonous, this unblinking focus on existentialist problems? Undoubtedly, but Sæterbakken's texts often boil over with orgiastic-burlesque *joie d'écrire* precisely where he repeats himself, where he touches a sore spot he has scrutinized many times before. The narrators of his novels are often choleric philosophers— Edwin of *Siamese* being the first in the series. Edwin is a Rabelaisian figure marked by Beckett-like pessimism who towers as "absolute ruler" over "the monarchy of [his] thoughts" in a darkened bathroom as he chews gum, waiting for his wife Erna to enter so he can vomit his bile all over her and the rest of the world. As critic Øystein Rottem wrote, "In the sub-genre of 'excremental modernism,' *Siamese* scarcely has a counterpart in Norwegian literature."[3] A backhanded compliment, to be sure, yet the prankster in Sæterbakken most likely appreciated the play on words.

He liked to quote Balzac's Vautrin, who claimed, "There are no principles, there are only events; there are no laws, only circumstances." If there is a common thread in Sæterbakken's writing, it is how little our moral bulwark can withstand at critical moments, when we are truly put to the test. Whether it comes to committing acts that level unforeseen consequences on a loved one or being complicit in atrocities, Sæterbakken wants us to realize that we should be careful not to paint too rosy a picture of the potential we carry within us. His poetics suggests that unstable kinds of literature, those without clear moral assumptions, can come closest to conveying the unruliness of evil, and, for a brief moment, help us to glimpse beyond the barriers, into the unfathomable.

This belief led to the character Sauermugg, who began to take on a life of his own after having done the talking in the darkly comical novel of the same name. Sæterbakken claimed that he gave the worst in himself an outlet in the form of this alter ego, who at times almost seems like an excuse for putting profanity in print. Sauermugg is somewhat of a social-democratic Céline, that is, essentially harmless, even in his most invective attacks. The man behind Sauermugg was aware of this dilemma (even as he continued to publish these monologues in literary journals and anthologies, an extended *Redux* version of the novel was published by Vertigo Förlag in Sweden), and could joke about how completely futile Sauermugg's belligerence would be, in a hyperliberal Scandinavian media culture characterized by its own kinds of repressive tolerance. Appropriately enough, in an interview with Morten Auklend, Sæterbakken claims that *Sauermugg* was inspired by none other than—hold on to your hat—Donald Duck's hometown Duckburg.

> I was rather inspired by Duckburg, which also has a sort of malleable size that can be one thing one day and something else entirely the next. You see, in one story, for instance, Duckburg is a tiny town with just a few streets (plus Scrooge McDuck's money bin), whereas in the next story the town is suddenly a booming metropolis, with bridges and skyscrapers and high-rise apartment buildings and towering statues, because the story required more situations, more people, more chaos. I think it's terrific when you can do what you want with realistic elements in this way, when such radical changes and strains can happen just like that. This is what Sauermugg is like: fluid, pliable, ever-changing, an evasive voice. Everything in him flows. Everything is left open.[4]

Or, as the French put it in the 1960s, the semiotic force of language threatens the symbolic order. Though he rarely spoke of it, much of Sæterbakken's thinking about literature was in line with discussions by Roland Barthes, Jacques Derrida, and Julia Kristeva on Georges Bataille's concepts of heterology, that is, experiences which cannot be assimilated through everyday language or societal consensus. Sæterbakken was in constant search for that which evades presupposition—not wishing to tame or to master it, but to be able to let it flow to us in the guise of literature, a kind of literature that tells us what it's like to stand there, if only for a fleeting moment, in the wind from outside.

The surroundings in the S Trilogy are generic and rather timeless, without very many benchmarks in concrete, present-day reality—which led the critic and author Gabriella Håkansson, in an essay about Sæterbakken's essay collection *The Evil Eye*, to challenge him to include a cell phone in his next novel. *Capital*, then, was the first in a series of works describing a more recognizably contemporary Scandinavia. Here, the bankrupt salesman Konrad Ofting, in a two-hundred-page courtroom monologue, rails against those in power as he puts forth his reasons for setting his own store on fire, and extends his accusations beyond the realm of fiction to a number of real-world executives.

It was three years until the release of Sæterbakken's next novel, *The Visit*, after which followed a surge of productivity, with the publication of at least one book a year, whether a novel, a collection of essays, or a translation. His most widely read novels were published in this period: *The Visit*, in which a defense lawyer's meticulously constructed life is disrupted by the arrival of an old friend, a weekend visit that lasts far longer and that forces him into a process of painful self-reckoning; *Invisible Hands*, in which an investigating detective gets involved with the mother of a lost fourteen-year-old girl, and in which the novel's crime elements reveal psychological dispositions in these characters, the realization of which leads to previously inconceivable thoughts and acts; and *Don't Leave Me*, a book on jealousy and self-destruction among teenagers, in which the story is told in reverse, and which features the only happy ending in Sæterbakken's authorship (too bad, then, that the ending is actually the beginning, and that the reader knows the entire time the glorious wreckage it all becomes). Finally, there is his last novel, *Through the Night*, which details a journey across Europe ending in a nightmare sequence in a haunted house where your innermost longings become true. All of these novels are characterized by their protagonist's own nervous voices, and their gradual understandings—however partial and flawed they may be—of their own anxieties and deep loneliness. "Show, don't tell" was never a mantra Sæterbakken could identify with—to the contrary, his protagonists spell it all out. As Sæterbakken once wrote in an homage to the ninety-year-old Ole Øvrebø, a writer of letters to the editor in *Gudbrandsdølen Dagningen*, the local newspaper in his hometown of Lillehammer, "All things considered, Norway is probably one of the countries in the world where there is least to gain from being subtle."

Sæterbakken always spoke with passion about art of all kinds, not only about Cărtărescu and Dostoyevsky, but also about Rutger Hauer and *Donald Duck*. He often lectured with particular enthusiasm on the topic of sad music. Like a devoted fan, he took great pleasure in making lists: his contribution to the anthology *Den beste låta* (*The Best Song*, 2009) is accompanied by a list of over a hundred songs that he recommends, and his essay "Why I Always Listen to Such Sad Music" is one of his most widely read pieces.[5] Never has Sæterbakken written so playfully—or with as much Calvinoesque lightness—as in his last book, a sixty-page essay on the album *Block to Block* (1981) by the Polish-Norwegian post-punk band De Press. His teenage love of industrial and new wave music having flared up again, the piece, written by a forty-five-year-old Sæterbakken in the summer and fall of 2011, is shamelessly nostalgic, and possesses a youthful, reckless energy found only in smaller doses in the writings of the younger, more gaudy Sæterbakken.

Sæterbakken was often called a contrarian outsider, a description that cannot be wholly denied. But what, amid all the hearsay, was a persona he cultivated himself, what was merely a role journalists created for him for their own gain, and what was a genuine effort on Sæterbakken's part to crusade against the compact majority? Whatever image we have of him, we should keep the following in mind: It may be impossible to find a Norwegian writer from the same period as well-connected within the literary infrastructure as Sæterbakken was. Whether he was writing an article for *Vagant,* an afterword to a new translation of a classic, serving as president of *Det litterære råd* (The Literary Council, official committee of the Norwegian Authors' Union) or as artistic director of the Norwegian Festival of Literature, teaching creative writing, or tirelessly engaging with editorial staff across Scandinavia, all of his work demonstrated a deep respect for literature as a phenomenon dependent upon literary communities and ongoing debate. To a large extent his essays consist of meticulously crafted introductions to authors and titles dear to him and lesser known to Norwegian and Scandinavian readers; his essays positively glow with the delight both of articulating how these titles reveal our most pressing existential concerns, and of the urge to make those same titles visible to like-minded people.

In 1995, his publisher, Cappelen (today Cappelen Damm), gave him the green light to start the anthology series *Marginal*. The series set out to cover various writers, one per issue, two issues per year, in the form of new essays by authors from Denmark, Sweden, and Norway, and published in their original languages. ("I'm really a unionist at heart," Sæterbakken told *Morgenbladet* in a 2006 interview, before going on to renounce "the artificial walls built up to separate the Danish, Swedish, and Norwegian literary public spheres"—walls that weren't as palpable in the era of Brandes, Ibsen, and Strindberg.) Issues featured Emmanuel Bove, Julio Cortázar, William Faulkner, Peter Handke, and August Strindberg. An issue on Gottfried Benn was in the works when Cappelen, for financial reasons, ended the series.

Sæterbakken, while serving as artistic director of the Norwegian Festival of Literature, caused a furor by inviting holocaust-denier David Irving to the public event, whose theme that year was "truth." The idea to summon Irving likely came from his impulse as a novelist to engage widely different, idiosyncratic narrators, only now he tried to do the same in the role of festival director: What better idea, for a festival dedicated to the exploration of truth, than to invite an individual found by several courts of law to be misrepresenting and manipulating historical evidence, that is, *to invite a liar*? ("The more internally conflicting voices there are in a literary work, the more exciting I find it," he once said in an interview). None of the people who publicly criticized Sæterbakken mentioned that he had spent several of his formative years immersing himself in the atrocities and repercussions of Nazism, which resulted in *The New Testament* and an outstanding essay, "Hitler: A Metaphor from Germany" (1994). Suspicions of his motivations took center stage, and the public reaction was nearly tantamount to a lynch mob. Sæterbakken, however, was too proud to remind anyone that he had already lent his—rather substantial—voice to Norway's debate of Nazism.

This calamitous event, seemingly so far detached from the inherent humanism often attributed to literary culture, might lead us to ask: What role does literature play in developing a given society's humanism, its respect for life and different ways of living and thinking? Sæterbakken always defended writers who take on the task of examining subjects that are neglected, unimaginable, or taboo, or who are aligned contrary to the values of their community.

His essays treat questions like these through readings of authors such as Céline, Conrad, Ján Ondruš, Gaétan Soucy, Nikanor Teratologen…and Adolf Hitler. They reflect on how one can understand and give voice to that which cannot be stated or explored through the accepted structure of the "events of classical narratives: home, conflict, defeating of monsters, home again, reunion."[6] Indeed, Sæterbakken lives up to Theodor Adorno's assertion that "the law of the innermost form of the essay is heresy": he strives to escape orthodox ways of thinking and unreflective devotion to everyday norms. However, the heresy underpinning Sæterbakken's writing isn't restricted to freethinking and cultural radicalism; the alluring yet ominous religious connotations of the term are also in evidence.

On the one hand, Sæterbakken advocates the freedom to strive for understanding, and to cast a keen critical eye on society's dead traditions, mechanical faith in authority, and convenient pretense. He also consistently prioritizes the individual's right to rise up against the collective good. On the other hand, his essays make it clear that the author struggles with a fascination with that which is outright destructive. When Sæterbakken analyzes depictions of evil in literature, the visual arts, and film, it often seems to stem from a belief in a sort of alchemy, a transforming love, a desire for insight that can expand the domain of humanism by challenging the widely accepted preconceptions. But he also doesn't hide the fact that evil possesses its own kind of seductive power—impulses and desires that we can only reluctantly acknowledge. At times, it even seems as though a cultural radical and a doomsday romantic are fighting for control over the author's drive to articulate and discern, which, in a similarly contrasting way, incorporates both hypotactical, literary language as well as popular stock phrases.

Again and again, these themes recur in his works, with slightly different emphases. "When we write, does our grammar house a benevolent spirit that governs us," he asks in his essay "Literature and Ethics," "that keeps us from losing control over ourselves, our humanity?" Jan Ondrus's poetry is described by Sæterbakken as engaging a "wild use of metaphor that moves with feverish—or intoxicating—authority and extends to the brink of the intelligible, perhaps in preparation for one final linguistic break."[7] On the driving force of Céline's writing, he notes: "By conquering the laws of musical language, he evades the laws of the social regime... To adapt to the sounds of language is to finally be in the position to speak freely..."[8] One text after another strives for a place beyond the categorical divisions of language and longs for insight which average prose cannot reach. The goal appears to be to experience the outside, to bear witness to this encounter, but without simultaneously deeming it agreeable and recognizable by employing a language whose words and expressions express, first and foremost, the "just and civilized" society's expectations for the world. It remains to be seen whether it's actually possible to realize this goal. Sæterbakken articulates the dilemma in "Literature and Ethics": "Are the building blocks of literary language so fundamentally essential to a text becoming an acceptable, readable entity that churches are the only possible resulting constructions, regardless of how grotesque the images we adorn them with are?"

His intense focus on the excesses of the universe, the arbitrariness of human existence, and the dizzying feeling of being left to ourselves—in other words, his insistence on confronting nihilism, tragic individualism, and the philosophical-literary canon of negativity and moral gray areas—could lead us to believe that Sæterbakken aligns himself with vitalistic beliefs which dictate that we live among violent forces we cannot control or foresee, but can only devote ourselves to or renounce. But no. In Sæterbakken, society is seen as being fashioned by human choice; in his lecture "To Write Is to Express as a Crime That Which Was Established as Law," which could even become a future reference text for leftist radicals, he offers an insistent message: All that has been created by the hands of man and that remains with us can also be refashioned.

So what do we end up with? A plethora of contradictions that will never be explained? Insoluble paradoxes and agonizing uncertainty? It's as if he is saying at times that, by acknowledging our own potential involvement in that which is contemptuous and unspeakable, we can transform the taboo into an asset. But with that, literature assumes once again a didactic objective; it becomes the instrument for human edification from which he distances himself in other of his central texts.

If, in Sæterbakken's novels, our search for people who breathe tranquilly, who rest, and who have reached their objectives, ends in vain, if his protagonists always drift from extreme to extreme, his essays show it is because this is his vision of life:

> Maybe finding peace isn't the point at all. Maybe our purpose is to live and express ourselves through the oppositional, the self-contradictory, the uncertain. To be sensitive enough to suffer inner turmoil is a prerequisite for all artistic endeavours. Nothing is created peacefully.[9]

And as he put it in "Literature and Ethics": "Literature is the place where we can speak freely about all of this."

Enthusiastic and Merciless

Henning Hagerup

Translated from the Norwegian by Benjamin Mier-Cruz

My first personal memory of Stig Sæterbakken goes as far back as about 1984. I was a magister student, as it was still called back then, in the Department of Literary Studies at the University of Oslo. Stig was only eighteen years old and had just debuted with his insanely talented collection of surrealist poetry, *Floating Umbrellas*. In addition to that, he had praised his own book lavishly in the magazine *Gateavisa*; rarely has anyone ever declared "I am a genius" in a more charming way. Of course it wasn't hard to find myself intrigued by such a guy.

He was good friends with the younger brother of my girlfriend at the time, and one evening the two young men visited us at the commune she lived in. We poured some wine and not half a minute later, Stig and I found ourselves in the middle of a lively discussion about Poe and Baudelaire, among others. If I remember correctly, it lasted most of the night.

What I noticed at our first meeting was the intense and passionate connection Stig had to literature. This isn't particularly unusual among writers, to be sure, but with Stig, it seemed as if there was an almost dreadfully close relationship between literature and reality: He required a deep and painful understanding of literature but also a corresponding solid commitment to understanding on the part of his readers—he considered great literature and art in general to be harrowing and scandalous at times, something that shakes us to the core intellectually and emotionally if we dare take it on. *Le plaisir du texte* was not at all a phenomenon unknown to him, but perhaps for him this pleasure was primarily a kind of joy mingled with fear. In keeping with this, his novels became a series of merciless confrontations with various accepted truths and prevalent attitudes as well as an exploration of burdensome, heated, more or less taboo-ridden ideas, emotions and human tendencies. His well-known literary affection for repulsive corporeal phenomena intensifies the general sensation of mercilessness and vulnerability in his books—everyone is isolated in their own decline and their own waste.

That his exceptional journal *Marginal* was forced to end after only five issues was not the type of scandal Stig liked to deal with. But things were up to the economy of the publishing industry and, with that, Norway's literary scene lost a distinctive, clearly profiled, and superbly edited journal that specialized in thematic issues surrounding individual authors. I hope the publisher will consider re-releasing the five issues in a single volume, making the many excellent contributions (Stig's own as well as others') once again available to a wider audience.

As an essayist and promoter of literature, Stig was strikingly consistent. He loved books that pushed aesthetic and ethical boundaries—or that destroyed them altogether; at the same time, there was a solid ethical basis behind his fascinations. His enthusiasm for Nikanor Teratologen is perfectly characteristic of him, but this is where he and I undeniably differ: a book like *Assisted Living* simply isn't something for an old, soft-hearted, leftist humanist like me; however, Stig's enthusiasm and insight is always infectious, and his literary critiques harbor what one might call a kind of "negative capability." While he can give me a pretty good idea about why I don't feel compelled to delve deeper into a book that he himself esteems, I can thoroughly enjoy reading his review of said book over and over. At other times, he can definitely get me to reassess my own opinion of a book, or he can pull something out of it in a way that makes it seem incredibly alluring; for example, he has given me the urge to familiarize myself with Gaétan Soucy. Furthermore, I like to think that Stig was able to laugh out loud, as well as in private, at *Don Quixote* and *Tristram Shandy*, and his interpretations of authors like Poe, Faulkner, Céline, Cortázar, Jarvoll, Cărtărescu are so precise and insightful that they inspire envy. He was also one of the writers who made the distinction between formal and informal essay writing seem utterly inadequate; Stig's point of departure is in itself formal, but he uses a wide range of informal methods and techniques, and the essayist's "I" sticks out prominently in his texts. If I hadn't known who wrote essays like "Good and Evil" (on the film *The Hitcher*) or "NO! NO! NO!" (on Céline), I most certainly would have guessed it was Stig on account of the angles of approach, linguistic style, and the strikingly recognizable voice.

In his collected essays *Dirty Things*, Stig writes of Cărtărescu:

> This is his central theme: the human being in contact with the excruciating universe. With some kind of sadistic joy, he opens the door time and again to the house of turmoil and melancholy in

which we all reside, whether we realize it or not—where the only difference is the extent to which we allow ourselves to be aware of it, the degree to which we let ourselves be afflicted and tormented by it and in certain moments, to revel in it and be inspired by it; in all cases, overwhelmed by it, and in the worst case, utterly crushed by it, succumbed to it.

Whatever led Stig himself to succumb, I certainly won't dare to comment on, but he had his reasons, and we must respect them. Now we are left with a great loss but also with a substantial and somewhat controversial body of work that will remain with us for a long time. And for my own part, I will never forget the image of the eighteen-year-old Stig Sæterbakken—so brilliantly gifted, so intelligent and sensitive, and surrounded by the light we can only exude when we are young.

Farewell, Stig. I wish we could have continued our conversation.

Holding Him by the Scruff of His Neck

Herdis Eggen

Translated from the Norwegian by Benjamin Mier-Cruz

Stig Sæterbakken died on January 25, 2012. The next morning, I found an email he had sent at 10:24 pm, a few hours before his death. He had just completed his work on *Selected Essays* and had told me that it would be a long time before he started something new. I was taken aback by the only word in the subject line. The single word was *After,* and when I opened the email, the message was clear: "Dear Herdis. You've held me by the scruff of my neck after all these years!"

There are few authors I've felt as close to as I have with Stig, and there is no one I've worked with for as long. It was 1987. I was brand new as an editor; he was a young writer who at twenty-three already had three poetry books under his belt, and now he was sending us his manuscript of what would become *Wanderbook.* I found Stig sullen and tense, and I worried that communication between us would be difficult. For his part, he was probably skeptical of the fact that an older (thirty-seven years old!), female editor was interested in his literary project. But I was frankly taken by the text of *Wanderbook,* and when Stig realized that we actually didn't have such different tastes in literature, he became more relaxed and our communication was more open. After the release of the book, I found a single orange carnation sitting in a vase in my office with a sweet note attached, and I was both relieved and touched. The orange carnation was a little nod; some of the font on the cover was supposed to be in orange, but something went wrong in production.

In hindsight, *Wanderbook* is somewhat typical of what would later become Stig Sæterbakken's signature style. The novel is lighter in tone, as the stories are narrated predominately in the oral storytelling tradition from the point of view of his childhood in Lillehammer. A folksy and restrained humor is also present:

> Karl's brother died two to three years back, from a stamp of all things. Wrote a letter to his sister, and he's about to lick the stamp

when it got stuck to his tongue, and 'e couldn't get it out 'cause it stuck in his throat and clogged his windpipe. Post mortem, that's what folk in the workshop said.

The book foreshadows the kind of writing to come, burlesque images of lizards popping out from behind their fathers' backs, stories of people on the periphery, like the one who goes by the name of Oedipus, or the young boy accused of having a gray dick. Fart jokes, sex at a very young age, and youthful innocence. *Wanderbook* was, however, perhaps more of a step toward prose and away from poetry (a genre he would never return to with the exception of reinterpretations) than a book indicating his future career.

Three years later, he debuted his first novel *Incubus*, and this time I was presented with the idea long before he sent the manuscript. Stig had come across a photography book, *Freaks*, which is about people with abnormal deformities, and that's where he got the idea for Magda, the intellectual hermaphrodite. Another book, by a Polish photographer, on black and white interiors, would inspire him several years later in "Skubínska cesta 64," a chapter in *Through the Night* about the house where hope turns to shit.

The main idea behind *Incubus* can't be said to have been fully delivered, but now his style was indicative of what would characterize the rest of his writing, and I was struck by how utterly beautiful his writing actually was and by his linguistic ability to describe any occasion. His style is poetic, burlesque, excessive, and not typical Norwegian.

The New Testament — his novel about young Lukas Landberg who, after a European odyssey, ends up on the hunt for Adolf Hitler's diaries — became the elephant in the room, the novel we never talked about in retrospect. A violent collision between our expectations of how the novel would be received and the unanimous criticism — not to mention the slaughter that sealed the novel's fate — that made the novel taboo for both the author and editor. Still, I tried discussing the novel with Stig a few times but was quickly dismissed by him saying it was a failure and had nothing worth discussing. Yet we had talked so much about it along the way. I had even been quite moved by a scene in which a horse slips on the rain-drenched cobblestones, by how vulnerable the majestic animal was. We used to laugh and gloat about his depiction of an omnipotent Lillehammer that was to organize the 1994 Olympic Winter Games. Today, I have to admit that *The New Testament* was neither then nor now a particularly successful novel, but it's still not without literary merit. A year later in *Morgenbladet*, a Norwegian newspaper, the literary critic Henning Hagerup posed the important question of what had become of the Norwegian critics' stance on this novel, and readers from Sweden and Denmark would eventually prove to be much more positively inclined.

Even if the novel was a colossal failure, it didn't lead to any break in his writing. Most editors have experience with books that "have" to come out in order to pave the way for whatever is to come, and so it went after this novel when the first sprouts of what would blossom into a prominent and distinguished career emerged. This started with the essay compilation *Aesthetic Bliss*, which was the culmination of essays he had written in various magazines over a five-year period, some of which were previously unpublished. In it, he discusses writing, film and art, which he also ended up critiquing in his later essay collections *The Evil Eye* and *Dirty Things*. Bret Easton Ellis, Julio Cortázar, and Lawrence Sterne are a few of the authors covered in *Aesthetic Bliss* along the films *A Clockwork Orange* (Anthony Burgess/Stanley Kubric) and the B-movie *The Hitcher*. There is also an interpretation of the Norwegian artist Per Inge Bjørlo's installation *Inner Rooms*, an essay he chose to also include in *Selected Essays*. One of the last essays he completed before he died was featured in a book on the art of Per Inge Bjørlo, published right before July 2011, and it revealed that Bjørlo was an artist who inspired him throughout the course of his career. The newspaper *Dagbladet*'s review of *Aesthetic Bliss* included a reference on the front page and an image of the author with the heading: "The Young Fog Prince"; still, the critic Østein Rottem, in his sarcastic and sharply polarizing review, had to admit that "it is actually the work of an exceptionally intelligent and well-read man."

His three "book-singles" published by Flamme between 2009-2011, with an essay making up each book-single, aren't about his writing, but instead address heavy, existential questions, as the telling titles indicate: "Yes. No. Yes"; "The Impossibility of Living"; and "The Terrifying."

His contribution to literature hadn't been one that was praised by critics, nor did he receive any awards until the very end of his career. Still, he was read and reviewed in journals, and his work was noticed and highly regarded in neighboring countries Sweden and Denmark. And then things started to get serious. Like pearls on a string, he came out with *Siamese*, *Self-Control*, and, most notably, *Sauermugg*, and from then on Stig Sæterbakken was regarded as a highly profiled writer in the contemporary literary landscape. The three novels that have since been deemed the S Trilogy posed no significant problems to our collaboration. Necessary cuts were made, word choice was discussed, as well as the descriptions of the characters, particularly Andreas Feldt in *Self-Control*, who was perhaps the only character one could question with regard to credibility and psychology. The natures of Erna and Edwin in *Siamese* and Sauermugg himself lay far beyond such questions.

In 1995, he also got the idea to start a literary magazine. Every issue of *Marginal* would focus on one author and consist of essays written by Scandinavian authors. There were five issues in all that covered William Faulkner, Peter Handke, Julio Cortázar, August Strindberg, and Emmanuel Bove. We had planned a ten-issue series, but without support from Arts Council Norway and poor sales in bookstores, "the publisher closed up the money bag," as Stig put it. Nevertheless, his work on *Marginal* was significant and fruitful to his career. He got to expand his interaction with other authors and intellectuals in Scandinavia; he got to discuss his own texts and the work of other authors with people he trusted and had confidence in.

Working with Stig was a vast and extensive undertaking that went well beyond editing his manuscripts. He kept me informed of whatever he was reading, the music he was listening to, and he often gave me books and cds to check out for myself. He shared personal stories with me. He told me about how he once got through an extreme case of writer's block by making repairs in his writing room and fixing up furniture, something he was good at. He told me about the nice garden where he dug holes and carried out extensive work, according to his wife Elizabeth's instructions. He enthusiastically described to me the wonderful summer vacations he spent in Italy with family and friends, and when he started taking Italian lessons with his daughter, Jenny, he would close all his messages with *Ciao* and *Ci vediamo*. He was very particular about food. Any time we met at a restaurant, it was never selected on a whim, nor was what we ate or the kind of atmosphere it provided by chance. I was always willing and shared his enthusiasm and aesthetic tastes, with the exception of whisky, which he loved but I thought was horrible. His joy and enthusiasm was nothing less when it came to literature. When he discovered Nikanor Teratologen's controversial novel *Assisted Living*, his excitement was genuine and never once revealed itself as empty praise; he delved deep into it, he made it his and gave an impressive lecture on it at the Nansen Academy during the Festival of Literature in Lillehammer; this also provided insight to an audience that still hadn't read the book. He would also later translate the Swedish book into Norwegian and subsequently received the critic's choice award from the Norwegian Association of Literary Translators. During his tenure as artistic director of the Festival of Literature in Lillehammer, he was proud and delighted to book such prominent authors as Mircea Cărtărescu, Herta Müller, and Gaétan Soucy; but not any less pleased that Antony and the Johnsons agreed to hold a concert there, or that Margaret Atwood wanted to participate via satellite and signed her books with a digital pen. As for the contemporary writers he most esteemed, such as Gaétan Soucy, he often became good friends with them, wrote essays on their books, and was dedicated to their work. Yet his curiosity could be just as unquenchable for classic authors like Samuel Beckett, Edgar Allan Poe (whom he also translated), and Georges Simenon, whose every Maigret novel Stig had read. That he also enjoyed *Donald Duck* was no secret.

His less charming sides were also evident; he could be abrupt, and he could be terribly arrogant. One year when I couldn't make it to the Festival of Literature, on account of a grandchild's baptism, I asked him if he really understood my priorities. His response was a sharp *no*. But the trust between us was solid, so I didn't pay much attention to it; instead, I knew the warm, loving Stig best. The man who was brought to tears whenever his laughter overwhelmed him.

Stig Sæterbakken was no typical Cappelen writer, to whatever extent such a writer might exist. In the nineties, Cappelen's fiction division reached its peak with several prominent authors on the bestseller lists and with a high share in the market. Stig was not among them; his work was placed under the misleading term "minor literature," and it was quite difficult for him to be invisible in such a large market; it hurt to receive less attention than writers whom he sometimes considered beneath him in terms of literary merit. But with the interest of a younger generation of authors, he got some vindication. When I used to visit creative writing classes to talk about our publication profile, among other things, they were often quite surprised to hear that Stig was one of our authors and not, as they assumed, at a smaller publishing house with a more targeted literary profile. And he certainly would have been well received at other publishers, but Stig knew that I was his woman at the press, that I ran his errands, that I considered his writing a high priority.

As an author, Stig was professional to the core. His manuscripts were always polished, so they were virtually free of mistakes before they were sent to us. He was orderly with respect to time; he was deeply involved in the design of the cover, both when it came to the image and font. He also gradually developed a ritual of the way he delivered his manuscripts. The first version would be delivered by hand and face-to-face in my office or at his home. Regardless of the place, this was followed by dinner where we could both celebrate his newly finished work and the fact that I didn't yet have any criticism for it. Indeed, Stig's enthusiasm for other writers and other writing styles could also show up in his own ideas, and in his own writing. And this is where my "grip on the scruff of his neck" came in to play, not so evident at the beginning of his career, but especially present in his last two novels *Don't Leave Me* and *Through the Night*. After having read the manuscript, I called him and spoke with what he called "your dead-voice," no less. I intuitively let my voice take on a neutral tone so as to not let myself be overwhelmed by his violent fervor, which at the time wanted nothing more than to ignore or dismiss by any means whatever might be problematic in the novel. It was difficult, but my "dead-voice' had its effect, and his excitement dissipated and frustration and anger overcame him, but after a few days of this, peppered with some surly emails, his mood gradually changed because he saw it necessary to go another few rounds. We rarely used a consultant, so it was just he and I and the text. (Elizabeth read it too. Even though we barely knew each other and never talked together about his manuscripts, we were always "damn united" in his eyes). Whenever the next version of his manuscript arrived, he had always made significant changes, much more than I ever expected. "Where I merely lightly indicated, you have taken an axe and cut out all of Montaigne," I wrote in an email to him. "Huh, huh, aren't you afraid of how resilient I am," he'd respond. And these were never superficial changes; he always went to the core of the text and saw for himself how it needed to change. Once the process was complete, he was satisfied and agreed that the changes had in fact made it a better book, and with the next manuscript, he invited me to be "his assistant in the darkroom." I thought all the messaging back and forth was tough and sometimes I had to speak in a lighter tone so that I could sneak my critical comments in little by little. He saw through it perfectly: "Cut the crap and come out with it," he demanded.

Through the Night, which I consider his best novel, was, however, the novel where this process was most severe. Parts of the text were taken out, not because it wasn't written well or was uninteresting, but because it had little relation to the whole of the novel (like the part about Montaigne). Over time, he realized it himself and by then there were no hard feelings. Just after *Through the Night* was published, I was present at his interview with Blå in Oslo. He said he knew he was a damn good writer when it came to the writing itself, but it was just that he could get so intoxicated by his own damn bad ideas sometimes, and I recognized this trait very well. We also had other discussions about his last novel; for instance, I wanted him to offer more reconciliation in the text, especially on the final page of the novel, but he only made subtle changes in that respect. I, for one, was uncomfortable with the violent darkness of the text and asked about his future writing plans, because he couldn't possibly get any darker than this. No, he responded, it can't possibly get any darker or else I'll drown in it myself.

A few months later, he chose to take his own life, and I, who got his message a few hours before it happened but didn't see it until the next morning, wonder if my hold on the scruff of his neck could have made any difference. There is no answer to that question.

Twenty-Five Years of Tenderness

Carl-Michael Edenborg

Translated from the Swedish by Benjamin Mier-Cruz

I am your Swedish publisher. This reason for this is because of my former girlfriend, author Gabriella Håkansson. She loves your books. She has written several essays and articles on your writing. In 2002, she convinced me to publish your novel *Siamese* in Swedish, the same way she convinced me to publish Nikanor Teratologen's novel *Förensligandet i det egentliga Västerbotten* (*Alienation in True Västerbotten*) a few years earlier.

She had to convince me, because I was unwilling. To begin with, your texts weren't exactly consistent with our press's specialization in erotic, violent, and extreme classics. But there was something else that stopped me. I think I already knew then that you and I are entirely too much alike.

I really tried to fight back. You assaulted me time and again. I object. We're too much alike. We are both only all too familiar with surrealism, small-town subculture, and new wave and industrial music. We love Joy Division, Throbbing Gristle, and Antony & The Johnsons. We read Edgar Allen Poe as children. We love the blackest humor; we idolize violence, horror, and filth. We've laughed at Hitler. You were introduced to literature by a book-loving working-class grandfather. I was introduced to literature by a book-loving working-class grandmother. We are practically the same age. We both have two daughters.

We are simply too similar. So I say no. You refuse to give in. I say yes. I regret it and say no. You say: Even if you reject me, I will always be a Vertigo author. So I say yes. We break up, remarry, and separate again.

There's a scene in the film *Seven* where Brad Pitt's older colleague Morgan Freeman explains to Pitt's wife Gwyneth Paltrow that he opposed having a child with his girlfriend because the world is such a terrible place. When he finds out that Paltrow is pregnant, he gives her the following advice:

> I'm positive I made the right decision. I'm positive. But there's never a day that passes that I don't wish I had decided differently. If you don't keep the baby, if that's what you decide, then never

tell him you were pregnant. But if you decide to have the baby, then...spoil that kid every chance you get.

Stig and I cannot bring ourselves to abort our children. We might regret it every day. But now we have to try to spoil them as much as we can. To be sure, these books are the perverse offspring of a dysfunctional marriage, and they are treated very badly in an evil world, yet we still try our best and give them as much tenderness and love as we can.

In the spring, I published your third novel at Vertigo: *Invisible Hands.* I can't lie: I was about to say no. The fact is that it was the folks at Bonnier who convinced me when they said: Okay, you can publish Stig's problematic books, and we can publish the somewhat more accessible ones. I was enraged enough to say yes to you.

But I struggled. When it comes to the text itself, I was irritated with the most common trope in your writing: your repetition, reiteration, variation after variation. Did you really have to say the same thing four times in every paragraph? I've gradually come to understand this as a hypnotic technique; it's meant to break through our defenses; it is ritual chanting:

> Everything she said had a detestable tinge of bluffing to it, of rehearsed responses, of tirades, of simply rattling something off: she had said all of this before, she'd said it a hundred times before, she showered my colleagues with it every chance she got, any time one of them was in reach of her.

Unlike you, I've been molded by hardboiled prose; I love Hammett and Spillane, and your repetition makes me yell: "Get to the point! End this already!" But at the same time, I realize there isn't a point. There is nothing, not a single Thing. There is just this empty cry, this grating voice that might seem meaningless and which constantly lapses into biting humor. And like the great humorist you are, you never laugh.

Your reiterations are like a horror film in which we kill the monster, the doorbell rings, and it's standing there again; we kill it, the doorbell rings, and it's standing there again. The monster never gives up. And you, Stig Sæterbakken, are the monster.

As humans, we lament isolation, loneliness, and alienation. We tell ourselves to strive for a higher purpose, intensity, and powerful emotions. We long for more reality. But once this reality hits us, when the planes meet the twin towers, when Edwin sticks one more piece of gum into his toothless mouth, when metal injures the body, then we want nothing other than illusions, dreams, biases.

The literary path to the Thing passes through meaninglessness, and when we rave with Sartrean disgust, we brush against the meaning, this Thing that psychoanalysis calls *the real*. It reveals to us that we, too, are real, that we are matter in a material reality—that we exist. And this is a deep wound of the most horrific and painful kind. In its most extreme moments, writing can lead us to this abyss that finally takes on the form of trauma.

The moment our loved one becomes a thing under our caresses, when our expressions of love sound hollow, when our bodies become meaningless objects—this is when solitude will be absolutely devastating. And your writing doesn't hesitate to inflict this horror on us. It's the same terror we experience in our worst nightmares:

Someone taps my shoulder.

I turn around.

No one is there.

I was the one who was tapping.

For twenty-five years, you have bravely fought against all kinds of attacks, hypocrites, moralists, priests, idiots, conformists, all who label you a demon, a provocateur. And you have defended yourself against all these charges in a thousand different ways.

You have said that your writing is an examination of society's boundaries, of the way morality functions. You've said that you want to shake up the reader, reveal ambivalences. You have said that you fight against prejudices and fixed attitudes. You have said that you want to change the world and change us. You said that you write to purify yourself and the reader to the point of a catharsis that will leave us refined.

But you lied.

Your critics were actually right: you are a demon. You don't know why you really write. You just can't stop. I think that your defense, your insistence that you're actually a kind person, is an attempt to hide a fundamental fact: Like all writers, you hope to destroy the world and annihilate us.

You write to tear us to pieces. You are Sophocles: there's no point to Oedipus's suffering, incest, eye-gouging, eternal suffering. You are Dostoyevsky, minus the painful afterword to *Crime and Punishment*. This is literature where everything has simply gone to hell with such a great force that we are utterly crushed.

It's often been said that you are interested in good and evil, in what is moral. But you yourself have written that, "the dichotomy of good and evil might be humanity's greatest bluff since the Ascension of Christ." Evil is the thing that essentially and quite vulgarly inflicts pain, what aches, what makes sure that it stings, throbs, and feels sore. Nothing hurts more than when tenderness conceals a sharpened knife.

The hypnotic chanting in your monologues make us defenseless, allowing you to strike. You lie in wait in the dark, and you knock us out, you tie us up in the cellar and torture us, you force yourself on us with an almost psychopathic, monological calm that arouses within us a terrible sense of dread but also a terrible love.

Your monologues hurt. You try to touch our unguarded hearts. You are vicious. Your writing is total destruction, a natural catastrophe. But what sets you apart from most authors who poison this hell on earth otherwise known as the "publishing industry" is that you recognize writing for what it really is: annihilation of the cosmos.

Your chanting monologues began with *Siamese*. You said after *Capital* that it was your last monologue, the same way you have claimed "this is my real debut" after almost all of your subsequent books. But your monologues continue in *The Visit* and *Invisible Hands*. And they go on in your new novel *Don't Leave Me*, despite the fact that it's written in the second person. It's like when Teratologen wrote his book of aphorisms, *Apsefiston*, and referred to himself as "it." It doesn't change a thing. In fact, the very fact that you aren't identical to the "I" that speaks makes the voice that much more dangerous.

You, Stig Sæterbakken, are a violent criminal, a pedophile, a serial killer, you are a kind of Hitler. But so are all the creepy, rotten bestselling authors of crime fiction. Only they don't know it. That's why they are the fascists. They place evil on the other side; they put up walls and fences; they affirm the worst in people.

You have said that you want to steer clear of the fully grotesque.

Because you know it doesn't hurt enough, it doesn't inflict enough harm; it makes the reader put up his defenses and look away, but you want to get inside us through our eyes, into our brains and our hearts with raging momentum.

You can accept that you hurt us, that you damage us, that you rip us to shreds, and that you make us cry. You can accept this because this is what you expect of literature yourself. You confess to an unforgivable crime. Yes, you can blame literature, you can keep your distance, you can claim that it's a free zone. But, no, you have violated significant sections of the agreement that makes literature entertainment. You assault the reader.

There are others who violate the contract. There are epistolary novels that include real names, the exposure of private personal information and public shaming. But all of that is trash. It's ridiculous. It creates more illusions than it destroys. They are founded on illusions of the self and language.

Your breaking of the contract is much more threatening. You don't actually despise your reader, and you respect your enemy. You know that it's a life-and-death struggle. You dedicate yourself to what Chantal Mouffe refers to as agony: a sympathetic antagonism; a loving misanthropy. Your fictitious characters with their macabre humor and their nostalgically bitter, feeble-minded monologues bring the reader closer to the Thing and thus closer to absolute dread.

You began your career as a surrealist. It was unplanned, unconscious, automatic writing, a flood of metaphors. It stopped after *The New Testament*. Maybe you knew then that this kind of violence isn't enough, that it's too blunt. You wanted to cause much more, deeper, pain. After a few years, your writing began anew with *Siamese*.

The novel was a turning point: Edwin is just a body that passes through everything. It's still ideal of surrealism, still the communicating vessels, still the automatic writing, still the unconscious composition where exterior and interior cease to be opposites. But the form is something else entirely.

The experience changed your writing. You are still Edwin and Sauermugg; you have opened the door to chaos once and for all and refuse to ever close it. You can empty out this well now, this dirty, corrosive water, from a place beyond all control and self-restraint.

So, a few years ago you wrote what you yourself called your first "evil" book: *Invisible Hands*, a text that leaves your reader filthy and bewildered.

No longer is your literature a free zone. Leaving behind the surrealists and Bataille, with their ideas of liberating imagination, liberating poetry, liberating literature, you have proceeded via a series of breakdowns and breakthroughs, and with a devastating blow, you forced literature back into the world, into the flesh of the world.

Speaking of force: I hardly need to mention that you are a man. Do we need to look at your texts through the lens of gender, at your interviews, at the all-male gallery of authors you refer to? Sterne, Strindberg, Ibsen, Beckett, Céline, Handke, Dostoyevsky, Burroughs, Bernhard, Le Clézio, Enqvist, Gombrowicz, Bataille and all the others in your library? You are, quite simply, a man. There isn't much to say about that. I can't even pretend to.

But these masculine texts with their solitary, narrating men do something that the traditional man can't do: they admit their weakness, their impotence, their lack of control. Time and again you have tried to create your own worlds, but they collapse. You live among the ruins of unfinished giant novels. In your manly omnipotence, you attempt to erect monuments, but they collapse on top of you, in pieces, leaving only a grating voice behind. And through your failure, you have won my love.

For, irrespective of genius and patriarchy, no one is excluded from an author's texts. Kafka is read by young girls and old men, the Japanese and Latin Americans. This isn't on account of some sort of universality; on the contrary, it's on account of something private, some form of friendship.

I think it's a literary version of Stockholm syndrome. Your texts arouse love for the perpetrator, that is, the original author. The reader is kidnapped, bound, but still, she loves the masked criminal, because he, too, is taking a risk with her. They form a bond, a gravely dangerous, unequal, dreadful bond. They cry together, they suffer together. Threatening to kill her seems to only add to their solidarity.

Maybe, even though it's contradictory to admit it, maybe there's simply something redeeming in thinking or feeling that the one doing this with me is sharing the experience. Maybe it's the special kind of relationship a reader can share with the writer.

You are bad, because you cause harm: you make us feel disgusted with ourselves, you make us cry with shame and doubt over the frailty of beauty. You force us to live by placing us face to face with our own defeat. You get us to love by showing us over and over again that it's impossible to do so.

It's no coincidence that in *Don't Leave Me* you portray a teenager. Like me, you are drawn to that time of dread, disgust, and filth. I think we both wonder why, and maybe come to the same conclusion. We idolized these moments because they were more real than the so-called reality we lived in. In our youth, we have dreams that can never be satisfied, a longing that is extremely perilous because it despises all restrictions.

You are an arch-romanticist because you're always trying to reach that eternal dream and at the same time you affirm the impossibility of it. Your love tears us to pieces. Your tenderness slashes open our wounds. Your pleasure rips us apart from each other. It's a world far from modernism's faith in poetry, love, and freedom.

But unlike the romanticists, you simultaneously make a serious attempt to break through isolation, you don't dwell upon romantic self-awareness of the impossibility of longing; you have, through a series of breakdowns and breakthroughs, reached a force that penetrates the hard shells.

You've made me disgusted with myself. You've made me cry. You have hurt me so much. I love you.

The Major Works of Can Xue

黄泥街 (1987) / *Yellow Mud Street* (1992)[1]

天堂里的对话 (1988) / *Dialogues in Paradise* (1989)

突围表演 (1988) / *Breakthrough Performance* (later retitled *Five Spice Street*, 2009)

苍老的浮云 (1989) / *Old Floating Cloud* (1992)

种在走廊上的苹果树 (1990) / *Apple Tree in the Corridor*

思想汇报 (1994) / *Ideological Report*

灵魂的城堡－理解卡夫卡 (1999) / *The Castle of the Soul: Understanding Kafka*

解读博尔赫斯 (2000) / *Decoding Jorge Luis Borges*

中国当代作家选集－残雪卷 (2000) / *Anthology of Contemporary Chinese Authors: Can Xue*

长发的遭遇 (2002) / *Changfa Meets with Disaster*

地狱的独行者 (2003) / *Lonely Walker in the Inferno* [on Shakespeare and Goethe]

残雪自选集 (2003) / *Can Xue's Selected Works*

从未描述过的梦境－残雪短篇全集 (2004) / *A Dreamscape Never Described: The Complete Short Stories of Can Xue*[2]

永生的操练 (2004) / *Drilling for Eternity* [on Dante]

最后的情人 (2005) / *The Last Lover* (2014)

暗夜 (2006) / *Dark Night*

残雪文学观 (2007) / *Outlook on Literature*

黑暗灵魂的舞蹈 (2007) / *Dance of the Dark Soul*

边疆 (2008) / *Frontier* (2017)

辉煌的裂变 (2009) / *Splendid Fission* [on Calvino]

美人 (2009) / *Beauty*

吕芳诗小姐 (2011) / *Miss Lü Fangshi*

新世纪爱情故事 (2013) / *Love Story for a New Millennium*

残雪短篇全集 *(2014)* / *The Complete Short Stories of Can Xue*[2]

瞒过之后，发现没人，就跪下去大啃一顿泥巴，嚼得满嘴泥沙，"没、没关系"地一间。

大前有过老孙头，后来没有了。

老孙头怎么没有的了？没人记得起来。

那些树呢？砍完，没了。

那太阳呢？总挂在黄天里。

〈二〉

一热，又一湿，好多好多小东西就都被逼出来了。叫着嚷着，碰着撞着，有翅子的就如直升飞机似的在阳光里飞上飞下，便围了，占领了"黄泥"的整个空间。在地上的阴处，各种各样的里面落里，没翅子的一小堆一小堆地滚动着，蠕动着。凭空怎么就长出这么多东西来了呢？大家都莫名其妙。或许"黄泥"的空气本就不同，比外面湿润多，也稠闷多，稠乎乎的，多些能孵卵东西，什么都长，长出的小东西又肉实，又活泼。第厕的房檐下先是长蜗牛，一串一串地长。后来忽然长出了一只巨大的花蛾，大得如同蝙蝠，飞起来呼乎作响。纺工车间主任老都带领了全车间的人去扑，扑过来，扑过去，眼见扑了下来，走近一看却什么也没有。扑打中撒下的粉迷蒙了许多人的眼，后来还发了一场红眼病。大家得出教训：长出的东西是不好加害的，和睦相处，倒落得个无病无灾。

Original manuscript from *Yellow Mud Street*.

acta poetica

Sjón

for Can Xue

black rice
we do not eat it

we take to the streets
scoop a raw handful into our mouths
spit it out
grain by grain
into the ears of strangers

(it stains our palms and teeth
like the pellets of ink
we swallow each morning)

black rice
we do not eat it

we plant it
in the ears of strangers

Dust

Can Xue

Translated from the Chinese by Annelise Finegan Wasmoen

We are dust in the wind. In the wind, our dance is disordered. We dance as randomly as we want. When the wind pauses, we scatter as we will onto the rooftops, onto the windowsills and balconies, into the flowerbeds, onto the roads, on the heads of the passersby and on their clothing. Sometimes we cluster and sometimes disperse, sometimes solidify into coarse flecks and sometimes turn into powder, without conforming to any law. Yet I, being a single particle of dust, have a secret: I know that every speck among us believes itself to be a flower. How strange that I seem to have known this secret ever since I entered the world. Why do they think they're flowers? Such wild presumption. Everyone knows that dust can't compare to flowers. Flowers are alive, they have beautiful contours.

Tonight the wind is blowing from the north. Our collective of dust twitches in the dark wind, one part condensing into a whip and beating the leaves of the trees while another large part changes into a mushroom cloud rising to the sky. The little girl behind the windowpane holds back her tears. We call out to her, silently: "We are flowers! We are flowers!"

The city is dust's proper home. We have never left the city. We enjoy sticking to the windshields in a thick coating, infuriating the drivers. This is no prank, but rather a means of communication. I often wonder, does the city make us cherish this dream that we are flowers, or are we actually flowers after all? The drivers don't believe we are. They roughly sweep us away with the wiper fluid so that we run down onto the concrete, then slide into the sewer. But, after a few days, we become dust in the wind again. We sweep across the city. We are everywhere, but we never stay for very long.

When the wind stops, I hear noisy murmurs all around. We murmur; no one can tell what anyone else is saying. Though I can't hear them clearly, I know they are always returning to their stubborn idea. None of us is upset at being deserted by the wind. We are too proud, falling from the air in the same way that humans disembark from a plane. Even if we land in a manure pit, our mentality does not change. We will always have ways of returning to power. Does the wind not exist for us? Look at my companions tumbling through the square like fighting ghosts! The wind blows from their direction, they are chasing the wind.

We can only live in this carefree way because we are small and have no physical strength. According to what the elderly among us remember, in the past our ancestors were majestic and stable, because they came from stones. The younger ones do not believe much in this kind of thing. How could rocks turn into powder? Besides, if stones have already turned into dust, can one still speak of majestic or stable? We have not investigated this issue of our forebears. It makes no difference, as this is how we live now. We may be degenerating, or maybe we are evolving. Stones can't be everywhere at once, especially not in the city. And there's another question: if we were stones before, why does each speck of dust think it is a flower? I only know this secret; I cannot say what it means. A carefree, as-you-will existence means not being good at deep thinking. In deciding where to go, we only think for a second and then decide. If we want to leave a given place, we think about it for half a second at most, then leave. However, this does not mean we lack continuity. Have you ever seen a tornado? Its shape is assembled from our carefree actions. Isn't that terrifying? The day we turn into a tornado we are extremely excited, and frightened, too.

The city is a giant melting pot and, since we live in the city, we become something like it. I cannot say in what way precisely we resemble the city, only that every one of us feels that we do. For example, we often greet each other by saying: "Hi, Three, I'm here now," or, "Hi, Little Four, I'm leaving." Isn't this manner like the city? Some of our elders call this "getting in everywhere," and they also say that it's the way of the city to get in by any means possible.

How did we come to the city, in the very beginning? Even the older dust won't say anything about it. Apparently you're allowed to think whatever you want on this subject. As for me, I believe that from the first day there was a city, we were there, too, because I cannot imagine a city without dust. Really, there could be nothing more natural. Take a look at how many of our small fellows collect on a pet dog and you'll understand. Sometimes we remain concealed. If we don't hide, our quantity is too incredible to describe. At such times, you can't even see the fingers of your outstretched hands, because we occupy every inch of space. We even believe that we are the city, a city of flowers. The people of the city have a name for us: the spirit of the plague. We take this as praise. Aren't the cleaners sweeping the streets in the early morning proclaiming our existence to humanity? We're happy to be cleared away. This is one of the means by which our race circulates. Life has meaning.

For the most part, we believe ourselves to have no memory. In the square, for example, we whirl in mid-air into a certain pattern, and then we slowly fall to the ground. After we fall to the ground we cannot recall what flower-like pattern everyone had formed in the air. It's as though we had always been an ordinary part of the concrete. We crowd together, lethargic and silent, sometimes dreaming of the sun, sometimes of dew. The only thing we never dream of is the chaotic dancing in which each speck follows its own whim. In fact, not having a memory is also a form of happiness, because the next time we are about to become some design in the air, there will be voices among us shouting aloud: "We are flowers! We are flowers!" At such moments, the sky and earth disappear, leaving only the brilliant shimmering of designs never seen before. They really never have been seen before, at least that's what we think, because we only remember what happened in the last few seconds. Sometimes it even surprises me: how did the dust gain this advantage? I know that everyone has doubts, but this doesn't prevent our future enthusiasm for the dance of chaos. At idle moments, I have quietly followed a forced line of reasoning: I trace our traits back to the legend of our origin. If we came from stones, the disappearance of our memory can be explained. I don't take this as a conclusion, but it's what I prefer to think.

I don't know why, in the midst of our disorderly whirling, I always hear voices beside me. "Five, which level are you on?" "Little One, up three and down again." "There's a hole here, let me take it." And so on. Our psychology is balanced, despite the intensity of the activity. Although, as one of the older ones has said, "Balance invites danger." Sometimes I launch a prank to shock everyone. I move intentionally in a straight line, charging in a horizontal direction, hurtling along. The results have been exceptionally good—in the general panic, something from the dark depths reveals its towering excellence. At these glorious moments, I hear low exclamations of wonder: "That is a flower. Oh, a flower." If asked what design we form, we naturally cannot say, because we have no memory. However, certain things happen that are similar to remembering. We call these things quasi-memory. Quasi-memory has never happened on the ground, instead, it always takes place in the wind. In the wind, we have seen bright points of light, heard the sound of wooden clappers, sensed a change in the air's speed, touched a kind of emptiness. All of this together makes us think of flowers. This is quasi-memory, and it makes the dust both solemn and excited.

I, along with a crowd of fellow dust, once had the experience of being held still. It happened on the wing of a cargo plane. That day—without knowing whose idea it was—the group of us landed on a section of the wing. I don't know what part of the wing, either, but once we stopped there we couldn't blow away. The plane's route was from the eastern to the western outskirts of the city, but we did not want to leave the city. It was nighttime. We pressed into a heap, waiting anxiously. The idea of a plane should have been beyond our experience, but the further beyond our experience something is, the more wildly we imagine it. Some fellows thought about it and then said what they thought, other fellows listened and then spoke up—you had something to say, I had something to say. Then we started to fight, raising a churning grey cloud. Luckily it was dark all around and no one discovered this scene. At daybreak, while we still were fast asleep and without any preparation, the plane suddenly took flight.

The shaking was frightful, but dust has an exceptional ability to stick to things and we managed to stay on the wing of the plane without falling off. It was not the vibrations that made us uneasy, but rather dullness and a sense of monotony we had never experienced before. The vast whiteness stretched in all directions with nothing visible in it and the insane machine roared. All of us regretted landing on this surface, where we couldn't move at random, and any thinking was dangerous. We were afraid our attention would wander, so we tried not to think of anything. We sensed that if we thought, we'd be finished—what people call "vanishing into outer space." While we shook on the plane's wing, it seems as though something happened. What happened? Naturally, the whole group of us forgot. I dimly remember there being raindrops. Was it raining? In short, the experience of being on the plane and the experience of being in the wind or on the ground was completely different. Nothing to be thought, nothing to be seen, and being unable to relax our vigilance. When I recall the effect this had on us, I want to describe it as "death," yet we all lived. Dust cannot die.

The plane finally descended. We remained stuck to the wing, having lost the ability to move, but only for a brief instant. When the first gust of southern wind came, we gathered into it. Floating along in the wind, we saw the cargo plane below with lingering fear. Even if it wasn't death, it was more terrible than death! There were people unloading the plane. What was packed into all of the small black cases? Could it be animal remains? For the mass of dust our faith in life was damaged by this fearful journey. We had never known things like this could happen. In a fundamental sense, we had been free of worry. This collective experience left a hole in our thinking and nothing with which to fill it. We tried as hard as possible to forget it. But who, while in a state of consciousness, can forget a specific event? And that was the most unforgettable event in our careers. We resumed a peaceful existence. Even so, there are often times, when we are still and quiet, that our thoughts turn to that event. Already we cannot remember everything that took place, we only remember a shining drop of rain, and we say, shuddering: "If we held on, would there be a turning point?" Or: "I imagined myself sitting among the clouds. It felt like I was bouncing along on a carpet of grass." Or: "Hey, Three, have any pebbles appeared?" Or: "I want to combine with something, but I am always squeezed out." Each of my companions comes out straightaway with a crazy idea. I know that everything they say has something to do with what happened that time. That raindrop! Before long the crowd of us scattered. This is also unavoidable—even though there was a shared experience that has been difficult to forget, it's only a blank space, which cannot act as a magnetic force holding us together. Each goes a different way, merging into another community.

For a time, for a long time, I floated along with the wind, as if waiting for an opportunity, and then I drifted onto the roof of a grocery market. I stayed there, where I could hear the seething sounds of speech. This is the city's energy, an energy that fascinates me. I pushed through a crack in the roof into the market's large main hall, dropping onto a crossbeam. Ha, these humans, each with his or her own way of thinking, not at all like the dust. I can see how all of them have their own plans in mind. Maybe this is why they fascinate me. The unreadable expressions on their faces and the varied speed of their movements contribute to an air of scheming. After years of living in the city, I have a certain estimation of human eccentricity. I've never made predictions about their behavior, and I don't draw conclusions. I tell my fellow dust: "When it comes to humans, all we can do is a little observational work."

At the rear of the market a crowd of people began to fight. Blood flowed from a man's forehead. I thought that he was going to die. He fell slowly. I nervously observed the scene from the crossbeam. Oh, he did not actually fall to the ground. Another man had grabbed him. The man who held him was sucking the blood from his forehead. His eyes widened in surprise. Then there was a turning point of profound significance: the man who had been bleeding suddenly grabbed the bare shoulder of the other man and bit it. The man who was bitten gave a rending cry. Blood ran from his shoulder and the man who had bitten him sucked greedily at this fresh, warm blood. The two men held each other tightly, tangled in a mass. The people nearby stepped back, isolating them inside of a circle and watching with surprise from its edge. "He's an experienced vampire, very skilled!" someone said. "His mouth isn't on the wound, he's losing focus!" another said, not agreeing with the first opinion. I don't understand why people give viciousness so much attention. I pay attention, but only out of interest, while for them, it seems more than just a matter of interest. They actually believe it to be somehow relevant to their own lives. Humans really are hard to understand. The entangled men had stopped moving, as if transformed into fossils. The onlookers sighed in unison, as if disappointed, and then slowly dispersed. Had the two troublemakers fallen asleep? A draft blew through the hall and I hastily leapt into the air, leaving the violent site. I do not like violence, but in the city where I live, violence often erupts. This is a drawback to the city.

Through the winding path of the air I came to a stage in a theater. Several of my companions had also paused there. The stage was empty, yet crowded with human souls. The ambience was loud and lively. I know human performances are not the same as our dancing in the wind. The greatest difference is that we have no memory, while humans remember. Look at these souls, these formless beings escaped from a play! How should they be categorized, where do they belong? One old man had an especially resonant voice that prevailed over the whispers of the others. Was he playing the role of a king? What was he saying? He kept rambling on about getting treatment for the corns on his feet. Do all kings have corns? However, his voice was magnificent, and with the resonance of the stage it made for a good effect. I was moved while listening to him, not on account of the corns, but because of his perfect voice. My compatriots were also touched. I heard them tumbling in the shadows, echoing in low voices the old man's trivial rambling.

The old king finally finished what he was saying. Another voice, a young woman's, cut through from the background. She was selling flatbread, shouting and even screaming as she hawked her wares. All of us could hear that she was threatening the customers, hinting that if they didn't buy her bread there would be deadly consequences. Yet her voice, too, was perfect. She kept moving, from the front to the back and from the left to the right. My compatriots were moaning, so moved that they almost fainted. One fellow next to me groaned over and over: "Quick, buy her flatbread, it's a wonder! Quick, buy it!" Although I was slightly moved, too, I thought he was making a display of himself. It was really too much, it disgusted me. So I leapt into the air, landing on the other side of the stage. The woman was still shouting, her voice growing more sorrowful, reminding me of long ago when I'd been on a thatched roof on the outskirts of town, where there were old ducks in a pond. Just when I began to feel sentimental, the woman's voice changed again, becoming indignant. She wasn't selling flatbread anymore. Instead, she was peddling children's toys. They must have been toy animals because they were making all kinds of animal sounds, and kicking up a riot! I saw some of my fellow dust over on the other side of the stage dancing madly in mid-air, roused by this woman. The king's voice entered in, still rambling about his corns, then growing more powerful, merging with the rest of the racket into one sound. It sounded as though they were discussing the fate of humankind. Were the souls really talking about the great affairs of humanity? I had a sense of urgency. I felt the signs of a tornado coming outside, so I followed an air current out of the theater and into the avenue beyond. Night was falling and the lights beginning to be lit, the dark blue of the sky was peaceful. Where was the tornado? It must have been an illusion produced by the ghosts. I dropped onto the cover of a streetlight, planning to rest for a little while on this warm spot.

But I had miscalculated. A dark shadow appeared in the circle of light under the streetlamp. The shadow did not leave, it just stopped there. "Hello, are you the king?" I asked loudly. The shadow did not answer, but only grew denser, and its head shook several times in a way that made it look like a man. To find something to talk about, I tried being sensational on purpose: "There's a tornado tonight!" He still did not move, only growing darker and thicker. I glanced at him, and then jumped up and down on the lamp cover in my fright, because I saw an abyss! On a major city thoroughfare, underneath a streetlight, such a ghastly abyss! I comforted myself, saying, this is only the shadow of a man. It was the first time I had seen a human shadow with an abyss inside of it, but from now on I should get used to this sort of thing. In the city there's something new every day, every month. Is anything too strange to happen there? Since he had stopped underneath me, I could see there was no chance of resting now. All right then. I waited for a gust and left in a hurry, riding on the wind. I tried hard to rise, to keep the shadow from following. I flew for a spell, and then alighted on the grass in a garden off the street. It seemed strange that this evening there would be so many neon lights making the night colorful and grotesque.

I was just about to rest when I heard someone's voice: "Something is always chasing me." Oh, it was that man again! His shadow fell on the grass. So he, too, was pursued by something. Then why was he chasing me? I didn't dare ask him. I was afraid his shadow would move toward me and swallow me. From a distance of several meters, I could also sense the shadow's abyss, and the shadow's edge was trembling. "Are you the king?" I asked, summoning all my courage. At the sound of my voice, the shadow's head disappeared, as if it had been chopped off. The headless shadow shifted to the west by degrees, moving further and further away. I felt safer and relaxed, settling in to rest. Yet I knew he had not left. A question occurred to me: Had the king followed my flight out of the theater, or had I flown out following him? Could he have been the current of air inside the theater when I thought there was a tornado outside? If he were, it meant that I'd already been to the abyss. The abyss wasn't frightening after all, it only looked frightening from the outside. This deduction excited me so much that, all at once, I felt myself turning into a dahlia, and I shouted aloud: "There's a tornado tonight! A tornado tonight!" I saw the shadow as it, startled, moved a little further away and stopped again, standing motionless like someone who can't make up his mind. Could the critical moment have arrived? Why was I so restless?

A time, a long time, passed, and still I didn't understand. A tornado couldn't be summoned by the thoughts of an insignificant speck like me—could it? As I faced the shadow directly the entire city's neon lights suddenly went dark. The streetlights were also black. I could not see him, but I knew he was there in front of me under the loquat tree. Then I heard a whistling sound from the distance coming nearer, the moans of my innumerable companions in a wild wind, a sound at the full pitch of freedom. I knew they were dancing their random dance. What was I still waiting for? Wasn't this what I had longed for? The wind was everywhere. I tumbled into it, and then I ascended. I do not know how high I rose, but I reached the inside of a cloud. My companions were all around me. I heard the sounds they made; no one was listening to anyone else and they were only interested in themselves, but I knew each took the whole body to be itself, and I knew that each one was striving to align its frantic motion to a strange rhythm. My fellow particles are too anxious! Naturally, I was throwing myself into the dance, too. Were we trying to form a dragon, or was it the wind trying to do so? Without us, the wind couldn't form a dragon, it couldn't take any shape. A piece of dust beside me cried. Unusual for someone to cry at a moment like this! "Why are you crying?" I asked him accusingly. "I'm crying for you, because you don't recognize yourself!" he shouted as hard as he could. "What do you mean, myself? Who?" "There, behind you." I turned around and unexpectedly heard the king's voice: "Something is always chasing me. Now I'm slowly pulling away from it." Such a speech at a time like this! How I longed to throw myself into the king's—the shadow's—arms! But where was he? The east was already brightening, the enormous dragon already formed, the city trembled in the early light of dawn. From the lowest stratum, gradually rising upward, gathering into a chorus reverberating through the heavens: "We are flowers! We are flowers…"

The Tenant of Room 801

Can Xue

Translated from the Chinese by Annelise Finegan Wasmoen

There is no moon tonight and the wind is high. I am reminded once again of the tenant of Room 801. Would he enjoy this sort of weather? Do changes in the weather have the slightest effect on him?

I moved back in with my parents one month ago, and for a month before that I shared my little apartment, its single bedroom and living room, with this man named "He."[1]

When he came in, I was sitting on the balcony doing nothing in particular.

"Hello. Who are you looking for?"

"I'm not looking for anyone. My name is He. This is a nice place you have."

He pulled an air mattress out of his enormous hiking backpack and started, with some effort, to inflate it. Puffing, then resting, puffing, then resting.

"Old He, do you live in this building?"

"What do you mean? How could I possibly live here?" His words showed some resentment toward me. "But what you say makes sense, I'll live here for tonight. You won't object, will you? I'll only take up a little corner. And I'm not boring, either. I come from Wulong Mountain."

"Wulong Mountain," the Black Dragon Mountain, as he spit out these syllables, a slight, chill wind seemed to blow through the apartment. I felt agitated. He had already finished blowing up the air mattress and was spreading blankets on top. The mattress lay in the corner closest to the kitchen. He was so thin, he really did not take up much space. I watched this man, thinking to myself: how had this happened to me? I couldn't figure it out. As for He, he lay down with complete composure.

"I've brought the fresh air of Wulong Mountain with me. A person needs a little bit of illusion, don't you think? I've always lived on the mountain."

I didn't know what to say. But he didn't seem to care that I didn't say anything.

Feeling slightly awkward, I went into the bedroom and sat by the bed. After a while, I heard something moving in the kitchen and couldn't help going to take a look.

Old He ate very little, little more than a bird. He was making noodles in my pot, sprinkling in a kind of green vegetable, as well as pork fat.

"This is called 'the least is the best.' Wild vegetables picked in the mountains with pork fat are enough extravagance," he said.

He ate the noodles standing beside the stove, then washed the bowl and pan efficiently.

Next he undressed in an orderly fashion and went to bed.

"Young Tong, don't answer if I cry out during the night![2] I've been living in the mountains for a long time, and sometimes I shout in my sleep."

Yet that evening was exceptionally quiet, and I, who have always had trouble sleeping, did not wake up during the night. Could it be the fresh air he had brought from Wulong Mountain? It must be a wild place, where ghosts and demons ran rampant.

During the day I went to work at the company where I sell health products, but I worried constantly about Old He. I was well past thirty, and I suddenly had a tenant for the first time, so my thoughts floated and scattered. You see, he hadn't said how long he would be staying at my apartment. Naturally, I didn't see the need to tell anyone. It would have been difficult to explain.

Ha! It turned out he'd cleaned and swept my messy nest, and made food. There was rice, a corn soup, steak, and broccoli.

"Old He, you're turning into my maid!"

"I'm restless here, I have to do something to calm down."

We ate dinner together. He immediately snatched the bowls, chopsticks, and pans to wash them. He had actually consumed very, very little of the meal. I had done most of the eating.

I inspected the apartment, discovering a number of arrows made out of red paper on the walls of the two rooms. There was one above my nightstand, for example.

"Old He, what are these signs you're making?" I asked him.

"They're directional signs. Since I left the mountain, no matter where I am, I always have to determine my position. Using Wulong Mountain as the point of orientation, I take the measurements mentally. Look, this arrow is shaking. Tonight there's a strong wind in the mountains. We will sleep well."

His words made me jittery. Could he be a shaman? The shamans had been driven from the city many years ago, and I had seen one only as a child. The shaman had not been very skilled, and all he could do was make the lids of the teacups fly up into the air.

Old He and I sat at the dining table drinking tea. I stood up to add more water. Suddenly I was kneeling on the floor—the boards tilted to a twenty-degree angle, then returned to normal. Maybe there was something wrong with my eyes. Old He, as if expecting this, caught hold of the cup in my hand, filled it with water for me, and placed it on the table.

"You say you live partway up the mountain? It must be a wild place."

"It's a wild mountain. What's there to be afraid of? I haven't been afraid of anything for a long time." He paused, and then said cheerfully, "Last night I slept incredibly well!"

I thought, I slept well, too. Was he the reason my insomnia improved?

Old He and I stood on the balcony, an open expanse of darkness before us. A gust of wind blew past, and I shivered. He was speaking. I could not hear a single thing he said clearly. I was suddenly afraid, without knowing why, and I retreated into the apartment, went to the bedroom, and shut the door.

I went to bed and turned off the lights. But his voice made its way into the room continuously. It felt like I was walking along the bottom of a river and hearing someone talking from above. When I first heard his voice, it gave me goosebumps, and I wrapped the blanket around me tightly. Later I finally felt drowsy and fell asleep suddenly. When I got up in the middle of the night, I heard Old He muttering three words over and over: "joy and happiness...joy...and...happiness!" But he wasn't shouting and yelling the way he had described to me. I sensed that he knew how to show restraint.

When I left for work he was still asleep. He slept in a very strange posture—extending his head toward the edge of the air mattress as much as possible, as if he were trying to separate it from his body. I couldn't guess the meaning of that sleeping pose. I turned around and shut the door of the apartment, only to discover that there was the symbol of the red arrow attached to the door. This arrow was moveable and the direction it indicated was also ambiguous. The arrow could have been pointing east, or it could have been west, or it could...I didn't want to keep trying to figure it out, because a feeling of dejection assaulted me. In the elevator I felt like I was suffocating. Old He, oh, He.

"Do you have a grasp on your location?" I asked him.

"No, I'm not sure at all. I'm always adjusting. Today I took down another arrow."

"Isn't this a difficult life?"

"But there's happiness. As long there's a possibility of happiness, everyone wants it, don't they?"

I thought to myself, I want to achieve happiness, too. But if my life were as floating and insecure as his, I would go crazy. Where had he come from that made him so assured in his belief? During the day he practically did not leave the apartment other than to buy groceries. He cleaned the rooms, cooked, and sat down for a cup of tea, "thinking" for a while, taking down an arrow, or changing its position, and suddenly achieving happiness. Then there was his speech that I couldn't understand: Was it, too, a portion of happiness?

"It's sometimes difficult," he sighed, "especially when I lose contact."

"Lose contact with whom?"

"With Wulong Mountain. I can't always receive messages. Once I stayed in a bicycle garage underground, where I hung arrows on more than a hundred of the bikes. But there are not many times like that. For the most part, I'm fortunate. You see how well I live."

I imagined him in the dark garage groping his way past bicycle after bicycle. The scene made me dizzy. I could never live like he did.

He turned toward the balcony, facing that stretch of darkness. No, it was not completely dark. There were a few stars. I sensed that the stars would not come out in front of him. He stood there and leisurely lit a cigarette. He was so sedate, no one could have made him waver. He listened to the sound of the explosions behind the heavenly spheres—one, two, three.

I went back inside the apartment and sat quietly, clearing my mind and preparing to go to bed.

Just as I reached out to turn off the table lamp, the arrow above the bedside cabinet started to rattle fiercely, the paper making rustling sounds. There couldn't be wind inside the bedroom, so how was this happening? I turned off the light, determined not to pay any more attention to it.

But in the dark, it made an even more energetic disturbance, like a whip cracking in the air. Old He, oh, He, I helplessly concentrated on him, hoping he would bring me quiet. How could I dare take down his arrow? I didn't dare get up, either, because the sound was too fantastic. I felt bursts of intermittent tightness in my chest. If the pieces of paper were not scraping against themselves in the wind, how could they make noise? It wasn't ordinary construction paper. Old He had brought it from Wulong Mountain. Now the whole room was filled with that sound. I didn't know how many arrows he had actually pasted up around the apartment. What a frightening man.

A sound of movement came from the balcony, it was He shutting the door. At the same instant the clamor in my room suddenly stopped. Yet I felt let down. Why? I'm not sure, it just seemed as if I was expecting a dangerous adventure, and had prepared to die, only to discover it was all a misunderstanding.

In this night as hollow as the grave, I could not fall asleep.

Old He, however, slept well. I could hear his even breathing.

The chrome doorknob reflected a little light. I focused my thoughts on that light in order to resist the black tide. He had already been here for five days, and this was the first time I had been sleepless since he had arrived. I had even believed he would be able to cure my insomnia. I had been so naïve.

Another two hours passed, at least. This sleeplessness was different than before. In the past, I spent the night in a daze, sometimes asleep and sometimes awake. Now I lay in bed with my mind exceptionally alert, not feeling the slightest bit drowsy. Should I get up and take a walk outside? As soon as this idea occurred to me, there was a noise in the living room, the sound of Old He getting up.

"Young Tong, do you want to go downstairs? I'll go with you."

I didn't turn on the light, fumbling instead to put on my clothes and shoes before heading out the door with him. In the elevator, I finally noticed that he was carrying a hunting rifle on his back. What was going on? "I'm a hunter," he said.

I wandered unsteadily around the housing complex with him. It was still better than tossing around in bed like a pancake being flipped. Later on we left the residential area for the patch of willows that lay in front of it and where I often went. With starlight filling the night sky, the appearance of the trees had changed entirely, their trunks and branches transformed into a dismal white color, making for a distressing atmosphere.

"A man who used to be my neighbor lives in the house under that bridge, the one with a tile roof," Old He said.

I was surprised, because I knew there was no bridge in the willow grove, not to mention a tile house.

Old He walked calmly along, sometimes pushing aside the twining entanglement of willow branches.

An onslaught of drowsiness struck me and I almost tumbled to the ground. Old He reached out and took me by the arm. He asked whether I could keep going. If not, I should go back to the apartment building. "It's fine," I answered, in a voice that sounded like the whine of a mosquito. The things that happened afterward became difficult to relate.

It seemed as though there really was a tile-roofed house in the forest. The owner was an elderly man with his head wrapped in a white turban. Old He and I sat in the old man's living room, which was bright and shiny in the lamplight. I began to doze, so they had me lie down on a large table to sleep. I kept being startled awake by the noise of Old He shooting his rifle. He would fire a shot, and then there would be a conversation with the old man in low voices. I couldn't quite hear what they were saying, but there were a few words they repeated so many times that I could make out what they were: "directional bearing." Was Old He using the rifle to take a directional bearing? I was too exhausted to think it through.

The rifle was now in the hands of the old man, who was taking aim. Opposite him at a distance of ten paces, Old He was leaning close to the white wall placing an "X" on it. I was wide awake now, and I saw that Old He's expression was grim.

The old man fired three times in total. The bullets were all swallowed by the wall. He put the rifle under his foot.

Old He ran over and grasped the old man's hands with words of gratitude.

"What's there to thank me for?" the old man asked, looking helpless.

"I have to thank you," Old He said staunchly. "Now I've succeeded."

The old man said, "Ah," and sat down in a chair, the expression on his face relaxing.

At this moment I heard, faintly, the sound of a bullet whistling through the air outside, like the echo of the shooting game inside. Old He had already heard it, of course. He was smiling, the slippery fellow!

My eyelids began to knock together again. Old He shouldered his rifle and pushed me, saying, "Go back to the apartment and sleep."

I was deadly tired, moving one foot ahead of the other, staring at the indistinct form of Old He ahead of me. Every time a bullet passed over us, he applauded with excitement.

We got in the elevator and I went to sleep leaning against the wall. Old He had to drag me out of the compartment.

I don't know how long I slept during the night, but in the early morning when I woke up I was in good spirits.

"Old He, can you lend me your rifle?" I asked him.

"What rifle?" He rolled his eyes. "I don't have a gun. I'm a pacifist."

I was on vacation. I had nothing to do, but I didn't want to stay at the apartment. Why? Was I afraid of Old He? No, that wasn't it. It was just that when he was nearby, I always felt a sense of urgency that I didn't enjoy. I couldn't stand it. To be sure, he had already torn down the arrows, and there was nothing making noise at night, but my insomnia was worse than in the past.

Before, when I didn't have anything to do, I would go play billiards in the game room. But now, even thinking of the game was tiresome. I went downstairs into the community area, where I saw several men with dark faces digging away at the foundation of the building, probably putting down wires, like electricity lines or internet cables. Their faces were as dark as Africans'. As I passed by, they stopped working and turned their strange dark faces toward me in unison.

"Hello," I said.

Their fright at my greeting quickly turned to expressions of disgust. One of them, a man with a head of long, dirty hair who seemed to be the leader, walked over and interrogated me: "Where are you going to go? The whole globe is a giant village."

He ordered me to go come over and look at the hole they were digging. I glanced toward the bottom of the pit and immediately felt my scalp tingling. There were so many different kinds of network cables in that hole, too many to ever count. And did all of these lines lead to our residence?

"All right, all right! You've looked enough!"

The long-haired fellow pushed me away, and the other men all began to laugh mockingly.

I remembered that there really were many inexplicable outlets in my apartment. I had seen them when I'd first bought it. Since I was too lazy then to ask about the outlets, I had forgotten all about them.

The long-haired man snarled toward my receding back, "If you don't contact him, he will still be in touch with you!"

I remembered the unreal night in the willow grove with apprehension: had it been one link of this "contact"? The old man in a white turban and the tile-roofed house would not be there during the day. I suddenly felt ashamed. I ought to be like Old He and finish what I started, but for some reason, for some reason…for what reason? That man had been right, the world is a global village. How could I bypass the spider's web of connections?

I walked into the willow grove and sat down on a stone bench. The weeping willows looked unwell, undernourished, with sparse branches like a little girl's scattered hair. Just then, I discovered that the soil under the old tree in front of me was being stirred upward. After a while a man dug out from underneath the ground. He shook the clods of soil from his body, patting his clothes with a towel. I recognized Old He's neighbor. I sat still, but he walked over to me.

He did not speak, either, and just sat facing me. Dust covered his body, neck, and hands.

How could an ordinary person burrow underground? I noticed that the look in his eyes was sinister. He might be a threat to me. I stood up, intending to go.

"Don't go, stay and talk with me."

His voice was sharp and shrill, not at all like what it had sounded like that other night.

"There are some things that once you stick to them, it's not so easy to extract yourself. Especially a character like Young He who's experienced many hardships. Who wouldn't be fascinated by him?"

The old man blinked, and used the towel to wipe the dust from his eyes. He seemed to be speaking about his own confusion, but his expression was obscene, making him look like a cockroach.

"And you, where do you actually live?" I asked him.

"A good question!" He grew cheerful. "I live wherever I want to! I decide based on different threads and clues. Sometimes I disappear from above ground, like I just did." He grew dejected. "I can't compare to Little He, he has more stamina than I do. I think he's a character."

My mind aflame, I made a determined gesture to bid him farewell.

"I used to be his neighbor on Wulong Mountain. But I missed my destiny because of one wrong decision. You shouldn't give up so easily!"

This was the advice he gave me.

I wandered around the residential area of the large apartment complex. In the garden at its center, I saw another small group of the dark men digging from a distance and skirted around them. My feet on the ground might as well have been standing on top of those network cables. I reflected that, of all of the people rushing around blindly, only Old He was able to orient himself. He was remarkable. He certainly was a "character." Naturally, Old He's neighbor, the old man, was also a character. Not just anyone can disappear from the earth's surface. What had it been like when these two men lived on the wild mountain? Did the old man leave because his willpower was weaker?

I ordered some food and a bottle of beer at a restaurant inside the residential complex, then sat down and began to eat.

At the next table there was another diner immersed in his meal. The light in the restaurant was too dim to see his face clearly. A moment later I heard him laugh coldly.

When I turned toward him again, curiously, he raised his head. It was one of the dark men I'd just seen, his dark face reflecting the light.

"You've been searching the apartment complex, we've been watching you for a long time."

His words made me nervous. What did he mean?

He stood up to pay his check and left. As he passed the widescreen TV, its antennae, swaying madly, followed his steps. This was no ordinary man. What did they think I was looking for? I had not known I was searching for anything. Who could make sense of it? There are some things that can never be understood.

I opened the door of the apartment and saw Old He bounce up from the air mattress. He obviously had been waiting for me the whole time. I don't know why, but I always felt that he was intimately familiar with my every action.

"There's a large-scale settling of accounts. You must have seen the dark people?"

"What kind of accounting?" I asked amiably.

"Like cutting the stomach open and inspecting every organ. They're a violent gang, and their leader discovered where I am."

"What are you going to do?"

"Me? I'll have to escape, of course, like a fish breaking a net. I've been through this many times before."

He sat on the blue air mattress deep in thought, with no anxiety visible on his face. I doubted he was exaggerating. Should I tell him about the dark-faced people digging ditches and burying the network cables? I kept my mouth shut, there were depths to this affair that I could not comprehend.

As the curtain of night lowered, Old He sat on the balcony again. When I passed through the living room and looked out toward the balcony, I was struck with panic. In the night sky in front of Old He there appeared a wheel of fire, a fiery ring suspended in the sky shooting out flame, as if it were someone infuriated. Old He smoked a cigarette, his silhouette unperturbed, and not looking like a fish struggling to escape the net.

I returned to my bedroom and inspected the same stretch of sky from the window without seeing anything. I said to myself: "Each person has an individual destiny. So I'll go to sleep. Though I hope Old He will be safe tonight and nothing will happen." Then I got into bed.

As I had anticipated, it was another sleepless night. The room was permeated by a whistling sound, one burst following another with intense, strident pressure. Then the noise would abruptly stop with a ghastly silence that was even more dreadful, like the earth had split into an abysmal breach. This repeated several times, lasting until after midnight. There was a split second when I heard myself shouting, "Save me."

Later, the tossing and turning ended, but I faintly sensed the menace lingering in the apartment, so I could not fall asleep. When the sky was about to grow light, I remembered that I didn't need to go to work that day, my nerves finally relaxed, and I fell drowsily asleep. I slept until noon.

When I got up, I saw that the living room was filled with irritating sunlight. Old He had gone out.

I discovered another problem: someone had split open the left side of the balcony. It looked extremely dangerous. I didn't dare go closer, but I called the building's maintenance management right away to come repair it.

"Room 801?" the man on the telephone said. "This isn't the responsibility of the building management. You have to be patient when something like this happens, instead of having a rebellious attitude." The abnormal fellow hung up the phone.

Oh, Old He. He had fallen, or flown away? I had to go find him.

I searched the bottom level of the apartment building, at the site where the dark-faced people had been digging. The ditch was already filled in and even covered over with the same sod as before.

"Young Tong, what are you looking for there?" Old He's voice came from above.

He was standing at the opening in the balcony waving to me.

My mood clouding over, I went upstairs.

"Look at what happened to the balcony," I said.

"Don't be depressed, I can get someone to come fix it. Last night was thrilling. I tied a rope around my waist, crawled out of the window, and climbed up and down the wall like a spider! They were furious because they couldn't find me, so they damaged the balcony. I couldn't let myself be captured by them...It's a question of freedom."

"Old He, I want to know, will my insomnia be cured?"

"Of course it can be cured! You must have faith. I don't usually misjudge people."

"Maybe, this once, you are mistaken. I'm completely worn out. Don't misunderstand, I don't want you to leave. I'm going to stay at my parent's house for a while, wait until my insomnia gets better, then move back."

He lowered his head and walked back and forth through the apartment, apparently thinking this over.

"You're not really just bored with our life together?" he asked, looking directly at me.

"No, not at all. I'm just too tired, it'll be better after some rest."

"All right." He was reassured.

I went back to my parent's house. They didn't ask why I was moving back in, since they were happy I was—my mother and father had been too lonely.

Probably because my exhaustion had been stored up for so long, I fell sound asleep the first night after returning home. I didn't have a single dream, only waking up once in the middle of the night, my mind so empty it was almost unbearable. But I got myself under control right away and went back to sleep until the next morning.

At dinner, my mother looked at me as if wanting to speak but holding back.

"Mom, was there something you wanted to ask me?"

"I was wondering, won't your tenant be pointed with you? He's not like us. Your father and I have you as our only son, we didn't have a choice in the matter. But for him, you're someone he has chosen. He came from that terrifying Wulong Mountain all the way to the city and chose you."

As my mother spoke, she kept her eyes lowered, as if she were embarrassed.

"Wulong Mountain isn't a terrifying place, it's just a wild mountain. He's not the only person who lives there either," I objected.

"Who else is there?" My mother's eyes brightened. "Who is it?"

"His neighbor, an old man. But he came down from the mountain a long time ago."

"It reminds me of when your father and I were young, when it was an age of revolutions. Who other than your tenant He would have the courage to stay somewhere like that his whole life? I hope he won't be disappointed with you. Information channels grow more advanced each day now."

"I came here to rest for a while, I'll go back there soon."

What I said happened to be heard by my father, who had come in from outside.

"Why are you rushing back? You should stay with us a little longer!" he said loudly. "The more obstacles you manufacture, the easier your communication with him will be!"

"Dad, who are you talking about?" I was startled.

"I wasn't talking about anyone. I was speaking generally."

What both of them said made me uneasy. Even my parents, it turned out, only cared about Old He's opinion of me, and what reason did I have for staying around the house? Besides, I had never revealed to them that I'd taken on a tenant. How had my parents gotten in touch with Old He? It was obvious that they both knew Old He, even though my father tried to conceal it.

"Are you often in touch with Old He?" I pretended not to care.

"Hmm." My mother lowered her eyes as she answered. "That man is an outstanding talent!" She actually used the word "talent" like this, in a way that felt extremely jarring to me. But I didn't want to continue questioning her, because it would look tactless.

I went to sleep as early as possible. The ruined balcony appeared again and again in my mind, every time with a dark shadow standing in the gap looking as if it were about to jump. I stared intently and listened closely, but only heard my father talking in the living room.

"Our child Tong is such a disappointment! How did he get this way?

He may as well not have come back. But if he hadn't, we would miss him even more."

My father also said a few things that were not in keeping with his dignity, and it made me irritable as I listened. Fortunately, his voice grew quieter. I didn't know what he and my mother were conspiring about, but I guessed that it was nothing that would interest me. What my father said made me remember something that happened when I was little and he'd taken me for a walk in the snow. A vast snowy whiteness, and we walked, and walked, then he suddenly abandoned me and ran away. I couldn't keep up with him and began to cry in shame. I stood in the same spot, turning into a snowman. A neighbor bundled me into his house and managed to bring me back to life. Why would I think of this now? Did that event have something to do with Old He? Maybe it was related. In today's world the information channels are so perfectly developed, no matter where we go, we mark out that touching pattern in the air overhead. What was Old He doing at this very moment?

Gradually, I became afraid of talking with my parents because they quickly changed the topic of every conversation to gossip about Old He. They didn't seem interested in talking about anything else. My mother bluntly brought up Old He while my father always spoke of him in twists and turns of insinuation.

Often, when the three of us sat together eating dinner, both of them started off chattering like a record player. So I tried as hard as I could to say little, going to wash the dishes when I finished eating, loitering in the kitchen, picking up a dishcloth and wiping a little here, a little there, and standing around for nearly an hour, at least. Then, loudly humming a march, I went into the bathroom and showered, finished washing and went into the bedroom, where I got into bed. I performed this show almost every day. My parents left me no other option, they kept winking as they said things like:

"Someone who cherishes an ideal is different than the rest of the crowd."

"I wish I could return to the period of my youth."

"I wanted to get in touch with him directly, but when I got to the entrance and saw an arrow stuck to the door, I got scared and backed away."

"I never imagined that the day we waited for would come. It's wonderful: our child Tong is here, he's here."

I didn't dislike what they said, I disliked myself. Once I opened my mouth, I would say insincere things, only to regret them. Apparently I was unable to talk about anything having to do with Old He. My two adversaries in conversation were too cunning, they would prod me in the ribs, or make me get upset.

In the end, I grew weary of this family life. Although my insomnia had taken a turn for the better here, what kind of sleep was that! An empty dreamland; waking up in the middle of the night as if I had been dead, filled with a nameless after-dread; and there were the pre-dawn cries of an old toad, sounding like it was shut inside of a cemetery, its croaks shaking the ground like an earthquake ... Naturally, living at my parents' house, my sense of urgency disappeared. Now, though, for whatever reason, I wanted to return to that urgent and pressured lifestyle. I would rather, as Old He had said, "breathe in the dense swarm of information every day." That kind of breathing was steady. And, at present, I was afraid of suffocating in my heavy sleep, or of my entire respiratory system becoming paralyzed.

But when I put on a very nonchalant appearance and mentioned to my parents that I wanted to move back to Room 801, their expressions showed that they were panicking.

"Go back right away? The day before yesterday I went by your apartment complex on my way food shopping. I went inside and looked up from the bottom of the building. Your balcony hasn't been repaired!" my mother said, raising her voice.

"Everything has been constantly changing," my father continued, with a look of concentrated misery. "I thought several times that I was going to have a heart attack. Now is not the time to fall ill, because our child Tong's problems still haven't been resolved. There's a mountain pressing on my heart."

I knew the two of them were afraid of being alone. Although they didn't need to be afraid. Even assuming I went back, wouldn't they know about everything I did? My attitude toward Old He was full of contradictions, and theirs was, too. I sensed that they hoped I would be caught up deeper in the situation, because then they would have more material to discuss, along with all kinds of prediction games to play, which was the thing they enjoyed the most.

There is no moon tonight and the wind is high. I remember Old He, the tenant of Room 801. Will my tiny little apartment compress and explode from the wild onslaught of information in the middle of the night? Will the windowsill cave in? I secretly admire the art Old He studied on Wulong Mountain.

I stand on a side street outside the apartment, staring fixedly at the iron mailbox I have known since I was a child, seeming to hear a nest of ducklings inside the mailbox talking in their sleep. An old man comes over. He had been my teacher in elementary school, but I have not seen him for many years.

"This mailbox has always been here, for the past fifty-three years," he says quietly.

"Yes, teacher. Do you know a lot about information and messages?"

"Young Tong, unless I'm mistaken, don't you suffer from insomnia? You are so young to have contracted this disease. But it could be a good thing, you shouldn't be pessimistic. There is sleepless information everywhere. For instance, inside this mailbox, late at night, there's the sound of footsteps, back and forth. The number of people chronically awake during the night is increasing."

My teacher quietly disappears at the end of the side street. He is like my dream of homesickness.

At my parents' house, my sense of unreality grows stronger every day. Did Old He transmit this sense of illusion to me? I cannot keep on staying here. Life is too short, I must seize every opportunity. Tomorrow, after breakfast, I will pack up my things and return to Room 801. Whether or not Old He is there, I will return to my own home.

In the darkness ahead of me, there is an old duck swaying side to side.

An Excerpt from *The Last Lover*

Can Xue

Translated from the Chinese by Annelise Finegan Wasmoen

The next day Joe took off from work. He began reading a book with only one page. The book was clothbound, with a drawing of a tall pine tree on the cover. Inside there was a single thick sheet of paper. This sheet could be unfolded to the length of the desk. The picture on the cover appeared to be of an anthill. The periphery of the anthill was densely written over with a miniature text, visible only under a magnifying glass. And once Joe looked with the glass, he discovered that he didn't recognize a single word. This book had sat on the lowest shelf of the last rack in a small bookshop on a noisy street in the city. When Joe went to pay for it, the elderly bookstore owner came over and told him the book was not for sale.

"It was on the shelf, but it's not for sale?" Joe was furious. He grasped the book tightly, almost afraid the shopkeeper would take it back by force.

"Fine, take it away, take it away! But don't regret it!" He walked away resentfully.

The book's price was unusually high, but Joe paid without hesitation.

Now he attempted to locate his own square in this anthill. Accompanying the slow movements of the magnifying glass in his hand, the floor under his feet began to rise and fall.

"Father, what are you doing in there?" Daniel shouted from outside the study.

"Be a good boy. Don't come in, it's a mess in here…"

Daniel evidently didn't dare enter. Joe sighed in relief and continued to wrestle with the book, which was flying around madly. At one point, he flopped down to the ground, his ear to the floor, and heard Maria's voice underneath the floorboards. She sounded irritable. Joe didn't care to listen to more, so he stood up, leaning against the wall. But he hadn't been on his feet two minutes before he fell down onto the sofa. He looked around from the sofa and saw that the anthill had disappeared from that remarkable book and turned into a blank white space. He felt as if the sofa were a small boat on the rippling water. Daniel pushed the door slightly open and stuck his head in. His neck and face looked fresh and healthy.

"The study is finally mad, too," Daniel said, looking pleased.

"Daniel, son, what are you planning to do?"

"Me? Don't blame me, this is because of you, you bought that book. And there's Mother…"

He closed the door, apparently to go downstairs. Joe was astounded: "Does Daniel really know everything?"

In the chaos of the study, Joe started to think calmly. A dove was cooing. There was an actual dove inside the heap of books on the floor. Had it flown in through the window or had Maria put it there? Many of the books were damaged, their pages strewn all over. Joe leaned against the wall and slowly moved out onto the balcony. Before his eyes a familiar scene reappeared.

Maria and Daniel sat among the bushes drinking tea. The two cats walked, stately, back and forth. The balcony was directly in the line of sight of mother and son. Joe waved to them, but they did not respond. Did they even see him? The room shook again with violent tremors. Joe feared he would fall from the balcony, and quickly went inside, crawling aboard the sofa, holding on with a death grip. "And so there are things as strange as this," he said to himself irritably.

Afterward the earthquake gradually subsided, although there were still aftershocks. The aftershocks continued until Maria called him to come downstairs and eat, when they finally disappeared. He went downstairs, disoriented, and sat at the dining table. Daniel wasn't there.

"Did Daniel go to work?"

"So you know everything after all."

"Of course. Doesn't he know everything about me, too? He's an ambitious young man. I just lived through an earthquake, damn it."

"Daniel and I saw. You were shaking with fear. But we couldn't have helped you, could we?"

A turkey was arranged on the table. Maria's face appeared almost bewitching in the rising steam, her cheekbones almost like two red halos. Joe couldn't make out her expression. It was as if she were covered by a membrane.

He had just finished eating and put down his chopsticks when an uninvited guest entered his yard. The man's head was wrapped in a turban. He seemed travel-weary. Maria told Joe that the man was his driver. Joe recognized the familiar face. It brought to mind the time he'd stayed for a night and day in the north at Mr. Kim's home. But when had Maria come to know the driver?

"I arrived a number of days ago, and I've been staying in the basement of the restaurant. You've seen me, you haven't recognized me, and you've walked away from me. At the time I was drunk, down on the ground, but one of my eyes was always open."

Maria called to him to put down the canvas bag he carried on his back, but he didn't, standing in the doorway instead.

"Mr. Kim wants you to come and relive old dreams with him," the driver said to Joe.

A vast pastureland floated up in Joe's mind, the mountain peaks piled with snow and the eccentric owner of the house halfway up a mountain. The driver stood in front of him without moving. His face under his turban was extremely handsome in the evening glow. Joe was drawn in by him, thinking that in the city one very seldom met a good-looking man like this one. Was he the descendant of a warrior from ancient times? But when Joe had first met him on the pastureland, he hadn't been handsome. Maria's eyes were fixed on the man. Joe remembered that she and this fellow had already been in contact, and jealousy unbidden leapt up in his heart. She, and him, and also Kim, what sort of connection did they share?

"How would I relive old dreams?" he asked.

"You're already reliving old dreams." His eyes were smiling.

"But I don't understand." Joe felt his whole body go hot and dry.

"I'll go now."

He walked from the yard, through the main gate, and disappeared into the golden sunset. Maria's face glowed.

Joe couldn't stay sitting at home. He went outside. He walked aimlessly and unconsciously reached the small bookstore, where he saw the fearsome shopkeeper. People came and went in the shop. With the dim lamplight, the people coming in all appeared furtive, but the bookstore owner sat haughtily on a high stool at the entrance. Over many years, Joe had bought many fine books here. Yet before it had been an ordinary little bookstore, doing a lackluster business. Who would have thought such a bookshop could survive in the city for so many years? Joe suspected that the bookstore owner might rely on an occasional shady transaction to support his livelihood. Joe had never spoken with the bookstore owner, who wouldn't cater to people, as if he really were someone important. Nevertheless, his shop contained some truly interesting books.

Today was a little strange. After Joe entered the shop, the electricity suddenly shut off. He was shoved back and forth, and a bookcase was knocked over. All the books fell out. The bookstore owner cursed in the dark. Fortunately the lights were soon restored.

"Wherever you go, there are earthquakes," the bookstore owner said, gathering the books.

Joe helped, thinking to himself, How did he know? After the books were gathered up, he was too embarrassed to stay and left the shop. But the bookstore owner called him back. From under his buttocks he drew out the book he was sitting on and handed it to Joe, saying it was especially for him. Joe's heart pounded. He hid behind a bookcase, opened the book, and saw a portrait of Kim. But it wasn't Kim. Another man's name was written underneath the portrait. He read from the introduction. The introduction said that in the book the author described the minutiae of his entire life. It also contained an extensive daily record. "Because someone is willing to publish it, I wrote everything without scruple," the author wrote derisively. Reading up to that point, Joe resolved to buy the book. The bookstore owner wasn't willing to accept money for it. He said the book was left by the author with instructions to give it to Joe as a gift.

"The author came?" Joe was disturbed.

"He didn't come himself, he sent his underling. Look, he's sitting over there."

In the obscure light, Joe saw the driver's handsome face. He was browsing through a book in a corner. Joe's heart palpitated. He thought, "It really is still him."

"Sometimes the people one meets by chance were already by one's side." The owner finished this sentence after he returned to his high stool, recovering his haughty look.

Joe thought the driver was smiling at him, but evidently he didn't want Joe to disturb him. He seemed to be looking for a book. Joe left the shop. In the light of the streetlamp, he couldn't help opening the book again, and so he saw the photograph of Kim a second time. When he'd calmed down, he discovered that the man wasn't Kim after all. It was only someone whose face had a similar shape. The man's expression was cold and stern, even a little cruel. Joe didn't like cruel men. But wasn't Kim a bit cruel? Joe thought this strange: he rather liked Kim. A fellow who could write down his personal secrets in a book this thick, and who moreover wanted to give the book to him. Joe shivered, although he wasn't cold. So this driver, was he the driver he'd met at Kim's? Perhaps this book was what he called "reliving old dreams." But the man in the picture didn't really look like Kim. Even the color of his hair was different: Kim had black hair, black like a crow's wings, and this man's hair was a lighter color.

Then Joe thought: Could he write a book like this himself? If someone would publish it, would he write all the trivial things that happened in his life into a book? This way of thinking stemmed from a kind of avarice. Joe wasn't sure whether he would be able to do it. He honestly disliked the countenance of the man in the picture. Pondering this question, he carelessly ran into someone's back. It was a black woman, the beautiful street cleaner.

"Good evening! Why are you reading in the street, sir?" she asked cheerfully.

"Excuse me." Joe's face and ears suddenly reddened.

"This time of day is so beautiful, especially in the bookshops where the light is dim. Don't you think so?"

"Yes, yes, you are so beautiful, that's how it is." He spoke at random.

The woman walked away, smiling. Joe saw his own awkward, distracted look in the shop window. He clamped the book under his arm and hurriedly walked toward home. Without intending to watch him, he saw the driver leave the bookshop and go in a different direction.

A Conversation with Can Xue

Annelise Finegan Wasmoen

ANNELISE FINEGAN WASMOEN: *Readers of your novel* The Last Lover *are sure to notice the book's setting in an abstracted, symbolic City B of Country A. What inspired your decision to set most of the novel in an unnamed Western nation? You have also given many of the characters names that are not Chinese in origin: Joe, Maria, etc. How would you explain the international nature of this novel and these characters to a curious reader?*

CAN XUE: While writing this novel, I was driven by a transcendent impulse: I hoped to achieve freedom through the portrayal of love and hidden human emotions. I have written fiction with foreign settings before. I believe that what I have depicted here is the essence of a kind of universal reality, one that is not at all influenced by national borders or by race. It is also a kind of ideal possibility, so that the further removed the setting and the scenes depicted in the novel are from the everyday world, the greater the effect the story produces on the soul through a sense of absence. I am, for the most part, the first reader of my own works, and I think that in this regard the novel achieves the goals set out for it. Today the world is becoming a global village, with attempts to build links of communication between each nation. But, in my view, each nation tends to emphasize its distinctiveness instead of realizing what is common to humanity. This is because of old ways of thinking (exemplified by nations such as America and China), and also because these nations lack a medium of communication. Providing one may be the particular significance of *The Last Lover*. Of course, I did not do this intentionally. Artists cannot do things like this intentionally. All artists can do is give a performance of freedom and deepen the ethical meaning for the unliberated souls of the world's peoples.

How would you describe the experience of reading your fiction in English translation? Is it different with a novel such as The Last Lover *that has an international focus?*

In my own experience, reading my works in Chinese and in English creates a different effect. But I also think that my works are perfectly suited for translation into other languages because they are concerned with questions that are engaging for people from different nationalities. Chinese is abstract, concise, and veiled; English is clear, fluid, and direct. The collision of these two completely disparate languages can at times produce unforeseen inspiration. In my fiction, I use an extremely narrow vocabulary, so I think that the greatest difficulty in translating it would probably be in capturing the subtle meaning within its sentences. I think your translation of *The Last Lover* is excellent in the technique by which it communicates some of my more obscure emotions to Western readers. I really enjoy this kind of translation. Although *The Last Lover* adopts an international setting, it has strong Chinese elements in its depths. I believe that a Western audience will gain many new experiences through reading it. I love Western culture and I am a thoroughly Westernized Chinese person. I hope a few thoroughly Sinicized readers will emerge in your country, too.

While the chapters of The Last Lover *shift between the interior lives of different characters, Joe's journey seems of central importance. Joe, the inveterate, obsessive reader, fails to separate the world of his reading from the world that surrounds him. Toward the end of the novel, Joe disappears into the world of his stories and Maria discovers this world embodied in Joe's study among the forest of books that have taken over his life. Is Joe's complete absorption in the world of stories—where narratives, settings, and characters merge indistinguishably—an ideal of reading or a parable of misreading?*

Joe is a man who lives in the world of the soul. A man who holds fast to his spiritual qualities. A man like Joe will always be plagued by the torment of an impulse toward freedom, living in constant apprehension as he tries to "verify the truth." At the beginning of the story Joe is pressured by his boss Vincent (who represents a deeper layer of Joe's intrinsic nature). When Joe says that he wants to leave his job in order to read more books, his boss says, "Haven't you made up your mind yet?" Matters of the soul cannot be put off for a moment. Later, Joe is pressured again by his client Reagan. Reagan makes a connection between the design of the clothing manufactured by Joe's company and death, reminding Joe of the brevity of life. The characters in *The Last Lover* are mirrors of each other. When one of them speaks to another, the second character often represents the inner nature of the first character. The beginning of the novel brings Joe's state of mind out into the open. A man in this state becomes the best of readers, because he must take risks in his struggle for survival. And reading literature, especially experimental literature, is a risk-taking kind of mental activity. As the story unfolds through this double existence, the boundary between what is inside and outside of books gradually disappears. Joe arrives at a house halfway up a mountain where he meets his customer Kim (a stern man from the East who has grasped the solution to the ultimate riddle of the realm of freedom), and at Kim's house he endures a night of strange passions. Joe then allows Kim to guide him toward a tense, cruel, and novel life of risk-taking.

The motivation for Joe's adventure comes from the death of love. Because love is also a form of continuous risk-taking, a continuous sense of novelty that nourishes the spirit. Modern man lives the greater part of life in an environment that lacks love, an environment which confines one's creativity. Passion can never be entirely satisfied, though. Joe is a discontented modern man, a true reader. With the enlightenment of literature he gradually sees a way out for his spirit and unknowingly begins the reader's enactment of freedom.

The theme of love pervades the novel, but in many ways The Last Lover *seems to be about people constantly moving away from each other, constantly leaving each other, particularly the three central couples: Joe and Maria, Vincent and Lisa, Reagan and Ida. However, as these lovers move further away from each other in space, their communication grows deeper. Does this form of communication at a distance relate to the novel's central parable about reading?*

You're right, the novel is a parable about the deep communication that takes place between each segment of the soul. Reading, writing, loving: these three forms of mental activity are really quite similar. Love requires distance, otherwise it suffocates. Take the relationship between Vincent and Lisa, or between Reagan and Ida, for instance. A spouse or a lover is your mirror: you see yourself in them, but the two of you are independent. You can never completely understand him, nor can he completely understand you. In a certain sense your understanding of him and his understanding of you is imperfect, very imperfect, and this is the inevitable result of your being two free beings. This is the perpetual contradiction of a free world.

The lovers become mystified and each has the impulse to explore his or herself. Whenever the narrative reaches this point, the plot descends into deep, unfamiliar landscapes where the image of two primitive forces wrestling with one another appears. In a state of tension the explorers push ahead into even deeper places in an attempt to make out the shape of the soul, and to learn the painfulness of love. At the same time, their resilience is constantly strengthened. The stronger love is, the more its pain can be alleviated. Very few lovers could live in peace with a girl like Ida, who sees dying for love as love's ultimate end. But Ida is a symbol of beauty, and beauty is sometimes ghastly.

Another recurring theme in the novel is the idea of a personal "long march," which takes place largely in dreams. What is the relationship between the historical "Long March" and this personal long march, between personal struggle and historical events such as the Luding Bridge crossing that are so central to the modern history of China?

The image of the "Long March" has a strong effect on readers and in my novel this symbol is transformed into an account of the battle of the inner soul. To me, this was an entirely natural selection. I am a Chinese artist: I have experienced the turmoil of wars in ancient times, and I have also experienced the long march of idealism. This "Long March" extends into the present, entering the realm of my art, evolving into an extremely individualized spiritual pursuit. The characters in my novel live, they want to pursue freedom and love, and this means that each of them must undergo a personal long march—the trial of being attacked by "enemies" from all sides; staking everything on a single fight; the abyss of darkness in primal chaos; being locked in battle with death; continual perseverance. History flows through the veins of each one of us, and artistic creation is meant to remake history, to construct a history of the mind of the modern individual.

After translating The Last Lover, *I would be fascinated to know more about your writing process. Did you write this novel from start to finish in a linear fashion, or did the stories of the central characters develop in parallel?*

My creative process is different from most. I have never worked out the plot of an entire work. I merely follow a general emotional impulse when I write. The strange thing is that inside of every piece of writing I produce in this way lies an intricate structure. This structure is metaphysical and only skilled readers can perceive it. I believe, in this sense, that I must be a "pure" artist. My feelings are tremendously creative; they sprint ahead regardless of anything else. But they also have an innate structure and purpose, so that in each piece of writing they spontaneously coalesce into a pattern of human nature. Both linear and parallel developments among the central characters appear in my fiction, but these are not planned out intentionally. These developments emerge from an explosive exercise in "creating something from nothing." We Chinese call this kind of thing "seamless construction." Everyone in China's literary circles knows that I write for an hour every day and that I neither reflect on nor revise my fiction. I just sit down and write, finish writing, and then let it be. In this way, I am not unlike the poets of ancient China, perhaps, but my writing process has also been strongly influenced by Western culture, with my powerful inner rationality promoting the eruption of my inspirations. This novel certainly has linear narratives and descriptive parallels, but what I would like to emphasize is that the novel is suffused with a kind of "vertical" (that is to say, "anti-gravitational") movement of growth toward the earth's core. This is an activity of recognition, but in a purely metaphysical rather than psychological sense.

In addition to your prolific fiction writing, you have published a number of works of literary criticism, including studies of Kafka, Goethe, Borges, and Calvino. Did you have any of these authors in mind when you were writing The Last Lover?

In my mind's eye the writers you mention all belong to the family of a global spirit. This family would also include, among others, Dante, Bruno Schulz, Shakespeare, Cervantes, Robert Musil, and the stories of the Bible. I also believe that the stories I have written and that my literary predecessors have written are one and the same story. It's precisely as Borges said: "All books are one book." But for a reader to enter this great book and discover its structure is as difficult as undergoing the Long March. As I write, these literary ancestors rise before my eyes, but I can only meet with them through my own efforts. If your creativity is not strong enough, their forms disappear into the darkness.

In writing about The Last Lover, *you describe your writing style as comprising vertical rather than horizontal description. I was particularly intrigued by your comment that readers might find this vertical style easier to accept in short fiction and more challenging in longer works. Would you have anything further to say about the experimental nature of your writing in* The Last Lover?

You are correct, writing a long form such as a novel using the "vertical" method of creation certainly results in a work that is more obscure, more difficult to grasp as a whole. Reading a novel like this one is hard work, even more tiring than reading philosophy. Because the depths reached by the senses far exceed reasoning. The description in every single sentence, every scene and every movement of the spirit, in every piece of dialogue, hides many different kinds of metaphor. For readers who are not familiar with the various levels of the psyche, my novel will be as inscrutable as an illegible book from heaven. In China, people call me a writer's writer, which is probably correct. I want to supplement this statement: my books are written for all readers who seek an elevated mental realm and who are not afraid of difficulty. Based on my own reading experience, once a reader comprehends a literary work of this sort, the work becomes a spiritual companion for his or her entire life. And with a long novel this proves even more striking.

The family in the garden at *The New Hunan Daily News*.
Can Xue is at the far right in front.

Can Xue at age 15 during the Cultural Revolution.

Can Xue with her son at 6 months, 1979.

Can Xue in Beijing.

The Shining World of Can Xue

Jonathan Brent

In 1981, my wife and I founded *FORMATIONS*, a literary magazine dedicated to publishing work largely from Eastern Europe and Russia, that, in my view, had been little read or understood. Soon, however, we began to seek out work from literatures of other countries under communist domination that expressed the bitter struggle for artistic freedom that artists and writers in those countries so often faced.

From the beginning, therefore, *FORMATIONS* had a political as well as literary interest that had been shaped, in looking back on it, largely by the fervid atmosphere of the Cold War that was then reaching its final stage. Like many in the West, I viewed the Cold War largely as a contest between freedom and un-freedom that reached from politics into the most private details of daily life, from the making of tanks and atomic bombs to the making of poetry and fiction. It was a world-embracing contest. In the East, imagination and creativity were threatened by repressive regimes, self-censorship, and isolation from world culture; and in the West by commercialism, kitsch, the mechanization and routinization of daily life; in short, a deadening of consciousness. *FORMATIONS* was my wife's and my small protest against the stupid brutishness of the East and the brutish stupidity of the West.

By the mid-1980s, we had begun receiving submissions of translations from around the world. One day, my wife opened an envelope that contained two stories by an unknown Chinese writer, Can Xue, in translations by Ronald R. Janssen and Jian Zhang. At once, I realized we had found something new. The prose, the imagery, the narrative style and voice were entirely familiar to anyone who had read Kafka, Bruno Schulz, Ionesco, or Daniil Kharms. But how did this voice find its way into Red China? As I read her stories, I became convinced that they contained nothing derivative or merely imitative. The power I felt in Can Xue's work came from an authentic experience of the modern world.

The horn of the purple ox that disappears into the back of Old Guan's head, the hut at the top of the mountain that does not exist, but which nevertheless is filled with rats and rattled by a powerful wind, reminded me of a story relayed to me by Jan Kott, a Polish essayist and theater critic. Kott had been part of a Polish delegation to Communist Red China after World War II and had been feted in Beijing in lavish style until one day he asked to go see the countryside. His hosts rejected this idea on the grounds that such a trip was impractical, if not impossible. Kott, however, persisted and eventually persuaded his Chinese comrades to take him to a village to witness rural life. They stopped the car in one such village to stretch their legs and were almost immediately besieged by legions of malnourished and bedraggled children of all ages, begging for food and money. When Kott asked, "Who are these children?" his alarmed and embarrassed Party handler stretched out his arm and said, "You see these children? In all of China such children do not exist."

Can Xue's writing springs from the murky landscape of that non-existence. Her father, a journalist, had been the victim of a political purge in the 1950s and the family was forced to move into "a tiny hut of about ten square meters at the foot of Yueyushan Mountain,"[1] where they lived on less than ten yuan a year per person—approximately sixty dollars. To avoid starvation, her father loosened grains from the small amount of steamed rice they bought daily at the communal dining room until he formed little piles that he would distribute to each family member. He grew pumpkins that never produced fruit and sweet potatoes that were nothing but a mass of vines and useless roots. Under such circumstances, Can Xue's elderly grandmother soon died. Somehow the rest survived. Can Xue inhabited the invisible world of Jan Kott's story. She could have been one of those children who did not exist.

I was very proud to publish the first collection of Can Xue's short stories in English, *Dialogues in Paradise*, at Northwestern University Press, but when I moved to Yale University Press in 1991, we lost touch (at the time Yale did not publish fiction) and it was not until 2006 that Can Xue reestablished contact and we were able to collaborate again to publish her work in English translation at YUP, this time *Five Spice Street* and *The Last Lover*.

As Kott's Chinese handlers demonstrated, the very act of vision can be political, and the political, psychological, moral, and aesthetic problem of seeing and knowing has remained at the center of Can Xue's work. Since *Dialogues in Paradise*, Can Xue has produced a body of writing that has consistently protested the comfortable certainties of perception and knowledge—Vladimir Mayakovsky's "blown-up lackey on [the] greasy couch" of consciousness,[2] regardless of whether that couch was in Communist

China or the United States. Can Xue is not a surrealist, much less a fantasist, despite the remote, often surreal, rural settings of her early short stories. She does not posit an alternative world, whether of fantasy, illogic, or irreality.

By 2007, her imagination had turned to the social world and quasi-urban landscape of Madam X, the election of people's representatives, trashy disquisitions on sex, photography, or social justice, and the antics of communal self-deception. Nevertheless, her literary aims had not essentially changed course.

Can Xue's narrative voice has remained a powerful corrosive against the sleepy world of prevailing assumptions about meaning and value—what can and cannot be seen—but its uniqueness derives from her deep love of her home. "I would like to be able to say," she writes,

> that my work shines with a brightness that penetrates every word in every line. I would like to reemphasize that it is the beautiful blazing sun in the south that has evoked my creation. Because of the brightness in my heart, darkness becomes real darkness; because of the existence of paradise, we can have the deeply ingrained experience of hell.[3]

She sets this beautiful, blazing brightness of life permanently against the official handlers of meaning, whether in the realm of culture or politics, whether in China, Russia, or the West, who tell us, "these children do not exist."

Sour, Salty, Bitter, Spicy, Sweet: On *Five Spice Street*

Paul Kerschen

In 1988, the final year of China's post-Mao, pre-Tiananmen "Culture Fever," the Shanghai Literature and Art Publishing House organized a conference in honor of two women writers. One was the realist Wang Anyi; the other was the unclassifiable Can Xue, whose first full-length novel had just been published to the same controversial reception as her earlier short work. Her oblique, nightmarish fictions had quickly gained notoriety, and once it became known that a woman was writing behind the pseudonym, criticism had turned personal. The author was said to be too individualistic, or simply too deranged, for significant achievement; her work was called neurotic and scopophilic, "the delirium of a paranoid woman."[1] Against such charges any author might have taken a conference as an opportunity for self-defense, but it is a mark of Can Xue's slyness that she chose to do so in the form of a fiction. Addressing her audience, she announced the happy news that in preparation for her lecture, a "male colleague" had given her guidance and even chosen her topic: she would be speaking on "Masculinity and the Golden Age of Literary Criticism."[2]

The colleague, in her telling, is affronted not to be giving the lecture himself: "Those people in Shanghai are really blind. How could they invite you there? What does a woman have to say? Such questions should be answered by men. And not any kind of men, but those who have deep philosophical knowledge about things and who have also maintained their masculinity." In his pique, he kicks apart Can Xue's tea table—a gesture she finds "well done"—and storms out. She is left to explain his masculine philosophy, which turns out to originate from his childhood in a bandit village where "eight hundred strong men and bewitching women with bound feet" are ruled by a sexually formidable grandfather. By this point in the lecture, the audience would have recognized that they were hearing a parody of Mo Yan's recent novel *Red Sorghum*, and by extension an attack on the dominant literary school of the day. All participants in the Culture Fever debates agreed that Chinese literature required a positive program, and one leading view was that it should emulate the rural mythmaking of Gabriel García Márquez, "seeking its roots" in order to "march toward the world."[3] In such an era of slogans, Can Xue's work could not but cause distress; whatever else it was doing, it was not marching toward anything at all.

The most immediate effect of this lecture was probably to offend the establishment. But for those of us now reading her first novel in translation, twenty-five years later, it makes a good key; for *Five Spice Street* is among other things an author's reflection on her newfound public position. The book was originally published as *Breakthrough Performance* (突围表演), a purposely self-conscious title for a debut novel. At the same time, 突围 suggests breaking free, an escape from entrapment or other immediate danger, and this raises the possibility that the escape itself constitutes the performance, that a kind of Houdini act is being staged. The plot follows a community's reaction to an outsider, an enigmatic woman whose so-called "performances"—scholarly, sexual, perhaps supernatural—are sometimes threatening, sometimes laughable, and never well understood. Whether they constitute any kind of escape, and whether they have anything in common with Can Xue's writing itself (which she often calls 表演, "performance"), are questions that the novel keeps in the foreground while deferring anything that looks like an answer. While it might be a fiction about writing fiction, its integrity depends on offering no positive program, nothing that could collapse into the kind of sloganeering that Can Xue mocks in her lecture. This imperative motivates its hazy narrative form, in which the protagonist is always seen obscurely and indirectly, and permits nothing—not even her bare existence—to be verified as fact.

Madam X is a stranger with an shadowy past. She has opened a snack shop on Five Spice Street (五香街), but otherwise holds back from the street's communal life. She shuts herself indoors to pursue activities variously called "performances," "research," or "miracles"; whatever these practices are, they are solitary and admit no clear description. Rumors abound concerning her: that she is a former government official in disgrace, that she exerts an occult influence on the people of the street, that she is having an affair with a Mr. Q under the nose of her complaisant husband. None of this is precisely proved or disproved over the course of the book, which holds itself to a collective, external narrative compiled from the observations, conjectures, and outright fabrications of the prying neighbors. Five-spice powder is a common ingredient in the kitchen, but as narrative it makes a less harmonious mélange; every part of it is contradicted by some other.

Like Yellow Mud Street (黄泥街) in Can Xue's earlier novella of that title, Five Spice Street is nominally part of a larger city but acts as a closed space. Apart from the initial irruption of Madam X and her family, hardly anyone arrives or leaves. The insular setting might recall the rural villages of Cultural Revolution "scar literature," though the cruelty and famine that appear naturalistically in that genre, and obliquely in *Yellow Mud Street* as decay and infestation, are absent here. What persists is a paranoid social structure of spyings and denunciations, meetings in dark rooms, insinuation in every speech. "In our discussions, we used to squeeze together…we lowered our voices, making them fainter than the buzzing of mosquitos. It was as if we weren't talking at all, just moving our lips. We could only guess what the others were saying… Only the in-group could understand the profound meaning of these movements." The subject of these meetings is invariably X, who has been branded a social problem in need of solving, a "dissident element," a "slut," a "counterfeit," a "loathsome spotted mosquito" sucking the community's blood. Yet over the course of the book, very little direct action is taken against her. The longer the vilification goes on, the more it comes to seem the obverse of the fascination—even desire—that so many characters covertly profess for her. "On Five Spice Street we all knew: whenever someone expressed contempt for a certain thing, that thing was what he or she secretly desired."

Yellow Mud Street is often taken as an allegory of life under the Cultural Revolution; certainly its juxtaposition of Maoist slogans with images of vermin and disease earned it heavy censorship on its first publication. Can Xue, who discourages political readings of her work, has described that novella as "not very mature," incorporating too much of the outside world.[4] The breakthrough (突围) that she attempted in *Five Spice Street* was to break free (突出) from the quagmire (or "mud-pit," 泥潭) of language and culture.[5] One way to gloss this would be to say that historical China—the squalid, dissolving landscape of *Yellow Mud Street*—is no longer her topic, not even allegorically. *Five Spice Street* places its questions of public and private identity at a more abstract level, and when snippets of historical language do intrude—whether as Cultural Revolution propaganda or Culture Fever's utopian pronouncements—they are made to play a more general role. When the officious Dr. A says that "in considering problems, one must not look at the surface, but must pierce to the essence with blade-like eyes," he expresses a recognizably Maoist thought.[6] Yet it is not only Mao's but any such overconfident method that founders on X's basic unknowability. If she has an essence, it is not graspable in the way that Dr. A imagines. What can be known is no more than what the novel shows us, a layering of incongruous surfaces.

Apart from Dr. A, the book offers two representatives of the public world as foils to Madam X. The first is the "much-admired widow," a matriarch who plays the same authoritarian role as the mothers in Can Xue's short fiction. The prime mover of Five Spice Street's public life, she takes it on herself to direct the "struggle" against the "adversary." Much of the evidence against X comes by way of her "unique powers of observation," which include breaking into X's house and opening her mail, and she administers ideological corrections to those who admit a prurient fascination with X, as well as to those who consider the X affair not worth their time. Her invective contradicts itself in the usual way of propaganda against adversaries: on the one hand X is dangerous, an immediate threat to be opposed by all means available; on the other hand X is powerless, negligible, beneath consideration.

The second foil is the actual narrator of the book, who does not immediately emerge as a distinct character since his duty to the collective forbids him to use the first person singular. For the street exclusive of Madam X he writes "we"; when he means himself, he writes "the writer"; after an early scene in which he is attacked for artistic pretensions, he humbles himself to "the stenographer." His task is to assemble the contradictory accounts of the X affair into what becomes the book's text, a "precious historical record." He glosses over difficulties with sheer propagandistic brio: "On our flourishing, colorful street, each resident enjoys full freedom to the best of his ability. Like a duck taking to water, everyone is relaxed and happy. Vehicles full of wonderful foodstuffs roll past…" In his telling, even the sinister nocturnal meetings acquire a nostalgic glow: "Many still sigh and say they wish time could reverse itself—if only it could stop in that moment filled with mysterious conviviality…they wouldn't mind having their lives cut short by a decade or two." The writer's aim is to "draw a diagram of the maze," "to string these diverse viewpoints together like pearls, bring them into focus, and achieve a static view, like the way the sun—before it sets—grasps the whole of the universe." Yet he recognizes the impediments to his task; for every question the "answers were maddeningly endless. Where one person saw a wild boar, another saw a dove, and perhaps a third person saw a broom." Before long he finds himself plaintively asking: "Is Madam X even a real person, or is she a figment of our imaginations?"

The absent center of *Yellow Mud Street* is one Wang Ziguang, a Godot-like figure of vague promise who was much discussed but never encountered. Madam X is a touch more substantial than this, but only a touch; from beginning to end she remains the unknown entity signaled by her name. The writer and his informants are chary of physical description, preferring to pass immediate judgment, and the profusion of direct quotations hardly provides the intended journalistic grounding since any one account of X will be immediately contradicted by some other. The book's first public meeting takes place with the simple object of determining her age and looks. She is said to be skinny, as befits so ghostly a figure (and contrasts with the widow's much-remarked breasts and buttocks), but beyond that nothing is agreed upon, and the disagreement soon provokes physical violence—not for the last time. The writer is left to give an ostentatiously contentless summary of X's qualities: "skin that's either smooth or rough, a voice that's either melodious or wild, and a body that's either sexy or devoid of sex." With the same specious precision he calculates that, since her age lies somewhere between twenty-two and fifty, there must be "at least twenty-eight points of view" on the matter.

In the presence of X vision is a barrier rather than a portal. A letter intercepted by the widow recounts that "The first time Mr. Q looked at X's face, he saw only one immense continuously flickering saffron-colored eyeball. Then he swooned and couldn't see a thing. To the very end of the scandal, he never got a good look at Madam X. He didn't because he couldn't. When Madam X was in front of him, all he could see was one saffron-colored eyeball." Even when X's eyes do not obliterate the rest of her form, they are usually obscured in some way: lacking pupils, or else clouded by tears. Early on it is asserted that "she didn't look at people with her eyes," that her eyes "had retired"; though she perceives physical objects, people are obscure to her. When the public intrudes into her house, she complains that oxen are wrecking her research— "There's always something coming in. Damn it!"—and her husband, who repeatedly serves as mediator, can only mollify her by reducing people to things. One intruder, he says, is "merely a rag drying on the clothesline"; another is a "dust rag…in the wrong place, and that bothered you. I threw it into the garbage."

Yet with mundane blindness comes otherworldly vision. Madam X's private activities are thick with mirrors and microscopes, trained on vistas of which the writer can catch only hints: "If you close your eyes, you'll see the spectacle of spaceships and the Earth colliding"; "a twig poked through a red heart and a blue heart and hanging in midair"; "she concluded that she was standing on a huge, creaking sheet of thin ice." The sexual affair with Q, if such it is, is conceived by X in purely mystical terms. Unable to see him, she employs a faculty "ten thousand times truer than seeing" to perceive a Q who has little in common with the Q seen by everyone else. In her vision he becomes a "peddler from afar," wearing a baize overcoat, with eyes of "at least five different colors."

The writer dismisses these descriptions as "double-talk." Yet they are one of the few points where the novel approaches the lyric quality of Can Xue's short fiction. In her stories, women often shut themselves inside houses; Xu Ruhua in "Old Floating Cloud" ends her adulterous affair by blocking her doors and windows and turning into a bundle of dry bamboo, while the nameless "I" of "The Things That Happened to Me in That World" secludes herself for an ecstatic encounter in an imaginary landscape of ice. The glacial scenery of X's own visions, as well as their ambiguous sexual content, certainly follow from this, but the point of view has changed. *Five Spice Street* inverts the visionary short fiction by restricting itself to externals, and showing only the reaction to a visionary whose visions are unknowable. Much of the opacity in the stories derives from the characters' inability to communicate; a barrier stands between them, and only allows them to soliloquize their obsessions at each other. In *Five Spice Street*, the barrier has contracted to surround X alone. Communication is possible in the public world, though it mostly consists of sloganeering and abuse; but when language encroaches on Madam X's private sphere it finds itself silenced.

Whatever the true extent of X's sexuality, the street's obsession with it testifies to much repressed desire. The most obvious satirical target is the widow, who boasts of keeping herself "pure as jade" although she makes clumsy seduction attempts on both X's husband and the writer. She vents her jealousy by calling X a "skinny monkey" without the sexuality of a "real woman," but this does not at all diminish the street's appetite for an adulterous affair, every detail of which they have invented. Having posited (and confirmed through "high-level telepathy") that X and Q's tryst took place in a granary, they spend an entire chapter on competing retellings which all turn out to be opportunities for sloganeering: one character is masculinist, one feminist, a third simply hopes to establish himself as a genius. Others are inspired to action over words. Various sex farces interrupt the main drama, often between comically mismatched parties (an old woman, a young coal worker), at one point drawing the entire street into an outdoor bacchanal, "sweating profusely and breathing hot and heavy like oxen." To the extent that X notices this, she finds it incomprehensible. "What the hell?" she asks her husband. "Did I ever give a lecture to those guys?" She is the catalyst for every event in the book, but always at a remove; she cannot be affected as others are, for she is not a person as they are.

A different kind of book would have us reject the writer's narrative, and the communal viewpoint he represents, as simply unreliable. Yet amid all his partiality and conjecture, the writer does display genuine insight: for one, he understand that Madam X cannot be imagined separately from the desires that the street has foisted upon her. She is "an assumption that might not be true—like a tree with massive foliage but shaky roots"; the "only true existence is the illusion, the foggy mist that aroused our enormous interest." It is only natural, then, that the street's tactics of surveillance, confrontation, and denunciation get no purchase on her. Only at the end of the book do they hit on an alternate plan, and instead of repressing her begin to acknowledge and even celebrate her. As a means of neutralizing her power, this turns out to be far more effective. In a political context, we would call such a move a co-optation; in a psychoanalytic context, we would call it a cure.

In a late attempt to draw his "diagram of the maze," the writer hits on the dialectical insight that X and the street are interdependent. "Without Five Spice Street, X would not have existed...We molded her...it was because of X that our good character and our noble sentiments had the chance to be revealed." Recast as a necessary stage in the street's historic development, X becomes explicable through rhetoric: "A mother can't casually abandon her child, even if that child is a rascal or a traitor." The figure of the mother heralds the most nightmarish moments in Can Xue's fiction, and the insidious talk of forgiveness sounds much like a dissident's forced confession. This essentially comic novel dispenses no such grim fate to X, but from this point forward her influence is seen to wane. It becomes possible to imagine her dissolving as she appeared, fading to a symbol and finally vanishing altogether, "returned to the womb." The first thing to go is the never-sturdy adultery plot, which abruptly resolves through the simple disappearance of both men. X's husband is said to have left her, while Q sticks himself in the crack of a tree and dries into a insect-like husk. Neither returns; but then, as the writer acknowledges, they were never substantial characters in the first place, "mere shadows — X's shadows, two parasitic vines."[7]

As it turns out, the easiest way to integrate Madam X into the community is to hang a slogan on her. The chosen phrase, "the wave of the future," is conveniently utopian; it acknowledges the fascination that X exerts ("everything she did is something we had been longing to do") but places her at a safe remove: "what Madam X does and is today is not at all related to real life. It's an artificial performance... To transplant her style into the context of present life would only create jokes." The supposed honor of electing her people's representative has no practical consequences, other than requiring her to turn two somersaults in public and have her picture taken, an imposition she had avoided as a pariah. In her last talk with the writer, she recognizes her incommensurability with the public world: "Her greatest wish was that the people would 'forget' her... she had come to understand that she was different from others. She wasn't a person but only the embodiment of a desire. Because it could never be actualized, this kind of desire could only upset people." It is a quiet irony that in confessing her lack of personhood, she comes to seem like a recognizable person for the first time.

In her disempowerment, X is driven at last to appeal to the community. When she applies for funds to keep her house from collapsing, her application is treated as an art object, universally praised, and set aside until her wall falls down. Subsequent applications are less comprehensible, "monotonous and dull, absolutely different from her earlier sexual exploits. Who had the patience to watch her doodling." Fortunately, the "wave of the future" requires little attention for the present. "Let posterity deal with it. Our responsibility is only to provide her with space, protect her work, and leave it for future generations."

The conclusion presents a fable on the dangers of canonization: while a counterculture may thrive on opposition, nothing is more deadly to it than indifference. Historical circumstances were not slow to bear out this lesson; within a few months of the novel's first publication and the author's bridge-burning Shanghai speech, the Tiananmen crackdown took place and Culture Fever came to an end. The most immediate changes may have been provoked by authoritarian pressure, but accounts of Chinese literature in the 1990s tend to agree that most of the avant-garde writers either turned to more lucrative realist fiction, or gave up writing altogether, because of their perceived irrelevance in the new mercantile order.[8] For her part, Can Xue simply continued to write, waiting out a period of obscurity in which Chinese journals rejected her work and many of her stories made their debut in Japanese or English translation. "Lots of them hate me," she said of Chinese critics in 2001, "or at least they just keep silent, hoping I'll disappear. No one discusses my works, either because they disagree or don't understand."[9] *Five Spice Street* was not reissued under its present title until 2002.

Notwithstanding the utopian language deployed at the end of this book, it is a story of diminishment and dashed expectations. Yet it concludes with a gentle, even wistful tone, as Madam X walks to the edge of the city and recalls a long-ago sexual encounter that never quite took place. If this unconsummated tryst is indeed what inspired the entire chain of rumor, then we have at last traced it back to its starting point in the imagination, a state of pure potentiality. Can Xue's own comment on the ending is that "although everybody seems to have failed in the story, I think that in a certain sense they have made it—in their discussions about sex; in their vulgar pursuing; and in their warm imaginations about Madam X."[10] Warmth lies in the inner world. Having followed the many-sided tale of X's scandal and rehabilitation, a reader able to rest in the inner world may find that warmth as well.

Editing *Blue Light in the Sky*

Declan Spring

I first became aware of Can Xue reading her stories published in *Conjunctions*. My friend, the jazz writer Ben Ratliff, was working at Henry Holt at the time, and he sent me a copy of her book *The Embroidered Shoes*. I became hooked, and went on to read the Northwestern University Press edition of *Old Floating Cloud*. I'll never forget encountering for the first time the novella *Yellow Mud Street*: the descriptions of filth and decrepitude, and the larger-than-life Doctor Wang. The novella seemed to be a veiled political commentary, but it was much more than that: a crazy, surreal work that could be compared to an abstract painting.

New Directions has a long history of publishing Chinese literature. James Laughlin began ND in 1936 at the instigation of Ezra Pound, who was fascinated with Chinese culture. Then, in the sixties and seventies, New Directions published Kenneth Rexroth's famous translations of ancient Chinese poets. David Hinton's translations of the Chinese ancients are also crown jewels of the New Directions list. Bei Dao and Xi Chuan are among the most important of our contemporary poets. And in terms of fiction, we've had great success publishing the Chinese authors Ah Cheng, Mu Xin, and Qian Zhongshu.

In 2003, Karen Gernant sent Barbara Epler—then our Editor in Chief, now our Publisher—a collection of Can Xue's stories that she'd translated with Chen Zeping. "The Chinese writer Can Xue has asked me to approach you with her work," Karen wrote. We had just published the Japanese author Yoko Tawada's *Where Europe Begins*, and Yoko encouraged us to publish the collection. Susan Sontag was also recommending authors to us, and she admired Can Xue's writing a lot. Once we made an offer and signed contracts, the editing began and the stories' order needed to be decided: the title story, "Blue Light in the Sky," would begin the collection, and "Mosquitoes and Mountain Ballads," the fabulous short story about the demise of Third Uncle with the swarming of mosquitoes, would end it.

Editing *Blue Light in the Sky* was one of my most rewarding experiences while working at New Directions, and I was really thrilled to receive an email from Can Xue recently saying she thinks it is one of her best works ever published. The biggest challenge for me in editing the translation was latching on to the style and hearing the voice. I might be wrong, but I think Can Xue emphasizes mood and story over highly stylized prose. Her voice is deliberately flat. Western literature draws on sources with which we're all familiar: the Bible, Shakespeare, Homer, Dante. Can Xue's biggest influences are writers like Kafka, Dante, Goethe, and Calvino, though I've read arguments elsewhere that her writing is rooted in emotion and landscape. I believe this is true. Her writing always conveys the constant threat of chaos lurking beneath. That said, the challenge of my job as editor was to see the arc in each story and make sure the sentences were correct, that the paragraphs flowed, and that the arc emerged clearly in each of the stories. As I said before, Can Xue's stories are to me like modern abstract paintings, demanding the reader's engagement in that particular way, and as an editor, I tried to help bring that out in the translation.

Some of my favorite stories in *Blue Light in the Sky* are "The Bizarre Wooden Building," "Night in the Mountain Village," and "My Brother." "The Lure of the Sea," however, may be my top favorite. One afternoon about three years ago, I was watching my six-year-old son and a group of his friends in Prospect Park (in Brooklyn, where I lived at the time). After a soccer game, the group of boys collapsed exhausted on a blanket. It was a hot day, and for some reason, I began to tell them the story of "The Lure of the Sea" with as much detail as I could. The kids were completely enraptured. I went on to tell them other Can Xue stories, and the afternoon passed quickly. It makes complete sense that Can Xue's stories (with their fable-like quality and unsettling unpredictability) would mesmerize readers and listeners of any age.

I've been happy to see Can Xue's reputation grow in the United States with more publications. A few years ago, right after Yale published her novel *Five Spice Street*, Can Xue gave an entertaining reading at the 92nd Street Y with Isabelle Allende. Hundreds of Allende's devoted fans swarmed the event, and it was satisfying to me that they were exposed to Can Xue, this wonderful author who writes like no one else. Can Xue is truly one-of-a-kind and deserves to be more widely read. As Bradford Morrow, the editor of *Conjunctions* and a novelist in his own right, said, "Can Xue possesses one of the most glorious, vivid, lyrical, elaborate, poignant, hellacious imaginations on the planet." We are very proud to have Can Xue's *Blue Light in the Sky* on our list.

Publishing *The Last Lover*

John Donatich

"Can modern man, in today's society, still fall in love?"

This seems to me the central question in the work of Can Xue. Granted, this might come as a surprise—that a writer who is so rigorously experimental and unapologetically demanding is obsessed with such a humanistic concern.

The phrase "fall in love" is especially operative here, suggesting a dynamic that not only illustrates but contradicts the cliché, for the characters in her latest novel, *The Last Lover*, propel themselves into love. While no less desperate than those capitulating to desire, these would-be lovers catapult forward. Whether or not their seductions are successful is immaterial; Can Xue challenges us to realize ourselves in the sheer effort of loving, in keeping in front of its satisfaction and behind its call.

I am privileged to be the publisher of Can Xue's latest novel to appear in English, *The Last Lover*, which takes place in City B of Country A, an unnamed, fictional Western country a bit like Kafka's "Amerika." Universal in scope, the book has the opposite impact of the international or globalized novel. Though its many characters come from different countries, they feel unspecific, outside national borders, de-tribalized. Here, in the heightened prose of this novel, cultural identity would seem trite. We are each of us merely a system of desires, a microcosm of the global village, atomic impulses that feel like our entire being but are subsumed within a greater process.

To say that the novel dives into the interior lives of its characters gives false credence to their existence. Can Xue sets out to show how these lives are impossible to manage, to control. She seeks a more intransitive relationship to the soul: to free oneself, to unburden: to lighten as well as to enlighten.

Joe, the manager of a clothing company, reads with a voraciousness that consumes the reality around him. Joe fails to distinguish between the world around him and the reality within his books. His wife Maria weaves tapestries and conducts mystical experiments with household cats and rose bushes. Reagan, who has sued Joe for making clothes blamed for the recent drowning of rubber factory workers, has an affair with Ida, a refugee from a country that has disappeared because of recent landslides. Vincent, a competitive clothing company owner, chases a woman in black who keeps disappearing. Earthquakes, mudslides, infestations, outbreaks: the chaos of the world is anchored only by the precision with which it is written. Surface reality is constantly subverted, but to call her narrative "non-linear" is too simple; it requires the reader's belief in straight lines to begin with.

"In the world I strove to create, the sun is a great burning flame, the character's actions exceed our anticipation, and each one of them drives death away with a singular performance," Can Xue has said about *The Last Lover*. "They are all moving toward the extreme end of the path to their own ideals." Reading Can Xue about her fiction is a profoundly different experience than reading her fiction; it feels more like the way a philosopher might think about her work: systematic, self-reflexive, threatening itself toward a closed system. Can Xue takes a Chinese materiality, the love of physical things and marries it to the abstractions of Western philosophy. On the surface, *The Last Lover* is a difficult novel. While it does have linear narratives and descriptive coherence, it is structured along a kind of vertical or anti-gravitational drive, escaping the downward pull of rationalism.

I first met Can Xue in Beijing nearly a decade ago. We ate in a hotel restaurant that was high concept in design; I could tell she was vaguely suspicious of it. I have no Chinese and her English was "halting," in her own words. I wondered how it would go. We sat down, ordered and before I knew it, four hours had passed. We covered favorite authors: Kafka, Nietzsche, Plato, Kant. She told me very little about her husband and son. About her writing habits, she said writes early in the morning in a single draft with very little editing. She smiles the whole time. Then she goes "for a punishing run, especially in the rain." Then she reads the rest of the day.

We keep up a fairly regular e-correspondence. She's a remarkable and generous reader, sending me sentences that touch her. Recently, she read *The Man Without Qualities* and sent me these lines by Musil:

> Art is subversive because art is love; it beautifies its object by loving it, and there may be no other way in this world to beautify a thing or a creature than by loving it. And it is only because

even our love consists of mere fragments that beauty works by intensification and contrast. And it is only in the sea of love that the concept of perfection, beyond all intensification, fuses with the concept of beauty, which depends on intensification.

This is the right context in which to approach *The Last Lover*.

The Tenant of the Soul: On "The Tenant of Room 801"

Deng Xiaomang

Translated from the Chinese by Annelise Finegan Wasmoen

Imagine for a moment how a person who lives alone in an apartment, if he has nothing in particular to do, would come to feel, as time passes, that his room is his inner world. We often call a man like this a "homebody" or an "introvert," someone who lives in his own little universe and inside of his own mind. In a certain sense every one of us, whether male or female, is a "homebody" at times, even though only a small percentage of people consciously choose a "home" life, or prefer to have one. It is the particular task of an artist to elevate the meaning of life as a "homebody" to the realm of human sensibility and aesthetics, yet this work also interests those who study the life of the spirit. However, the "home" of the artist does not mean the room where he lives, but refers instead to his correspondingly sealed inner world, meaning the artist's soul, and within it, he does not have nothing to do, but is instead intensely and constantly engaged in his own undertaking, which becomes almost a necessity. As an artist devoted to his own creative pursuits, he is never alone. In his self-consciousness there is an "I that is We, and We that is I," and, moreover, "Self-consciousness achieves its satisfaction only in another self-consciousness."[1] The "Room 801" depicted by Can Xue is a room of the soul. The "Old He" who bursts in unauthorized represents the artist's inner being, another self who is not, although strange, seen as an outsider.

Old He, as "I was sitting on the balcony doing nothing in particular," charges into "my" apartment, and then introduces himself by saying: "I come from Wulong Mountain." What is "Wulong Mountain," the Black Dragon Mountain? Where is "Wulong Mountain"? It must be a mysterious place, since at the mere mention of its name "a slight, chill wind seemed to blow through the apartment," so that "I felt a little agitated." Wulong Mountain brings "fresh air," it is an "illusion," and "a wild place, where ghosts and demons ran rampant." As the place where Old He used to live, within the domain of "my" soul, Wulong Mountain represents the human libido or instinctive desire. Old He, who was dispatched from the realm of instinctive human desires, turns out to be extremely sober and rational, with a calm and efficient manner. As soon as he arrived, Old He "cleaned and swept my messy nest," taking responsibility for preparing food and washing dishes for the both of them, almost turning into "my" maid. Old He's task is to make "directional signs" by putting arrows made of red paper all over the apartment. In order to determine his own position, "Using Wulong Mountain as the point of orientation," he will "take the measurements mentally." Old He, who comes from the irrational "wild mountain," says, "I haven't been afraid of anything for a long time"; he is like a shaman, with everything apparently under his control, as well as someone who "knew how to show restraint"; but he does not have a grasp of his own position: "I'm always adjusting." The arrows he pastes up are moveable, while "the direction [an arrow] indicated was also ambiguous. The arrow could have been pointing east, or it could have been west." Irrational impulses constantly require his rational attention and *Sorge*, or care. Rather than saying he is showing the direction, it would be more accurate to say that his signs follow the direction of the pulse of desire. If there were no such signs, the libidinous drive would disperse into the ether, coming to nothing; or, more precisely, the sign makes the libido take form. Thus, although this kind of work is "difficult," "there's happiness," that is to say, Old He believes himself capable of making the libido take form, and when he does it, this makes him feel "joy and happiness" in his dreams. The true difficulty was when he "lost contact" with Wulong Mountain, a time when Old He was lost and had to grope blindly, confronting "a stretch of darkness," and all he could do was paste a number of unreliable arrows everywhere. But Old He's willpower is strong, "no one could have made him waver," and his continual torment is even "frightening." "I" cannot live without the suffering of his tossing and turning, and when the racket Old He is making suddenly stops, "I felt let down. Why? I'm not sure, it just seemed as if I was expecting a dangerous adventure, and had prepared to die, only to discover it was all a misunderstanding." Surely, when an artist uses his (or her) reason to search out the primitive instincts of the inner mind, he is making a life-saving leap and experiencing a life-or-death risk that, even if he wanted to, he could not stop.

This type of searching sometimes relies on "reconnaissance by fire." When the narrator cannot sleep during a "night as hollow as the grave" and wanders outside, Old He brings a rifle and accompanies him, leading him into the willow grove and to his "former neighbor," the old man now wearing a white turban. Old He takes a "directional bearing" by firing his gun, although, in the end, it is the old man's three shots that lead to the response of the bullets whistling through the air for which Old He thanks him. Evidently, the old man has a closer relationship to Wulong Mountain than Old He: he is the embodiment of the libido. As the libido, he can suddenly "[dig] out from underneath the ground" without any forewarning, and he can also "disappear from above ground" at any time. He lives in no set place: "I live wherever I want to." However, as even the old man acknowledges, he is controlled by Old He: "I can't compare to Little He, he has more stamina than I do. I think he's a character." Besides, he exhorts "I" by saying, "I used to be his neighbor on Wulong Mountain. But I missed my destiny because of one wrong decision. You shouldn't give up so easily!" Then, "I" finally understands: "of all of the people rushing around blindly, only Old He was able to orient himself. He was remarkable. He certainly was a 'character'." These two "characters," Old He and the old man, are a pair of contradictions within the inner being of an artist, one representing the manipulative ability of rationality, the other representing the primitive life force that can erupt at any moment, and the two of them cannot exist without each other.

Once the narrator, who spends all his time at "home," leaves the apartment, he encounters a group of dark men who are digging ditches and burying wires at the foundations of its walls, network cables that all lead to his residence. This reminds the narrator of the countless threads of connection he still has to the outside world, even though he stays at home all the time. It's exactly as the long-haired man says to him: "If you don't contact him, he will still be in touch with you!" The eyes of the entire outside world concentrate on his dwelling because Old He has arrived and everyone wants to understand what his intentions are, and what he is seeking. Using Old He's words, this is a "large-scale settling of accounts," "Like cutting the stomach open and inspecting every organ. They're a violent gang, and their leader discovered where I am." Ever since Can Xue began to publish her fiction, people have been speculating about what her works are actually trying to say, with both general readers and literary critics trying to put the question to rest by fixing her in a conceptual framework. This "leader" represents the eyes of the world, and this gaze is like "a wheel of fire" that appears in dark night, "a fiery ring suspended in the sky continuously shooting out flame, as if it were someone infuriated." This forces Old He to make an "escape like a fish breaking a net," using a rope lowered from the window in the middle of the night to climb, as he says, "up and down the wall like a spider! They were furious because they couldn't find me, so they damaged the balcony. I couldn't let myself be captured by them... It's a question of freedom." The gaze of the world is the external motivator of Can Xue's writing, and just as Old He says of breaking out of his entrapment: "I've been through this many times before." He (or she) even enjoys this escape rather than being tired by it, because this is the ultimate opportunity to embody an author's "freedom"!

Undergoing this kind of escape with Old He proves too exhausting. The narrator wants to return to his parents' home for a while and wait until his insomnia is cured before returning. Old He agrees. But life at his parents' house is not easy, either. In fact, his parents are overjoyed at his returning home not only because they are lonely, but also because he is "someone [Old He] has chosen," since "they both knew Old He," and, besides, "my parents, as it turned out, only cared about Old He's opinion of me." To make him stay longer, his father even says philosophical things such as: "The more obstacles you manufacture, the easier your communication with him will be!" Returning home and leaving Old He unexpectedly brings him even closer into line with Old He's strategy.

Of course, his parents are also conflicted when it comes to this issue of his return, on one hand hoping "I" will follow Old He, and, on the other, hoping their son will remain at their side. In fact, this is another form of compulsion caused by living in the conventional world. If, for example, the coercive force the dark men exercise on "I" is external and compulsory, the parents use an internal force that is tender and stifling. They use sentimentalism as a means of guiding "I" toward the understanding that worldly tenderness is only a temporary resting place, one that allows more abundant energy to invest in creative activity. Therefore, once "I" resumes sleeping normally, he discovers that this kind of sleep leaves him feeling hollow, in a state not unlike death:

> An empty dreamland; waking up in the middle of the night as if I had been dead, filled with a nameless after-dread... Naturally, living at my parents' house, my sense of urgency disappeared. Now, though, for whatever reason, I wanted to return to that urgent and pressured lifestyle. I would rather, as Old He had said, "breathe in the dense swarm of information every day."

That kind of breathing was steady. And, at present, I was afraid of suffocating in my heavy sleep, or of my entire respiratory system becoming paralyzed.

This feeling is precisely the effect the parents want to achieve, because they don't want their son to spend all his time intoxicated by dreams and having nothing to do: "I sensed that they hoped I would be caught up deeper in the situation, because then they would have more material to discuss, along with all kinds of prediction games to play, which was the thing they enjoyed the most." It seems that all of this has been meticulously arranged by Old He, with everything from the dark-faced men's spying to his parents' urging him to stay becoming the "information" Old He uses to realize his intentions. Not only do the dark men say "The whole globe is a giant village" as they are burying the network cables, the parents, too, say "Information channels grow more advanced each day now," while "I" exclaims: "In today's world the information channels are so perfectly developed, no matter where we go, we mark out that touching pattern in the air overhead."

Naturally, all of the information and messages are pointing toward Old He. Thus "I" prepares to return to his own Room 801, to return to Old He's side. "Will my tiny little apartment compress and explode from the wild onslaught of information in the middle of the night? Will the windowsill cave in? I secretly admire the art Old He studied on Wulong Mountain." This art of Old He's commands all information, and the source of his information encompasses both space and time. "I" meets his former elementary school teacher on the street and the teacher tells him that the nearby mailbox has been there for fifty-three years, continuously delivering all kinds of information: "There is sleepless information everywhere. For instance, inside this mailbox, late at night, there's the sound of footsteps, back and forth. The number of people chronically awake during the night is increasing." Yet all of these messages, after leaving Old He's grasp and the self's Room 801, become unreal. "At my parents' house, my sense of unreality grows stronger every day. Did Old He transmit this sense of illusion to me? I cannot keep on staying here. Life is too short, I must seize every opportunity. Tomorrow, after breakfast, I will pack up my things and return to Room 801. Whether or not Old He is there, I will return to my own home." The final sentence of the story indicates that returning to his own "home" (meaning the inner self) is a precondition: when there is a "home," Old He will eventually arrive. Many storms will find this "home," but "I" is no longer afraid, and even longs be at this center of information, to "breathe in the dense swarm of information every day," "seize every opportunity" of throwing himself into a "pressured lifestyle." In truth, when "I" establishes this view on life, "I" has already realized that "I" is Old He, even though he still seems to be, like that "old duck" walking ahead of him, "swaying side to side" and walking none too steadily.

Can Xue's story "The Tenant of Room 801" reveals the soul's inner composition. Strictly speaking, this is the theme of all of her writing, and the source of her work's enchantment. In China, there has been literature depicting the conflict between different realities (such as *Romance of the Three Kingdoms* and *The Water Margin*), and there has been literature describing the conflict between the soul and reality (such as *The Dream of the Red Chamber*), but very seldom has there been literature that depicts the conflict between souls, and there has never been literature that describes the soul's interior. This is the fundamental reason why we have difficulty deciphering Can Xue's fiction. The Chinese soul lacks a solid structure and volume, whereas this kind of form and content is found everywhere in classical Western literature, from Dante, Shakespeare, and Goethe to Dostoyevsky, Tolstoy, Sholokhov, Kafka, Calvino, and so on. Can Xue, influenced by the essence of Western literature, started composing works about the profundity of the human soul, and through the experience of several decades of demanding exploration has discovered that the human heart truly is a bottomless abyss. In this regard, the Chinese people, who lack belief, may even have a greater and more spacious capacity for such an inquiry than Western peoples. This also explains how Can Xue's unfailing creative inspiration has persisted over thirty years, without yet showing any signs of decline.

Notes

SCREAM IF YOU WISH, BUT FLY!

1. *Suomenkielinen sekakuorokapple*, for soprano, baritone, and mixed chorus. The title translates as "Finnish piece for mixed chorus."

2. The work referred to is *Im Traume*.

CREDO

1. Elmer Diktonius, "Min Dikt" ("My Poem"), 1921.

IN MUSIC, OF MUSIC, TOWARD MUSIC

1. Though this essay takes the form of diary entries, they are not drawn from Saariaho's personal journal.

2. At which *Je sens un deuxième cœur*, for viola, cello, and piano, was performed.

FIVE ACTS IN THE LIFE OF AN OPERA COMPOSER

1. Quoted in Roubaud's *La Fleur inverse: essai sur l'art formel des troubadours*, Paris, Éditions Ramsay, 1986, p. 99. This English translation originally from the Provençal by Barbara Smythe in *Trobador Poets: Eight Selections from the Poems of Eight Trobadors* (London, Chatto & Windus, 1911), p. 11.

A CONVERSATION WITH KAIJA SAARIAHO

1. This interview was conducted on Wednesday, February 13, 2013, at the composer's home in Paris.

THREE CONDUCTOR'S PERSPECTIVES ON KAIJA SAARIAHO'S MUSIC

1. Interviews conducted with the help of Aleksi Barrière.

2. Phone interview conducted in English and Finnish on January 12, 2013. Esa-Pekka Salonen's conducting of *Château de l'âme* (with Dawn Upshaw), *Amers* (with Anssi Karttunen), and *Graal théâtre* (with Gidon Kremer) can be found on a 2001 Sony Classical SK 60817 audio CD.

3. Symphonic works are pieces that conform to the classical model or to

the essential characteristics of the symphony genre.

4. Interview conducted in French at the Calouste Gulbenkian Foundation in Lisbon on January 20, 2013.

5. Interview conducted in English via e-mail on February 10, 2013.

A Conversation with Anssi Karttunen

1. This interview was conducted at the cellist's home in Paris on February 25, 2013. Originally from Finland, Anssi Karttunen belongs to an elite group of internationally renowned cellists. He imparts his brilliance and unique style across a repertoire as vast as it is varied, ranging from classic pieces to the most contemporary works (with over 135 creations — including 24 concertos — to his name). He has been collaborating with Kaija Saariaho for over thirty years.

Kaija Saariaho and Musical Research at IRCAM

1. Given the constraints of space, it is not possible to include an extensive list of citations. For more specific details and references concerning this period, please consult *Le Passage des frontiers: écrits sur la musique* by Kaija Saariaho, ed. Stéphane Roth (Éditions MF: Paris, 2013).

Graal théâtres

1. The episode is from "La Science des rêves," the opening section of "L'Enlèvement de la reine," last of the four tales included in the first version of *Graal théâtre* (Gallimard, 1977). Four more tales were published in 1981, and a further four added in the definitive edition, of 2005.

2. "Lancelot is in love with Queen Guinevere, but he is at the same time the object of the love of the knight Galehaut" — Jacques Roubaud, interview on the Gallimard site (http://www.gallimard.fr/catalog/entretiens/01057096. HTM).

The Impossibility of Living

1. From Teratologen's *Assisted Living*.

2. A conservative Norwegian paper.

3. The son to a friend of the Sæterbakken's. Robin, who is also mentioned, is his father.

4. From *Kierkegaard's Writings, VI: Fear & Trembling/Repetition* (Princeton: Princeton University Press, 2013), p. 132.

SOME AUTOBIOGRAPHICAL NOTES

1. From *Traveling Yesterday* by Peter Handke

2. A collection by Ole Robert Sunde.

3. The main character of Sæterbakken's *Capital*.

THE WIND FROM OUTSIDE

1. The title of this article is borrowed from a monograph on Georges Bataille by Helge Pettersen.

2. From Sæterbakken's essay "Handke and the Serbs—and Us."

3. From the final volume of *Norges litteraturhistorie. Vår egen tid 1980-1998* (1998) (*The History of Norwegian Literature: Our Present Time, 1980–1998*).

4. *Prosopopeia* vol. 1, 2002.

5. This essay was made available in English for the first time in *Music & Literature* no. 1.

6. From Sæterbakken's essay "Literature and Ethics" (2001).

7. From Sæterbakken's essay "The Exorcist" (1999).

8. From Sæterbakken's essay "NO! NO! NO!" (2008).

9. From Sæterbakken's essay "Good Day, Sir, Alter Ego" (1997).

THE MAJOR WORKS OF CAN XUE

1. The novellas "Yellow Mud Street" and "Old Floating Cloud" were translated into English and published as a single volume, *Old Floating Cloud*, by Northwestern University Press in 1992.

2. Four collections of Can Xue's short stories exist in English: *Dialogues in Paradise* (Northwestern University Press, 1989), *The Embroidered Shoes* (Henry Holt, 1997), *Blue Light in the Sky and Other Stories* (New Directions Publishing, 2006), and *Vertical Motion* (Open Letter Books, 2011). Each of these volumes is assembled from various Chinese collections.

THE TENANT OF ROOM 801

1. *He* or *Hé* 何 is a Chinese surname distinct from the English personal pronoun "he." When not used as a name, *he* is an interrogative pronoun (what, where, why).

2. *Tong* or *Tóng* 童 is a Chinese surname. When not used as a name, *tong* can also mean "child."

THE SHINING WORLD OF CAN XUE

1. Can Xue, *Dialogues in Paradise,* translated by Ronald R. Janssen and Jian Zhang (Evanston, Ill: Northwestern University Press, 1989), p. 1 & ff.

2. Vladimir Mayakovsky, *Cloud in Trousers* (1916), translated by Jonathan Brent and Lyudmila Sholkhova, *Web Conjunctions,* 2013.

3. *Dialogues in Paradise,* p. 13.

SOUR, SALTY, BITTER, SPICY, SWEET: ON *FIVE SPICE STREET*

1. The quote is from Cheng Yongxin's editorial note in his anthology *Selections of New-Wave Short Stories in China* (中国新潮小说选, Shanghai shehui kexueyuan chubanshe, 1989). Lu Tonglin summarizes this and other dismissals in *Misogyny, Cultural Nihilism & Oppositional Politics: Contemporary Chinese Experimental Fiction* (Stanford University Press, 1995), pp. 77-78.

2. 阳刚之气与文学评论的好时光. The text of this speech was reprinted as an epilogue to the first book-length edition of *Five Spice Street* (突围表演, Shanghai wenyi chubanshe, 1990), but has not been fully translated into English. I rely on the translations in Tonglin, pp. 102-103, and Xueping Zhong, *Masculinity Besieged?: Issues of Modernity and Male Subjectivity in Chinese Literature of the Late Twentieth Century* (Duke University Press, 2000), pp. 146-148.

3. 寻根文学 is usually translated as "root-seeking literature." Jing Wang, *High Culture Fever: Politics, Aesthetic and Ideology in Deng's China* (University of California Press, 1996) discusses this slogan as well as 中国文学走向世界, "Chinese literature marching toward the world," and includes a rare dissenting view by the writer Li Rui: "I did not know if Chinese literature ought to or would march toward the world. Neither did I know if the world is truly in need of Chinese literature as anxiously as what Chinese people wishfully thought it should be."

4. Interview with Laura McCandlish, 2001 (http://u.osu.edu/mclc).

5. Interview in 残雪文学观 (Guangxi shifan daxue chubanshe, 2007), p. 36. Here and elsewhere, Annelise Finegan Wasmoen has very kindly shared her glosses and insight on Can Xue's original wording.

6. Xiaobin Yang, *The Chinese Postmodern: Trauma and Irony in Chinese Avant-Garde Fiction* (University of Michigan Press, 2002), p. 137.

7. Q's very name testifies to his lack of independent personhood. The names translated "Madam X" and "Mr. Q" appear in the original as 女士X and 男士Q. While 女士 is a common title for a woman of unspecified age and marital status, the parallel 男士 is not a usual title for a man, and has the effect of making Q seem a second-order creature derived from X. Xiaobin Yang's translation of the names as "Lady X" and "Gentleman Q" might capture a bit of this sense.

8. For one case study see Kang Liu, "The Short-Lived Avant-Garde: The Transformation of Yu Hua" MLQ: Modern Language Quarterly 63.1 (2002), pp. 89-117.

9. Interview with Laura McCandlish.

10. Interview, "The Aesthetic Activity in Modern Fiction" (http://web.mit.edu/ccw/can-xue/files/CanXue-Interview.pdf).

THE TENANT OF THE SOUL: ON "THE TENANT OF ROOM 801"

1. Georg Wilhelm Friedrich Hegel, *The Phenomenology of Spirit*, trans. A. V. Miller (Oxford: Clarendon Press, 1977), p. 110.

Notes on Contributors

Gry Bakken is a translator based in Bygdøy, Oslo.

Aleksi Barrière is a French-Finnish stage director, author, translator, and theater scholar. Together with conductor Clément Mao-Takacs, he has founded the music theatre collective La Chambre aux échos, which is interested in the gray areas of interdisciplinary performance.

Jean-Baptiste Barrière is a composer and multimedia artist. He worked at IRCAM beginning in 1981, directing Musical Research, Education, and Production, and left in 1998 to concentrate on personal projects focusing on music/image interactions.

Jonathan Brent founded *FORMATIONS* magazine in 1981 with his wife, Frances, and was Director of Northwestern University Press from 1981 to 1991. From 1991 to 2009 he was Editorial Director of Yale University Press. Brent is now Executive Director of the YIVO Institute for Jewish Research. He is also the author of two books on Stalin.

Florence Delay is a French academician and actress. She is the author of many books, including *Minuit sur les jeux* and *Riche et légère*, which won the Prix Femina in 1983. With Jacques Roubaud, she compiled a series of ten plays about Arthurian legend, *Graal théâtre*, between 1977 and 2005.

Carl-Michael Edenborg is a Swedish writer who has published five of his close friend Stig Sæterbakken's novels at his small press Vertigo. Edenborg's *The Parapornographic Manifesto* was released in the U.S. in 2013.

Herdis Eggen is Senior Editor for Norwegian Fiction at Cappelen Damm, where she was Stig Sæterbakken's editor from 1987.

Scott Esposito is the co-author of *The End of Oulipo?* (Zero Books, 2013). His work appears widely, including in *The White Review, The Point, Drunken Boat, Tin House, Bookforum, Southerly*, the *Times Literary Supplement*, and the *Washington Post*. He is a Senior Editor to the journal of translation *Two Lines*.

Paul Griffiths was born in Wales in 1947. A music critic for thirty years, he has published several books on music, as well as librettos and novels.

Henning Hagerup is a literary critic and translator. He is the author or co-author of a number of books, among them a collection of essays, *Vinternotater* (*Winter Notes*, 1998).

David Harrington is a violinist and the founder of the San Francisco-based Kronos Quartet. He is also the Artistic Director of the non-profit Kronos Performing Arts Association (KPAA), whose mission is "to continually re-imagine the string quartet experience." KPAA has commissioned more than eight hundred works for string quartet.

Camilla Hoitenga is a widely traveled flute soloist who collaborates with composers, visual artists, and writers. Classically educated in Michigan and Illinois, she is based in Cologne, Germany.

Anssi Karttunen leads a busy career as a soloist and chamber-music cellist, performing extensively with many of the finest orchestras and musicians around the world. He is the artistic director of the Musica Nova Helsinki Festival.

Stina Katchadourian was born in Helsinki, Finland. A writer and literary translator, she lives in Stanford, California, and spends her summers on an island in the Baltic. Her latest book is *The Lapp King's Daughter*, a memoir from Finland's arctic war against the Germans.

Paul Kerschen is author of *The Drowned Library* (Foxhead Books, 2011). He studied and taught at the University of Iowa and the University of California-Berkeley, and now writes and develops software in California.

Karl Ove Knausgaard was born in Norway in 1968. His six-volume novel *My Struggle* has won many international literary awards and has been translated into at least fifteen languages. Knausgaard lives in Sweden with his wife and three children.

Daniel Levin Becker is reviews editor of *The Believer*, the author of *Many Subtle Channels: In Praise of Potential Literature* (Harvard, 2012), the translator of Georges Perec's *La Boutique Obscure* (Melville House, 2013), and the youngest member of the Oulipo. He lives in San Francisco.

Audun Lindholm is a literary critic and the editor of the Norwegian journal *Vagant*.

Amin Maalouf is a Lebanese-born French author whose works have been translated into many languages. He received the Prix Goncourt in 1993 for his novel *Le rocher de Tanios* (*The Rock of Tanios*). He was also been awarded the Prince of Asturias Award for Literature in 2010. He has lived in France since 1976.

Derek Mahon is widely regarded as one of the most talented and innovative Irish poets of the twentieth century. His most recent books of poetry include *An Autumn Wind* (Gallery Press, 2010) and *Life on Earth* (Gallery Press, 2008).

Susanna Mälkki is a Finnish conductor. In May 2013, she was appointed Principal Guest Conductor of the Gulbenkian Orchestra, and in September 2014, Mälkki was chosen as the next Chief Conductor of the Helsinki Philharmonic Orchestra, effective autumn 2016.

Sverre Malling is a Norwegian artist whose work resides in major collections in the Astrup Fearnley Museum and The Norwegian National Museum of Arts, among others.

Clément Mao-Takacs is a French conductor, pianist, and composer. He is the founding artistic and musical director of the Secession Orchestra and, with Aleksi Barrière, is the co-founder of music theater collective La Chambre aux échos.

Ernest Martinez-Izquierdo is Honorary Conductor of the Navarre Symphony Orchestra of Pamplona and Principal Guest Conductor of the ensemble Barcelona 216.

Daniel Medin, co-editor of *Music & Literature*, is an associate professor of Comparative Literature and English at the American University of Paris.

Benjamin Mier-Cruz is a Visiting Assistant Professor of Scandinavian and German Studies at Augustana College. His most recent translation is Stig Dagerman's *A Burnt Child*. He is the recipient of the Susan Sontag Prize for Translation.

Saint-John Perse, pseudonym of Alexis Leger (1887–1975), was a French poet and diplomat. He was awarded the Nobel Prize for Literature in 1960.

Jacques Roubaud is one of the most accomplished members of the Oulipo. He is the author of numerous books of prose, theater, and poetry, and has long been a professor of mathematics at the University of Paris X Nanterre.

Kaija Saariaho is a Finnish composer internationally known and recognized for her works involving electronics. Her music has been commissioned and performed by leading ensembles worldwide.

Stig Sæterbakken (1966–2012) was one of Norway's most acclaimed contemporary writers. His novels include *Through the Night*, *Siamese*, and *Self-Control*, all of which are published by Dalkey Archive Press.

Esa-Pekka Salonen is a lauded composer and a world-renowned conductor. He is currently the Principal Conductor and Artistic Advisor for London's Philharmonia Orchestra and the Conductor Laureate for the Los Angeles Philharmonic, where he was Music Director from 1992 until 2009.

Stokes Schwartz is a translator who teaches film studies at Illinois Wesleyan University.

Peter Sellars is an opera, theater, and festival director as well as a professor in the Department of World Arts and Cultures at UCLA and Resident Curator of the Telluride Film Festival. He is the recipient of a MacArthur Fellowship, the Erasmus Prize, the Sundance Institute Risk-Takers Award, and the Gish Prize.

Sjón is a celebrated Icelandic novelist, poet, librettist, and lyricist. He won the Nordic Council's Literary Prize for his novel *The Blue Fox* and his latest, *Moonstone–The Boy Who Never Was*, was awarded the 2013 Icelandic Literary Prize. His novels have been translated into thirty languages.

Edith Södergran (1892–1923) was a Swedish-speaking Finnish poet. She released four volumes of poetry during her lifetime.

Declan Spring is Vice President and Senior Editor at New Directions Publishing. He has been working there since 1991.

Jan Steyn is a critic and translator of literature in Afrikaans, Dutch, English and French. He currently lives in Ithaca, New York.

Annelise Finegan Wasmoen is an editor and a literary translator. Her recent translations include stories by Jiang Yun, Lu Min, and Wang Meng, as well as Can Xue's novel *The Last Lover*.

Sophie Weiner is a French-to-English translator from Baltimore. She has contributed to publications dedicated to art, literature, cinema, and fashion.

Deng Xiaomang is professor of philosophy at Wuhan University. He is one of China's leading Kant scholars.

Can Xue, pseudonym of Deng Xiaohua, is the author of many novels, volumes of literary criticism, and short works of fiction. Formerly a tailor, she began writing fiction in 1983. She lives in Beijing.

Jeffrey Zuckerman is digital editor of *Music & Literature*. His writing and translations have appeared in *Best European Fiction, The White Review,* and the *Los Angeles Review of Books*.

h a r k

à Kaija Saariaho

Paul Griffiths

a jar shook

kairos

a jar shook

kairos

kairos

as air soars

kairos

risk or oasis

kairos

risk is oasis

*kairos**

---

* *"Kairos,* personified Opportunity… In literature, *Kairos* also encompasses time (differentiated from Chronos) and the seasons" (Oxford Classical Dictionary).